WHITE BORDERS

The *History*
of RACE *and* IMMIGRATION
in the UNITED STATES
from CHINESE EXCLUSION
to the BORDER WALL

REECE JONES

BEACON PRESS
Boston, Massachusetts

BEACON PRESS
Boston, Massachusetts
www.beacon.org

Beacon Press books
are published under the auspices of
the Unitarian Universalist Association of Congregations.

24 23 22 21   8 7 6 5 4 3 2 1

This book is printed on acid-free paper that meets the uncoated paper
ANSI/NISO specifications for permanence as revised in 1992.

Text design and composition by Kim Arney

Library of Congress Cataloging-in-Publication Data
Name: Jones, Reece author.
Title: White borders : the history of race and immigration in the United
States from Chinese exclusion to the border wall / Reece Jones.
Description: Boston, Massachusetts : Beacon Press, 2021. | Includes
bibliographical references and index.
Identifiers: LCCN 2021020957 (print) | LCCN 2021020958 (ebook) |
ISBN 9780807054062 (hardcover) | ISBN 9780807054123 (ebook)
Subjects: LCSH: United States—Emigration and immigration—Social aspects. |
United States—Emigration and immigration—History. | United
States—Emigration and immigration—Government policy. | United
States—Race relations.
Classification: LCC JV6475 .J66 2021 (print) | LCC JV6475 (ebook) |
DDC 305.800973—dc23
LC record available at https://lccn.loc.gov/2021020957
LC ebook record available at https://lccn.loc.gov/2021020958

CONTENTS

LIST OF TABLES

PROLOGUE

"**Y**ou. Will not. Replace us. You. Will not. Replace us."
With torches in hand and rage in their voices, hundreds of white men marched along tree-lined red brick sidewalks through the stately grounds of the University of Virginia on the evening of August 11, 2017.[1] Their destination was the towering Rotunda at the center of campus where Richard Spencer, a leader of the white nationalist movement and one of the organizers of the event, was planning to give an impromptu speech. Dressed in matching uniforms of khaki pants, tucked-in polo shirts, and fashy haircuts—shaved tight on the sides and slicked across the top in the Hitler youth style—the white nationalists belted out chants in an aggressive, forceful cadence. "One people. One nation. End to immigration. One people. One nation. End to immigration." Even more ominously, like an anthem they sang "Blood and soil," the English translation of the Nazi slogan, *Blut und Boden*.[2] As they neared the iconic dome of the Rotunda, Thomas Jefferson's architectural masterpiece and a World Heritage Site, the evocation of "You. Will not. Replace us" morphed into "Jews. Will not. Replace us."

After passing through the Greek columns of the Rotunda, the white marchers streamed down the north steps into the red brick plaza below, itching for a fight. They found one in the form of a few dozen counterprotesters encircling the statue of Thomas Jefferson at the center of the plaza, with arms interlocked as if to protect a fragile idea. The counterprotesters were mostly young, mostly women, along with a few Black men. They chanted, "No Nazis. No KKK. No fascist USA," but their small numbers in the vast space of the Rotunda dissipated their voices, making their grip on Jefferson's legacy seem plaintive and tenuous. They eyed the growing mass of white nationalists warily, as more and more hyped-up men spilled into the plaza.

The location of the standoff could not have been more appropriate. As Thomas Jefferson stood aloof above, two different visions for the future of America, both of which Jefferson himself had set in motion, collided at his feet.

———

The Jefferson statue on the north plaza of the Rotunda was sculpted by Moses Ezekiel in 1910. Ezekiel was born in Richmond in 1844, and, as the Civil War got under way, he became the first Jewish student to enroll at the Virginia Military Institute.[3] At VMI, his roommate was Thomas Jefferson's grandnephew, Thomas G. Jefferson. They served together in the Confederate Army during the war, and the younger Jefferson died in battle as Ezekiel held him in his arms. Ezekiel fought for the Confederacy until the bitter end, hunched in the trenches at Richmond as the city fell in 1865. After the war, he completed his degree at VMI and then moved to Europe to pursue his interest in sculpture, studying in Berlin before settling in Rome, where he lived for the remainder of his life.

Largely forgotten today, Ezekiel was one of the preeminent sculptors in the world at the turn of the twentieth century, but his most famous works are monuments to the Confederacy. The majority of the seven hundred Confederate statues that dot public spaces across the United States were not built immediately after the war but rather between 1890 and 1950, at the height of the Jim Crow era, as the antebellum white order was resurgent across the South and the entire country. These monuments still stand in thirty-one states, far beyond the eleven that were part of the Confederacy.[4] Ezekiel sculpted a statue of Confederate general Stonewall Jackson for the grounds of the West Virginia State Capitol, a memorial titled "Virginia Mourns Her Dead" on the VMI campus, and the Confederate Memorial at Arlington National Cemetery, which was dedicated in 1914. With his connections to the Jefferson family and the South, he was the obvious choice for the Thomas Jefferson statue on the campus of the University of Virginia.

Despite Ezekiel's Confederate bona fides, the design of the statue at the Rotunda focuses entirely on Jefferson's universalist writings. Jefferson penned some of the most famous lines of the Declaration of Independence, including the idea that "all men are created equal" and have an inalienable right to "Life, Liberty, and the Pursuit of Happiness." In the statue, Jefferson stares thoughtfully into the distance, standing atop the Liberty Bell and holding a copy of the Declaration of Independence. At the base are four figures representing Jeffersonian ideals of Justice, Liberty, Equality, and Religious Freedom. The religious freedom side of the statue even includes a tablet listing God-Jehovah, Brahma, Atma, Ra, and Allah. This inclusive version of Jefferson's legacy represents the dream of what the United States has to offer, where freedom and equality are protected for everyone regardless of their race, religion, or place of birth.

Thomas Jefferson, however, is also a foundational figure at the core of another version of the United States, one that is based less on the idealistic words that Jefferson wrote and more on how he actually lived. Even as he wrote that all men were created equal, Thomas Jefferson continued to hold hundreds of slaves in bondage at Monticello, his picturesque hilltop estate overlooking Charlottesville. Slaves built the elegant grounds of the University of Virginia, including the famed Rotunda where the Jefferson statue now stands. In this other version of history, the United States has always been a white country. It was founded by white men, for the benefit of white men, and a series of laws have been enacted over the centuries to maintain white supremacy. Slavery remained legal for almost a century after Jefferson wrote that all men are created equal. Jefferson's actions show that it is a misunderstanding of his words to think that he meant anything other than *only* all white men are created equal.

As Roger Taney, the chief justice of the Supreme Court of the United States, wrote in the *Dred Scott* decision in 1857 that denied citizenship to free African Americans, "The unhappy black race were separated from the white by indelible marks and . . . it is impossible to believe that these rights and privileges were intended to be extended to them."[5] The United States' first naturalization law in 1790 restricted citizenship to a "free white person." The Jim Crow era maintained white supremacy for almost a century after slavery was officially banned, in an era in which the veneration of the Confederacy grew and the country enacted strict, racially based laws on who could immigrate. From this perspective, the United States was a white country until the 1960s, when the civil rights movement and the 1965 Hart-Celler Immigration Act, which allowed for substantial increases in non-European immigration to the United States, fundamentally changed the character of the country.

―――――

The Unite the Right rally in Charlottesville in August 2017 was organized to protest the removal of a statue to Robert E. Lee, the commander of the Confederate Army. The Charlottesville City Council voted in February 2017 to remove the Lee statue from a city park and to change the name from Lee Park to Emancipation Park. However, the rally was also meant to symbolize the emergence of a unified movement, which Richard Spencer had termed the alt-right, to protect the white legacy of the United States from racial justice and immigration. The night before the main protest at the Lee statue, the rally organizers, Spencer and a Charlottesville native named Jason Kessler, scheduled the torchlight march through the University of Virginia, culminating with a speech by Spencer at the Jefferson statue on campus, staking a claim to both Lee's and Jefferson's legacies. As the white nationalists gathered beforehand in a parking lot, Kessler's round face was lit by the glow of a tiki torch as he explained the symbolism and purpose of the march: "The torches are to commemorate the fallen dead of our European brothers and sisters. Like Robert E. Lee. Like Thomas Jefferson." He continued, "Right now we are in a civil rights struggle to save white people from ethnic cleansing. Our monuments are being torn down. They are being removed and replaced. And our people are being torn down and replaced through immigration policy."[6]

At the Jefferson statue on the north plaza of the Rotunda, the flickering tiki torches created an eerie yellow glow as the situation devolved into chaos. Despite being outnumbered by a factor of ten to one, the counterprotesters stood fast, preventing Richard Spencer from getting to the statue. Scuffles broke out. Inexplicably, the police were nowhere to be seen, so the security for the white nationalists tried to keep the groups apart. The white nationalists circled menacingly and chanted, "You! Will not! Replace us! You! Will not! Replace us!" Suddenly it was not a general statement but a threat directed at the group of human beings standing only feet in front of them. After holding on for another few moments, the will of the counterprotesters broke and they ceded the Jefferson statue. The white nationalists swarmed it, shouting, "Heil victory" and "Heil Spencer."

Apparently not having thought to bring a microphone or any lighting beyond the tiki torches, Richard Spencer stood on the dark side of the Jefferson statue and attempted to give his speech, but he was largely drowned out by the commotion. He said, "Hey, alt-right, alt-right, we own these streets. We occupy this ground. We won." After pausing for a few cheers, he asked, "What in the hell are we doing out here? What in the hell are we doing risking our lives? We are risking our lives for our people, for our ancestors, for our future. That's what we are doing." A smattering of applause was barely audible amid the surrounding din. "Do you think antifa can defeat our throng? Our group?" Before he could continue the thought, one of his associates interrupted, telling him that they were not allowed to stand on the base of the statue. Spencer shrugged. "All right, off the statue. Out the way we came." With that, he ended his brief occupation of Thomas Jefferson's legacy.

WHITE
BORDERS

TWO VERSIONS OF HISTORY

A s the first chords of Neil Young's "Rockin' in the Free World" rico-cheted off the red marble walls in the lobby of the office tower, the candidate appeared on the mezzanine above, like a king greeting his subjects. His wife stood a few steps behind in an elegant white dress, graceful but tentative, seemingly using all her strength to resist fidgeting. In an over-sized blue suit with a red tie, he gave a thumbs up and mouthed "Wow" as he took a half step back to marvel at the whole scene. He waved, gave two thumbs up, then turned and indicated for his wife to head to the escalator to the main floor. Stone-faced, she stepped onto the golden escalator to descend slowly into a new reality. The devoted crowds of supporters that would eventually dominate his rallies had not yet found their candidate. There was not a single red hat to be seen. The people lining the railing above the escalator were mostly tourists in jeans and office workers who seem to have stumbled onto the spectacle on their lunch break. A few have awkwardly pulled "Make America Great Again" T-shirts over their jackets and dress shirts. As the candidate inched down the escalator, he stiffly waved as his signature golden jumble of hair slipped out of view. The candidate's daughter waited, awkward and alone, by the lectern as Neil Young chanted about a woman leaving her child at home to buy a hit of drugs on the street. The candidate's other children, three sons and a daughter, stood off the stage to the side, barely visible in the dark, shifting their weight from one foot to the other. The crowd in front of the stage consisted entirely of reporters, who smirked as they craned their necks to take in the odd scene, seemingly not knowing where to focus their attention. The candidate did not appear again for almost a minute as the smattering of applause largely died out, but Neil Young carried on singing about how the kid left by the drug-addicted mom would never be cool. Eventually, the candidate strode past his children waiting in the dark without a glance and lumbered onto the stage. He paused to take in the scene again and wave, then kissed his daughter and mouthed, "Hey baby, good job." Even before he was completely in front of the microphone, he started to comment on the crowd size: "Wow, whoa! That is some group of people. Thousands"—reports at the time estimated dozens—"This is beyond anybody's expectations. There has been no crowd like this." He then zeroed in on what would become the singular issue of his campaign. In the first minute of his speech, even before officially announcing that he was running for president, he said, "The US has become a dumping ground for everybody else's problems. . . . When Mexico sends its people, they're not sending their best. They're not sending you. They're not sending you. They're sending people that have lots of problems, and they are bring those problems with us [sic]. They're bringing drugs. They're bringing crime. They're rapists. And, some, I assume, are good people." He continued for another forty-five minutes, clearly off script and at times talking about whatever popped into his mind. He finally ended the speech by pledging to "Make America great again."[1]

Donald Trump's racist campaign for the presidency of the United States seemed to come out of nowhere, and the news reports after his announcement did not know what to make of the shambolic event. The golden elevator ride! The rambling, incoherent, conspiracy theory speech! The nonsensical campaign slogan! Many observers assumed he had already sunk his campaign with his racist language. In the week after the announcement, a series of business partners ended their relationships with him. NBC and Univision dropped the Miss USA and Miss Universe pageants. Macy's and Serta Mattress stopped carrying Trump-branded lines of products. The celebrity chef José Andrés withdrew from a deal to run the restaurant in Trump's new hotel in Washington, DC. Reince Priebus, then the Republican National Committee chair, asked Trump to tone it down because it could tarnish all of the Republicans running for president.[2]

Trump knew better and made the border wall his campaign slogan as he impugned Mexican immigrants as rapists and criminals, even as undocumented immigration to the country was in decline. He called for a complete shutdown on Muslim immigration to the United States, and he repeated the Nixon-era racial dog whistle of "law and order" to raucous rallies. Many commentators were caught off guard and scoffed at the idea that these positions were anything more than a strategy to rally his base, saying Trump would not actually ban Muslims, build a wall, or stop all immigration in the unlikely event that he actually became president.

For others, the election of Donald Trump was not a surprise at all. Instead, it was the culmination of a carefully orchestrated effort to move what had become fringe views about race and immigration back into the mainstream of American politics.[3] A single charitable foundation, the Colcom Foundation, established by the late Mellon heir Cordelia Scaife May, gave $63 million to anti-immigrant groups during the 2016 election cycle.[4] Scaife May and her brother Richard Mellon Scaife were deep-pocketed donors for conservative causes, and Scaife May held a strong conviction that overpopulation through immigration threatened the environment in the United States. When she died in 2005, her fortune went to Colcom, which she set up to support environment conservation, population reduction, and anti-immigration groups. It has over $420 million in assets in 2021.

Most of the extreme anti-immigrant groups that the Colcom Foundation funded during the 2016 election were established by a single man, John Tanton, an ophthalmologist from Petoskey, Michigan, who believed that "for European-American society and culture to persist requires a European-American majority."[5] In an oral history in 1989, Tanton explained, "I found virtually no one was willing to talk about this! It was a forbidden topic. I tried to get some others to think about it and write about it, but I did not succeed. I finally concluded that if anything was going to happen, I would have to do it myself," which he did. Over the past forty years, Tanton founded a fleet of organizations to pursue his vision of a white America protected by strict immigration laws, including the Federation for American Immigration Reform (FAIR), the Center for Immigration Studies (CIS), the Immigration Reform Law Institute (IRLI), and Numbers USA. These innocuously named groups, which are referred to collectively as the Tanton Network, hid their white nationalist ideology as they produced reports, gave interviews to the mainstream media, and testified before Congress about the need for strict immigration laws. Tanton, who died in 2019, has been called the most influential man in America that no one has ever heard of.[6]

Several of the groups in the Tanton Network are designated as extremist hate groups by the Southern Poverty Law Center, but the influx of tens of millions of dollars from the Colcom Foundation over the past fifteen years allowed his network to establish credibility. These groups used their growing influence to fight sanctuary city laws, promote "show me your papers" bills in state legislatures, stop bipartisan immigration reform bills, undermine the Deferred Action for Childhood Arrivals (DACA) program, and unseat prominent moderate politicians. In the 2016 campaign, they finally found a presidential candidate willing to run on their anti-immigrant agenda.

The Tanton Network also served as a pipeline for staff into Trump's campaign and his administration. Among the many key figures with close ties to these clandestine anti-immigrant groups are Trump's campaign manager and senior advisor Kellyanne Conway, who was a longtime pollster for FAIR; former attorney general Jeff Sessions, who was a keynote speaker at FAIR events and was awarded the FAIR Franklin Society Award in 2007; Kris Kobach, who chaired Trump's voter fraud commission and served as legal counsel for FAIR, IRLI, and Numbers USA; and most significantly senior advisor to the president Stephen Miller, who was the keynote speaker at a CIS event and who cited their reports to justify the administration's immigration crackdowns. With the election of Donald Trump, anti-immigrant extremists suddenly found themselves at the levers of power in the United States as many more mid-level staffers from these fringe groups flooded into jobs in the Department of Homeland Security, the Justice Department, and the White House.

Although the United States is often mythologized as a nation of immigrants, the mainstreaming of anti-immigrant politics was, in reality, a reversion to the ugly norm of the past.[7] The use of immigration and citizenship laws to pursue an exclusionary agenda did not begin with the presidential campaign of Donald Trump or John Tanton's network of anti-immigration groups. It did not begin with the 1965 Hart-Celler Immigration Act that made Mexican labor migration illegal or the 1924 Johnson-Reed Immigration Act that President Calvin Coolidge said would "keep America American" by completely banning Asian immigration and severely restricting immigration from everywhere except Western Europe. It did not even begin with the United States' first immigration laws in the 1870s and 1880s that banned Chinese immigrants from coming to the United States, which Senator John Miller of California introduced into the Senate by saying "of [the] Chinese, we have enough and would be glad to exchange those we have for any white people under the sun."[8]

Since the arrival of the first Dutch slave ship in 1619, the English colonies that became the United States were based on the dual foundation of open immigration for whites from Europe and racial exclusion of slaves from Africa, Native Americans, and, eventually, immigrants from other parts of the world. Racial exclusion was enshrined in the first naturalization law in 1790, which limited citizenship to a "free white person," and racial exclusion has played a central role in who could live and work in the United States through the present day, as immigration restrictions have become the mechanism to protect a fleeting vision of a white country.

WHITE BORDERS

The argument of this book is simple: immigration laws are about racial exclusion. They were created in the nineteenth century to protect an imaginary version of the United States as a white country, and they continue to be used through the present day for racial purposes. They have racial impacts on who can enter the country, and they are enforced through racial profiling by immigration agents who track down, arrest, and deport people based on their skin color and place of birth. The mainstream consensus that the United States needs immigration laws is, at its core, a white supremacist position rooted in the fear of what has been termed over the generations "the passing of the great race," "race suicide," "suicide of the West," "death of the West," "white genocide," and "the great replacement."[9] Immigration restrictions are a mechanism for protecting the numerically small but politically powerful white population and culture of the United States. Those who support severely restricting immigration to the United States are worried that immigrants will replace white people as the dominant group in the country.

This statement is likely to upset some readers who have grown up with the idea that the United States is based on the creed that all men are created equal and that it is a nation of immigrants, where diversity is its strength. For many people, passports, citizenship laws, borders, and immigration restrictions do not evoke racial exclusion in the same way that slavery and segregation do.[10] Borders are assumed to be part of the normal functioning of a country, but that has not always been the case. The United States did not have any national rules about who could enter the country until 1875, although there were state-level restrictions in some places. The first US national immigration laws were specifically designed to stop Chinese immigration into the country. Anti-immigrant positions are often shrouded in the seemingly progressive language of protecting the jobs of American workers, protecting the environment from exploitation, or simply upholding the rule of law. However, these smokescreens obscure the underlying logic of racial exclusion. The internal documents of the Tanton Network confirm that their leaders recognize that these justifications are necessary to make palatable what are, at their core, rules to prevent nonwhite people from entering the country.

There is a surprising amount of agreement about the racial history of the United States between anti-racists and white supremacists. The very first line of the *New York Times'* 1619 Project, which reframed American history through the lens of slavery, is "Our democracy's founding ideals were false when they were written."[11] This factual statement upset many mainstream commentators who called it revisionist history.[12] However, white supremacists describe the history of the United States in a very similar manner. Jared Taylor, a friend of John Tanton and the founding editor of the white supremacist magazine (and later website) *American Renaissance*, makes this point abundantly clear. In a 2012 article titled "What the Founders Really Thought about Race," Taylor quotes directly from a series of American leaders including George Washington, Thomas Jefferson, James Madison, Abraham Lincoln, and Harry Truman. With quote after quote, the piece shows "the record from colonial times through the end of the Civil War is therefore one of starkly inegalitarian views. . . . Until the second half of the 20th century, it would be very hard to find a prominent American who spoke about race in today's terms."[13]

The difference is that anti-racists want the United States to finally live up to the universalist language of the founding documents, while white supremacists want to return to the racial beliefs and practices of the founders. That was the debate in the Civil War, the Reconstruction era, and during the civil rights movement, and that is still the debate we are having today, even if many prefer not to face that reality. Indeed, when

Donald Trump and his supporters pledged to make America great again, they were actually talking about making America white again.

THE HISTORY OF RACE AND IMMIGRATION

White Borders tells the story of racial responses to immigration throughout the history of the United States. It begins with the arrival of the first nonwhite immigrants on US shores during California's gold rush. While the United States was actively attempting to increase immigration from Northern and Western Europe, as soon as a different group of people began to arrive, Americans developed mechanisms to exclude them. In the 1870s, the slogan was "and whatever happens the Chinese must go," and the Chinese Exclusion Act of 1882 did exactly that: exclude non-white immigration from China. By the 1890s, a wide range of different immigrants sailed to American ports who did not look like the Northern Europeans who were the first wave of settlers. V. S. McClatchy, the newspaper publisher, president of the Associated Press, and virulent anti-Asian campaigner, embodied the growing animus toward immigrants through his writings and testimony before Congress as he pushed for a ban on all Asian immigration. Politicians set out to stop the new arrivals, and scholars promoted the superiority of the Nordic race through eugenics and race pseudoscience. In the 1920s, President Calvin Coolidge campaigned to "keep America American" and signed into law the Johnson-Reed Immigration Act of 1924, which banned Asian immigration and severely curtailed immigration from anywhere outside Northern Europe. Senator David Reed of Pennsylvania, the coauthor of the law that is commonly referred to as the national origins quotas, wrote an article that ran on the front page of the *New York Times* under the title "America of the Melting Pot Comes to an End." Reed concluded, "Our incoming immigrants should hereafter be of the same race as those of us already here."[14]

In the 1930s and 1940s, Adolf Hitler and the Nazi regime took eugenics to its grisly conclusion with the Final Solution and the murder of 6 million Jews and other minorities, which forced a national reckoning in Germany with the consequences of racial pseudoscience and a disavowal. In the United States, there was never a complete reckoning with the race science that justified the 1924 national origins quotas. As the middle section of the book demonstrates, although the underlying pseudoscience was disproved, the immigration policies that were created based on eugenics persisted through the 1960s. Obscure foundations like the Pioneer Fund continued to provide money for eugenics research and white supremacist causes. Even as the Immigration Act of 1965, which was passed as part of the civil rights movement, removed the discriminatory national origins quotas, Senator Ted Kennedy pledged that the racial makeup of America would not be affected: "Our cities will not be flooded with a million immigrants annually. . . . The ethnic mix of this country will not be upset."[15] Kennedy's pledge turned out to be wrong, and a new anti-immigrant movement emerged in the 1970s at the intersection of environmental population control efforts and white supremacy, mirroring the eugenics and white supremacist coalition of the 1920s.

The final section of the book explains how John Tanton, a small-town ophthalmologist in upstate Michigan, built an anti-immigrant movement from scratch by founding dozens of different organizations and courting donors like Cordelia Scaife May, who was one of the wealthiest people in the United States. Even as the Tanton Network of anti-immigrant groups including FAIR, CIS, and Numbers USA eventually distanced themselves from Tanton's racist writings and affiliations, Scaife May's funding dramatically increased their influence in Washington, DC, and around the country. The Tanton Network built alliances with conservative politicians like Colorado representative Tom Tancredo and Alabama senator Jeff Sessions. They also spread their anti-immigrant message through right-wing radio hosts and like-minded media figures such as former CNN and Fox Business host Lou Dobbs and Steve Bannon, then chief executive at Breitbart News, as they looked for a presidential candidate that could take their anti-immigrant campaign to the White House. They found him in 2016, when Donald Trump ran for president on a pledge to build a wall to stop an invasion of "criminals, rapists, and murders" from crossing the border. As president, he enacted a Muslim ban and sought to stop all immigration to the United States in order to put "America First" and "Make America Great Again." Even though Trump lost in 2020, the fact that over 74 million people voted for him demonstrated that his brand of nativism continues to be a potent force in American politics.

The fear of "the great replacement" connects the Chinese exclusion laws of the 1880s, the "Keep America American" nativism of the 1920s, and the "Build the Wall" chants of the 2010s. The great replacement is often associated with the French author Renaud Camus, who started using the term in the late 1990s to describe a conspiracy theory that globalists wanted to replace white, Western European civilization with non-Europeans.[16] However, Camus was simply adding a new name to an old idea that had existed in the United States for centuries. The first Ku Klux Klan, which terrorized African Americans in the South in the years after the Civil War, feared that Reconstruction would replace white dominance in business and government. The anti-Chinese agitators in the 1870s and 1880s feared that Asians would replace whites in the West. The nativist movement and the second Ku Klux Klan in the 1920s feared that immigrants from around the world would replace the white Nordic population. The segregationists in the 1960s feared that the civil rights movement would replace the political power of whites. The anti-Muslim movement of the early 2000s feared that sharia law would replace American law. The anti-immigrant movement of John Tanton and Donald Trump in the 2010s feared that Mexicans and other immigrants would replace white Americans across the United States. From race suicide to white genocide, each era had its own name for the great replacement, but the fear of immigrants replacing whites was the driving force each time.

The words of the handful of senators who argued against the United States' first immigration laws provide an inspiration for what another version of the country could be. In 1882, as the Senate considered the Chinese Exclusion Act, Massachusetts Republican senator William Frisbee Hoar spoke eloquently of "the right of every human being who obeys equal laws to go everywhere on the surface of the earth." Foreshadowing Martin Luther King Jr.'s famous speech eighty years later, Hoar said that immigration restrictions should be based on only "an inquiry into the character of the individual applicant, and not by looking at the color of his skin."[17] Despite the moral clarity of Senator Hoar's words, his injunction has been ignored for over a century as the United States has used immigration laws as a proxy for racial exclusion at the border.

White Borders tells the story of how it happened.

CHAPTER 1

GO WEST, YOUNG MAN

O n the morning of January 24, 1848, James Marshall was building a sawmill on the American River, in the Sierra Nevada foothills, when something shiny caught his eye in the channel below. The thirty-eight-year-old Marshall and a small team of carpenters had arrived at the remote site a few months earlier, after leaving behind the high walls of Sutter's Fort, the only European-American settlement in the vast Central Valley in the Mexican province of Alta California. They trekked forty-five miles upstream through Native American lands and towering redwoods before settling on a site near the Native American village of Coloma, where steeper terrain provided the perfect location for a mill. As they began cutting timber and shaping the channel, Marshall could scarcely have imagined that in a few months his name would be in newspapers across the United States and around the world.

Marshall was born in 1810 on his family's Round Mountain Farm in New Jersey. His great-grandfather John Hart famously signed the Declaration of Independence, but his parents were not particularly well known or wealthy.[1] Coming from humble beginnings, Marshall apprenticed as a carpenter as a young man. When he turned twenty-one, restless for opportunity and adventure, he made his way west. Like many before him, the journey was filled with hardships and poverty, and he stopped along the way in towns like Crawfordsville, Indiana, and Warsaw, Illinois, to use his skills as a carpenter and save enough money to continue. In 1835, he arrived in the frontier state of Missouri where he tried his hand at farming on a government homesteading reserve called the Platte Purchase, but he struggled during several years of regional crop failures and famine. After falling gravely ill to malaria and suffering through fevers for six years, he finally continued west on May 1, 1844, in search of a different climate. Marshall joined a wagon train with only a horse, rifle, hatchet, knife, and blanket to his name.[2] He stopped at Fort Hall, which is today in the state of Idaho, and the Oregon Country before traveling the Siskiyou Trail, a Native American path running from the forests of the Willamette Valley past the snowcapped Mount Shasta to what is today the Central Valley of California. In order to survive, Marshall adopted the lifestyle of the nomadic trappers of the Pacific Coast and finally arrived at John Sutter's fledgling fort in July 1845 dressed head to toe in buckskins.

At the fort, Marshall found that Sutter, the first European to settle in California's Central Valley in 1839, was desperate for more hands in the sparsely populated area. Sutter gave Marshall some cattle to raise and a parcel of land along the Little Butte Creek. However, the Mexican-American War began in 1846, and Marshall's latest attempt at settling down proved to be short-lived. He impulsively joined John Frémont's California Battalion of the US Army, and when he returned to Sutter's Fort a year later, as the conflict in California ended, he found his cattle gone, possibly dead from neglect but more likely stolen. "Penniless," as he would later describe his situation, Marshall again relied on his skills as a carpenter and hatched a plan with Sutter to build the mill up in the foothills.

On that January morning, Marshall made his way around the mill inspecting the previous day's work. The night before he had opened the spillway under the mill to allow the current to cut a deeper channel, which stirred up sediment and dislodged smaller stones. As he gazed down at the flowing water, the low winter sun caught the edge of a sparkling object. Climbing down the ladder to get a better look, Marshall crouched on the rocky bank and plunged his hand into the cold mountain water, feeling around until he grasped the object. As he snatched a piece of gold out of the river, Marshall exclaimed, "I have found it!"[3]

James Marshall's discovery inspired one of the largest mass migrations in human history. Hundreds of thousands of people made their way to the remote Pacific Coast from across the United States and as far away as Europe and China in search of gold and filled with dreams of wealth and prosperity. The United States did not have any federal immigration laws at the time, and everyone was free to come. Most were welcomed.

However, the arrival of Chinese immigrants sparked a resentment that escalated into spasms of horrific violence, including the largest mass lynching in US history in Los Angeles in 1871. In the coming decades, anti-Chinese activists would barnstorm around the United States proclaiming that "whatever happens, the Chinese must go!" while politicians argued that the Chinese posed a grave danger to the white race in America. In a fit of racial exclusion, the open door for immigrants was soon slammed shut through the passage of discriminatory laws.

THE 49ERS

These monumental debates about the fundamental character of the United States were still decades away when James Marshall scooped that piece of gold out of the American River in 1848. Sutter and Marshall initially tried to keep the discovery a secret as they searched for more gold. Certainly, the representatives of Mexico and the United States who signed the Treaty of Guadalupe Hidalgo only a week after the find did not know of it. The treaty ended the Mexican-American War and transferred Sutter's Mill along with the entire state of Alta California from Mexico to the United States. In all, the United States took half of Mexico's territory, including the current US states of Arizona, Nevada, New Mexico, Texas, and Utah as well as parts of Colorado, Kansas, Oklahoma, and Wyoming.

Word of the discovery reached the small coastal village of San Francisco in May 1848 when a traveling merchant named Sam Brannan showed off a vial of gold dust at a saloon. Within days, half of the residents of San Francisco headed for the hills to search for their own fortune. The find was reported in East Coast newspapers in August, and President James Polk, looking to build more support for the colonization of the West Coast after the war, announced the discovery in December in a speech to Congress. By early 1849, the lure of riches in California sent prospectors from the eastern United States on their way to California. Eighty thousand fortune seekers set out for the wild, unknown Pacific Coast that year, increasing the European-American population eightfold and resulting in the name "the 49ers," which lives on through San Francisco's football team.

One of the 49ers was James McClatchy, a young immigrant from Ireland, whose son Valentine Stuart would become a prominent newspaper publisher and the president of the Associated Press, a perch he would use to lead the charge on a complete ban on Asian immigration to the United States at the turn of the century.[4] James McClatchy's early life had not foreshadowed that such an influential future might be possible for his family. He was born outside Belfast, Ireland, in 1824, and both his parents died by the time he was sixteen. Left without other options in Ireland, James and his two siblings took their chances on a boat bound for America.

Despite open immigration policies, the US population did not grow much in the early decades after independence. Many British loyalists left instead for Canada. In 1820, there were 8,385 new immigrants in the United States, and in 1830 still only 23,322.[5] Immigration began to increase in the 1830s as population growth and the enclosure of rural common lands in Europe sent masses of people into the slums of London, Glasgow, and Hamburg and eventually onto boats bound for New York and Boston. Most of these early immigrants to the United States were of the same English and German ancestry as the earlier colonists. In the decade of the 1830s, 143,000 people arrived. The McClatchys were among the 599,000 people who migrated in the 1840s, at the front end of the tidal wave of Irish immigrants driven to America by the Great Potato Famine.

With a shock of red hair, James was full of energy when he arrived at the ports of New York. Passports did not exist in 1841, so he took the opportunity to lie about his age, saying he was twenty in order to make himself more appealing to employers.[6] James marveled at the dizzying life of New York where wealth and opportunity were evident in the upscale neighborhoods. However, in the rapidly growing city, most new immigrants found themselves living in haphazardly constructed slums, while scam artists roamed the filthy streets looking to take advantage of immigrants' naive optimism. Tenements on the east side of Manhattan were the densest place in the world, with 290,000 people per square mile.[7] The immigrants, desperate for work, often found themselves being exploited by the businesses and new factories of the industrial era. Wages were low and many of the basic protections for workers that are taken for granted today, such as minimum wages, eight-hour workdays, weekends, and worker compensation for injuries, were still decades away. As James took jobs as a baker and a delivery driver, events were unfolding on the other side of the continent that would propel his life in consequential directions.

After waiting the required five years, James was naturalized as a US citizen in 1846 and soon dove into politics. Having experienced poverty as a child in Ireland, he was a critic of the enclosure of common lands to create private property that was occurring across Europe and North America, and he passionately advocated for the poor, a mission that would continue throughout his life. James found that he shared this interest with Horace Greeley, the editor of the *New York Tribune*. James became friends with the influential editor, who was a decade his senior, and took a job at the paper in 1846.

In the 1840s, Greeley was emerging as a key voice for reform in what was becoming the primary city in the United States. Greeley had a knack for writing pieces that were pointedly political and moving but also plainly stated and accessible to less sophisticated readers.[8] He was a workaholic and a stickler for grammar and spelling who attributed his eccentric behavior to the myth that as a baby he had not breathed for a full twenty minutes after he was born. He founded the *New York Tribune* the same year McClatchy arrived in New York, and Greeley used his new platform to argue against slavery while promoting the writings of his friends such as Henry David Thoreau and Ralph Waldo Emerson. A biographer later wrote that Greeley "helped fuel the Second American Revolution, transforming the liberty of the first American Revolution into the freedom and equality forged in the fires of Civil War."[9] At the end of his life, Greeley briefly served in the US House of Representatives and ran for president in 1872, in a failed bid to oust Ulysses S. Grant. He was the nominee of the Liberal Republican Party, in an alliance with the Democratic Party, but he only won Texas, Kentucky, Tennessee, and Maryland, which gave him 66 Electoral College votes to Grant's 286. Greeley died before the Electoral College met, so all of his electors voted for someone else.

It was on Greeley's famous advice to "go west, young man," that James McClatchy set out for California in February 1849, with a dream of striking it rich. Anything seemed better than the dirty, crowded existence in New York, and the *Tribune* agreed to pay him five dollars per article he wrote while documenting his journey. With high hopes he could secure a quick fortune in California, James departed in February on the schooner

John Castner, one of the first boats to leave that winter, blissfully unaware of the pitfalls that lay in his path.

THE JOURNEY WEST

Just getting to California was a daunting task in the 1840s, with the plight of the Donner Party a few years earlier seared into the minds of Americans. The intercontinental railroad would not be built for twenty more years, so for many the journey meant joining a wagon train on the California Trail. The overland route required months of grueling travel through lands that would become the states of Nebraska, Wyoming, Idaho, Utah, and Nevada. Disease, starvation, and inclement weather were a constant risk. The Donner Party was caught by an early snowstorm in the Sierra Nevada Mountains in 1846 and were unable to travel the final stretch of the California Trail to Sutter's Fort, which was tantalizingly close but completely cut off by drifts of heavy snow. Rescue parties from the fort attempted but failed to reach the families who had set up makeshift camps by Truckee Lake, leading to a winter of starvation and death. Thirty-nine people died, and most of the remaining forty-eight resorted to cannibalism to survive. The newspaper reports about the horrors of the Donner Party slowed migration to California in the years before Marshall struck gold. While in 1846, about 1,500 people made the trip, it declined to 450 in 1847 and only 400 in 1848.

Given this preceding tragedy, James McClatchy's party of prospectors looked for alternative routes and ultimately opted to sail part of the way. The Panama Canal was still decades away from opening, so sailing to California required crossing the malarial jungles of Panama on foot or going all the way around South America. However, there was a third option: sailing to Brownsville, Texas, and then trekking overland through Mexico. On April 20, 1849, McClatchy filed a story with the *Tribune* from Mazatlán about the novel route, warning of its difficulty. He recommended his readers to "not give up any employment worth having" and if they did go, to steel their nerves before the trip. He suggested that for anyone but the hardiest travelers it might be a better choice to sail around South America or go through Panama. If they did take the Mexico route, he implored them to not only buy a good-quality mule but also keep their pistol exposed on their hip at all times to warn off any thieves. Nevertheless, the dispatch has an air of relief to it, as if the worst was behind him.

In Mazatlán, James's party bought a schooner called the *Dolphin* from another party of prospectors who had sailed up the coast from South America. The fact that the other party was selling it and buying a different ship for the final leg of the journey to San Francisco should have given James's party pause. They quickly discovered why when they set sail. The *Dolphin* had a leaky, shallow hull that was not designed to face the waves and wind of the Pacific Ocean. Coupled with an inexperienced captain, they made little progress each day and at times were even pushed back toward Mazatlán. Their situation further deteriorated when they discovered that the freshwater barrels in the hold were contaminated by an oil in the wood.

Frustrated by the slow progress and worried about dwindling supplies, McClatchy and most of the passengers opted to disembark and walk the remaining distance up the Baja California coast to San Diego, the same desolate and dangerous routes taken by migrants today. Without mules to carry them, their shoes were shredded by the sharp rocks within days, and the searing summer heat forced them to consume much more water than they anticipated. Parched and without supplies, they ate cactus, rattlesnakes, and rodents as they staggered north, finally arriving in San Diego after twenty-six days, sunburned and sobered to the reality of the wilds of the Pacific Coast.[10] Miraculously, they all survived. The *Dolphin* limped into the San Diego port a few days after them, but James and his fellow trekkers made the wise decision not to reboard the vessel. It was lost at sea a few weeks later on the next leg of the journey to San Francisco.

After recuperating from the harrowing brush with death in the desert, James made his way to the new town of Sacramento that had grown up around Sutter's Fort. He finally arrived in August 1849, seven grueling months after he had left Horace Greeley and his other friends in New York. Once again, McClatchy found himself in a boomtown like the one he had experienced in New York, but in Sacramento there was no infrastructure yet. The masses of prospectors arriving in California that year drove the population from 150 in April to six thousand in October. The muddy and deeply rutted streets reeked of dung and dead animals. Churches and saloons alike sprung up to lure in the new arrivals, and land was scarce after speculators bought up large chunks and then charged exorbitant prices. Devastating floods swept through the unplanned town in 1850, and a cholera epidemic in the fall killed seven hundred people, 10 percent of the population.

McClatchy quickly understood that the dream of finding gold was a mirage. James Marshall himself was never even able to capitalize on his find, and within a few years he retreated to a hermit's cabin in the woods to lead a solitary life. Nonetheless, for McClatchy, Sacramento proved to be a place with a myriad of stories to tell and very few reporters to tell them. He used his newspaper experience to get a job with the *Placer Times* and built his reputation by reporting on the contentious process of turning the unruly gold rush boomtown of Sacramento into an orderly state capital. James cycled through jobs at several other papers before 1857, the same year his first son, Valentine Stuart, was born, when he took over the *Sacramento Daily Bee* newspaper. One of James's first stories was an exposé on financial misdeeds by the California state treasurer that led to the impeachment of the official.[11] James settled into his role of editor and built the *Bee* into the premier paper in California's capital.

THE LOS ANGELES MASSACRE

The tragedy of the Donner Party and the ordeal of James McClatchy's band of prospectors made clear the perils and length of the journey from the eastern states, but it was a much shorter trip for ships from China to reach California, and soon new trade routes opened up across the Pacific. The Opium Wars and famine in southeastern China, particularly around Hong Kong, made life challenging at the time, and some young Chinese men opted to test their luck in prospecting on the other side of the Pacific Ocean. In 1830, the US Census recorded only three Chinese people living in the country.[12] In 1851, 2,716 people arrived from China, while in 1852 it shot up to 20,026. The Chinese were free to immigrate to the United States, but what they found in the wilds of California was not an open and welcoming country.

Frustrated miners from the eastern United States blamed their lack of success at finding gold on the increased competition from the Chinese. An 1855 report in the *Annals of San Francisco* laid out the common perception of the Chinese: "The manners and habits of the Chinese are very repugnant to Americans in California. Of different language, blood, religion and character, inferior in most mental and bodily qualities, the Chinaman is looked upon by some as only a little superior to the negro, and by others as somewhat inferior."[13] The Chinese were accused of undercutting the wages of whites, bringing vices of prostitution and opium, and possibly being the vanguard of a Chinese invasion of North America.

Initially, the state of California instituted a series of laws designed to discourage Chinese immigration, even as the constitutionality of those laws was questionable. In 1849, the US Supreme Court had struck down immigration laws imposed by Massachusetts and New York in a ruling known as the Passenger Cases, finding that only the federal government could impose restrictions on immigration. The California laws included rules to prevent Chinese entry but also to make life difficult for the Chinese already in California. For example, in 1852, California passed a law that levied a monthly tax on foreign miners and greatly reduced their profits, driving them to work in other sectors such as opening laundries, restaurants, and shops. Many Chinese gathered in San Francisco, establishing Chinatown as a friendly neighborhood in the unfriendly city. As the lack of gold slowed the gold rush in the late 1850s, many of the Chinese opted to stay and found work in construction jobs. In the 1860s, the US Congress funded railroad companies' efforts to connect the Pacific Coast to the East, and Chinese workers were critical to the effort, accounting for 90 percent of the Union Pacific labor force.[14] They were paid less, worked longer hours, and were given more dangerous jobs than white Americans, but the wages were still better than what they could get in China, so more workers continued to arrive. By 1880, there were 105,000 Chinese people in the entire United States, which amounted to only 0.2 percent of the total population. However, people from China were clustered in California and represented 10 percent of the state's population at the time.[15]

The antagonism toward the Chinese boiled over in Los Angeles on a cool October evening in 1871. As the sun went down, Dr. Chien Lee "Gene" Tong was finishing his day's work in his small storefront office in the Coronel Building. As the only Chinese doctor in the city, Dr. Tong stayed busy treating a wide range of ailments using traditional Chinese medicine. He was well respected throughout LA but chose to live and practice medicine in a worn-down building in the Chinese quarter. The tight alley was known for its gambling halls and brothels and was lined with squat white windowless adobe buildings, which contrasted with the newer two-story brick warehouses on the adjacent Los Angeles Street.[16] In 1871, Los Angeles was not yet the sprawling metropolis it is today. The 1870 census only counted 5,728 people, of which 172 were Chinese.

There was tension in the air that evening as Dr. Tong tidied his office before heading to his residence in the same building. Over the preceding days, two rival Chinese businessmen, Yo Hing and Sam Yuen, were engaged in an escalating conflict that had resulted in multiple police visits to the Chinese quarter. On the evening of October 21, Jesus Bilderrain, one of only six police officers in Los Angeles, was having a drink in Higby's saloon when he heard a gunshot. He rushed to the Chinese quarter to investigate and found a man named Ah Choy, who had only been released from police custody an hour earlier, lying in the street with a gunshot to his neck. As Bilderrain tended to Choy, the businessman Sam Yuen and an associate came out of the Coronel Building and shot at, but missed, the police officer. Bilderrain gave chase and ran into the building. Moments later, he staggered back out without a hat or pistol and with a gunshot to his shoulder. A local rancher, Robert Thompson, came to the officer's aid and soon charged into the Coronel Building, where he was met by a volley of shots. He crumpled and fell back into the street and said, "I am killed." He died an hour later while being treated at Wollweber's drugstore a few blocks away.[17]

As word spread of the shootings of Bilderrain and Thompson, a mob of five hundred people, almost 10 percent of Los Angeles's population, descended on the Chinese quarter looking for revenge against the Chinese. They were "determined to clean them out of the city," as the first *New York Times* report about the incident put it.[18] After seeing the size of the crowd and their growing rage, the remaining Los Angeles police officers melted away. The chief of police reportedly retired to bed for the night. The Chinese residents, including Dr. Tong, barricaded themselves in buildings along the street. By the time the mob arrived, the men involved in the original shooting had already fled the area. Only innocent bystanders remained, but the mob was whipped into a frenzy and out for blood. White men grabbed axes from a nearby dry goods store and methodically chopped holes in the roofs of the buildings and then shot randomly inside. As wounded Chinese men stumbled out of the buildings, a woman watching the riot began to shout, "Hang them!" and offered some twine for a noose. A ten-year-old boy ran back to the dry goods shop and returned with ropes. The boy then climbed up on the awning of a nearby wagon shop on Los Angeles Street to hang the rope for a lynching.

Dr. Tong hid in his shop in the Coronel Building hoping to avoid the carnage surrounding him. When the mob found him and dragged him out into the street, he begged for his life, wagering that his station in society would spare him. He desperately offered $3,000 ($65,000 adjusted for inflation [AFI]) cash and the diamond ring on his finger if they showed him mercy. Instead, a man in the crowd shot Dr. Tong in the mouth to get him to shut up and tried to take the ring off his finger. It was stuck, so he just cut off the whole finger. Dr. Tong's desecrated body hung from the wagon shop roof partially naked because someone else had removed his pants in search of the $3,000 he mentioned. When there was no more space on the wagon shop roof, ropes were rigged up on two covered wagons out front. In just a few hours, all of the Chinese businesses in the city were looted and destroyed, and seventeen Chinese men had been lynched. When the dust settled that night, the Los Angeles Massacre of 1871 was, and still is, the largest mass lynching in the history of the United States.

"BY WHITE MEN, FOR WHITE MEN"

Back in the bustling city of New York that James McClatchy had left behind, the rising anti-Chinese sentiments on the distant and still sparsely populated West Coast in the 1850s to 1870s did not resonate. In the 1850s, there was a brief nativist movement called the Know-Nothings, who demonized the Catholicism of the new Irish immigrants, but Horace Greeley and other newspaper editors were preoccupied with the issue of slavery in the lead-up to the Civil War. The founding paradox of the United States was yet to be resolved as the idea that "all men are created equal" rubbed up against the horrific reality of slavery and white supremacy. As Horace Greeley wrote in 1854 in the *New York Tribune*, "We are not one people. We are two peoples. We are a people for Freedom and a people for Slavery. Between the two, conflict is inevitable."[19] As Greeley predicted, the differences between North and South proved intractable and the Civil War began in 1861. As the war raged, President Abraham Lincoln framed the conflict in the moral terms of emancipation. The

Union forces of the North won but only after the deaths of over 600,000 people, or 2 percent of the US population at the time.

After the Civil War, the idea that the United States was primarily a white country faced an inflection point. In the years before the Civil War, there was a concerted effort to protect the idea that America was only for whites. In 1857, the US Supreme Court decided in the *Dred Scott* case that even free African Americans were not eligible for citizenship in the United States. Roger Taney, the chief justice of the Supreme Court, wrote in the decision that "it is too clear for dispute that the enslaved African race were not intended to be included, and formed no part of the people who framed and adopted this declaration [of Independence]."[20] In 1860, Jefferson Davis, at the time a Mississippi senator and soon to be the president of the breakaway Confederate States of America, said that the United States was founded "by white men, for white men."[21]

The defeat of the Confederacy seemed to signal a new beginning. The institution of slavery ended and a society with equality for all, as was promised in the founding documents of the country, was momentarily visible on the horizon. In quick succession, the Civil Rights Act of 1866 declared everyone born in the United States citizens, the Thirteenth Amendment to the Constitution banned slavery except for prisoners, and the Fourteenth Amendment guaranteed equal protection under the law. In 1870, the US naturalization law was revised to include "aliens of African nativity" and "persons of African descent" in the description of who was eligible for citizenship, although the phrase "free white person" remained in the law well into the twentieth century.

Despite these changes, there was a countereffort to protect the white social order that had begun to slip away. The first way the white order was protected in the years after the Civil War was through a system of forced labor that looked a lot like slavery. Justices of the peace across the South used vagrancy laws to round up Black men who were often simply traveling from one place to another.[22] When they could not pay the fine, they were put in prison and then, based on the exception to the ban on slavery for prisoners in the Thirteenth Amendment, they were loaned out to farms and factories to work in poor conditions as slaves. By the 1880s, Jim Crow laws institutionalized segregation across the South under the notion of separate but equal, which was upheld by the Supreme Court in the

1896 *Plessy v. Ferguson* decision. Segregation maintained white dominance through the 1960s until it was challenged in the civil rights movement.

The second way the white order was protected was to encourage free Black people in the United States to leave. The American Colonization Society was founded in 1816 with the mission of helping freed slaves return to Africa. The colony of Liberia on the West African coast was established to provide a home for former slaves, and it was supported by Thomas Jefferson and James Madison, who even served as the society's president in the 1830s. Even as Jefferson occasionally contemplated an end to slavery, he did not envision a mixed-race America, writing in his *Notes on the State of Virginia* that "when freed, he [the slave] is to be removed beyond the reach of mixture."[23] After the Civil War, the idea of sending former slaves back to Africa gained credence, and the society was funded by the Freedman's Bureau. Over the years, the American Colonization Society provided logistics for thirteen thousand freed slaves to sail to Liberia; the organization did not actually disband until 1964.[24]

The third way the white order was protected in the post–Civil War era was to make sure no more nonwhite people could come to the United States. In the early 1870s, almost a century after the country was established, the United States still lacked any federal laws that limited immigration, although California and a few other states were testing whether state-level immigration restrictions were constitutional. However, that was all about to change as the western states' fears about Chinese immigration seeped into eastern political debates about race in the United States. Maine senator, two-time secretary of state, and three-time presidential candidate James G. Blaine explained in 1879, "I supposed if the admonitions of our own history were anything to us, we should regard the race trouble as the one thing to be dreaded and the one thing to be avoided." For Blaine, it was madness to "deliberately sit down and allow" another race problem to emerge through the arrival of the Chinese. Instead, he counseled another option: "It is a good deal cheaper . . . to avoid the trouble by preventing the immigration."[25]

— CHAPTER 2 —

LEWD AND DEBAUCHED

With her hair pulled back and dressed in her best gown, Chy Lung boarded the *SS Japan* in Hong Kong on July 25, 1874, in preparation for the long sea journey to San Francisco. The Pacific Mail Steamship Company began regular trips between San Francisco and Hong Kong in 1867, bringing overcrowded ships full of Chinese laborers to the United States and depositing a few American missionaries in Hong Kong on the return trip.[1] The voyage across the vast Pacific Ocean was long and monotonous, often taking more than a month to complete. There were comfortable cabins on the upper decks with viewing platforms to take in the fresh sea breezes and multiple dining halls, but Chy Lung and most of the Chinese passengers opted for steerage berths below decks. Steerage was much cheaper and provided a venue for cooking familiar foods together, rather than partaking in the expensive cuisine provided by the ship's kitchens.

Accounts of the journey by Americans on board often emphasized the exotic nature of the Chinese passengers in dehumanizing terms. A *New York Times* correspondent described the two hundred Chinese men on an 1861 journey saying, "Most of them seemed to be of the lowest class, filthy in their habits, covered with vermin, and with no more baggage than a couple of bamboos." The correspondent recounted a fight that broke out between two Chinese men that initially spiraled out of control. Stopping the melee "for the first few minutes was beyond the power of man, for the whole hive of Chinamen were yelling, screeching, fighting, scratching and biting like so many wild animals." Order was restored, the correspondent writes, when the white crew intervened, "but Anglo-Saxon muscle finally prevailed, and finding a more vigorous enemy had taken the field, the original combatants yielded."[2] This was the milieu that Chy Lung was about to enter as she sailed across the Pacific in the summer of 1874.

Chy Lung's ship, the *SS Japan*, could carry fifty first-class passengers and 908 steerage passengers in triple-stacked open bunks around the engine. Even with the large steerage capacity, the captains of the Pacific Mail Steamship Company often squeezed in more to maximize their profits. In 1873, the *SS Japan* was cited by authorities for carrying 451 passengers more than its capacity during a voyage from Hong Kong to San Francisco.[3] Chy Lung's voyage was mercifully nowhere near as crowded. There were six hundred Chinese passengers aboard the *SS Japan*, of which eighty-nine were women. Most of the women were traveling with their husbands or family, but Chy Lung was one of the twenty-two Chinese women traveling alone.[4]

When the *SS Japan* arrived in San Francisco on August 24 after the thirty-day voyage across the Pacific, Rudolph Piotrowski, the commissioner of immigration for the state of California, boarded the vessel at the docks. Almost a century after the Declaration of Independence, the United States did not have any federal immigration laws, but that was about to change. However, several states, including California, established their own immigration rules. California had recently amended the state code to give immigration commissioners like Piotrowski vast authority to search for contraband in the luggage of passengers but also to exclude people that were deemed undesirable in California. The list of potential reasons the commissioner of immigration could deny entry to noncitizens was long: anyone who is "lunatic, idiotic, deaf, dumb, blind, crippled, or infirm, and is not accompanied by relatives who are able and willing to support him, or is likely to become permanently a public charge, . . . [has] sickness or disease, . . . is a convicted criminal, or a lewd or debauched woman."[5]

Rudolph Piotrowski was an immigrant from Poland himself and, at 6'6", an unusually tall man for his era. He stooped his head as he moved around the interior of the vessel. Piotrowski surveyed the crowd of Chinese but quickly focused his attention on Chy Lung and the twenty-one other unaccompanied women. After cursory questions, he decided all of them were "lewd or debauched women" and denied them entry into the city and, by extension, the entire United States. There was no hearing or other recourse for the women except for the ship's captain to pay a $500 ($11,700 AFI) bond per person that would be held by the state for two years to ensure that the women were never arrested or became charges of the state. The statute governing the inspector was curious because it allowed the inspector to personally keep 20 percent of all fines they levied, providing a clear incentive to detain more people.[6]

John Freeman, the captain of the *SS Japan*, declined to pay the bond that would have allowed Chy Lung and the other women to be released. The less costly option for him was to take them back to Hong Kong on what would be a mostly empty return voyage anyway. However, the next morning a local business owner named Ah Lung, who had likely arranged for the women to come to San Francisco to work for him, had a lawyer file petitions for a writ of habeas corpus for the women. As that was adjudicated, the San Francisco sheriff had no other option but to move the women off the ship. The *SS Japan* then departed San Francisco and safely made its return trip to Hong Kong. A few months later it would burn at sea and sink somewhere between Yokohama and Hong Kong on December 18, 1874.[7]

RESTRICTIONS ON THE POOR

As Chy Lung and the other women sat idly in the San Francisco jail in the fall of 1874 while the habeas corpus petitions made their way through the courts, there were no federal immigration restrictions in the United States, but there was a long history of nativism and local and state limits on immigration. From the time when the first Europeans set foot in the Americas, early settlements and colonies established their own rules to prevent the entry of other people, most frequently targeting Catholics, the poor, and the infirm. The California statutes were the latest, and the last as it would turn out, in a long string of similar local- and state-level legislation.

Within a few years of establishing the Massachusetts Bay Colony in 1630, the Puritans enacted a law limiting the entry of "strangers . . . with intent to reside." The governor of the colony, John Winthrop, wrote in a court document in 1637 defending the law: "If the place of our co-habitation be our owne, then no man hath a right to come into us without our consent. . . . If we are bound to keep off whatsoever appears to tend to our ruine or damage, then may we lawfully refuse to receive such whose dispositions suite not with ours and whose society (we know) will be hurtful to us."[8] In the 1640s and 1650s, towns in the Massachusetts colony were given the right to eject strangers who were not able to support themselves economically in a set of laws that mirrored the poor laws that had limited the movement of workers in England since the late 1500s. In 1647, Massachusetts also made entry without permission a crime for Jesuit priests, who were thought to be encouraging Native Americans to fight against the colony. The punishment was banishment for the first violation and death for the second.[9] Quakers were banned in 1656 under threat of whipping and death if the law was violated. Laws were passed in 1700 and 1722 that placed the onus on ship captains to provide a bond for any infirm or ill passengers that arrived to ensure that the costs of their care were not borne by the colony.[10]

From the start, it was not all immigration that worried the leaders of the colonies. Instead, they encouraged some people to come while preventing others. The Massachusetts colony passed laws to encourage more Protestant immigration, which was reinforced by the British government's Plantation Act of 1740. In the lead-up to the Revolutionary War, the British government tried to limit immigration to the colonies, a fact that was mentioned twice in the Declaration of Independence. The rebels accused the king of England of having "endeavored to prevent the population of these States; for that purpose obstructing the Laws for Naturalization of Foreigners; refusing to pass others to encourage their migrations hither," and later, "For cutting off our Trade with all parts of the world." In essence, one of the key complaints of the American Revolution was that the British were closing the borders to the colonies in order to weaken them.

After the United States was established, the Constitution prevented Congress from instituting any limits on the entry of people into the United States until 1808. The Constitution guaranteed free movement, but the clause was primarily designed to protect the slave trade from any restrictions.[11] The Tenth Amendment of the US Constitution leaves all issues not explicitly reserved for the federal government as the domain of individual states. Since the Constitution did not address immigration after 1808, many interpreted that to mean that immigration rules were up to the states, and several began to enact their own regulations about who could enter their territory. Most of these state-level immigration limits were similar to the earlier colonial bans and focused on denying entry to the poor and the sick, who were seen as a drain on state resources and therefore undesirable. The impetus for many of these laws was not about limiting immigration per se, but protecting state coffers from expenditures to care for the sick or the poor.

The cities of Boston and New York were the primary ports on the East Coast and received the vast majority of new arrivals from Europe. New York and Massachusetts were also the two primary states that attempted local immigration restrictions.[12] In 1820, Massachusetts passed "An Act to Prevent the Introduction of Paupers, from Foreign Ports or Places" and in 1837 "an Alien Passenger Act."[13] Between the 1830s and 1880s, the state of Massachusetts expelled fifty thousand people back to Ireland, but that accounted for less than 1 percent of those who arrived in the United States over that period. None of the other colonies had nearly as many arrivals as Massachusetts and New York and therefore they did not enact any limits. New Jersey even positioned its ports as a way around the New York limits, allowing people to disembark in New Jersey and then head across the Hudson River to Manhattan.

In the South, a completely different set of fears drove early immigration regulations. Although the importation of slaves to the United States ended in 1808, slavery continued in the South through the Civil War. There were already slave rebellions happening in the Caribbean, and slave owners were concerned that people arriving in port cities could sow the seeds of rebellion. These fears increased after the successful revolution in Haiti in 1804. One of the first slave rebellions in the United States was led by Denmark Vesey, a free Black man who lived in Charleston, South Carolina. In 1822, he was accused of planning a rebellion in which he would lead a group that would kill slave owners, free the slaves, and then sail together to Haiti. The plot was discovered and Vesey and other alleged planners were tried and executed.

The South Carolina legislature became concerned that other free Blacks could organize similar rebellions as they networked with free people in the North and in the Caribbean. Consequently, the slave laws were rewritten to ban free Blacks from returning to South Carolina if they left. In 1822, South Carolina, followed quickly by Georgia and Virginia, instituted a ban on "Negro seamen" at its ports and required the local sheriff to jail any free Black seamen that arrived until the ship departed.[14] The ship's captain was obligated to pay the cost of the incarceration, and if they did not, the man could be sold into slavery.

This arrangement was immediately contested in the courts. Henry Elkison was a British citizen who was placed in jail when he arrived in Charleston in 1823 by the local sheriff, Francis Deliesseline.[15] The British government paid for the litigation and argued that an 1815 trade agreement between the two countries guaranteed the right of free movement for all British citizens regardless of their race. The lawyers for South Carolina argued that it was a state's rights issue, just as would be argued in defense of slavery itself in the lead-up to the Civil War. A US federal court ruled in favor of Elkison in the first instance of the commerce clause of the Constitution being used to invalidate a state statute. However, the ruling also found that federal courts did not have the authority to grant a writ of habeas corpus for a state prison, so Elkison remained in jail until his ship left the port. Although the statute was invalidated, South Carolina opted to ignore the ruling and continued to lock up free Blacks at its ports through the Civil War.[16]

The question of whether individual states or the federal government could make immigration laws first came before the US Supreme Court in 1837. A captain of a ship was fined $15,000 ($440,000 AFI) for transporting people who were deemed inadmissible by the state of New York. He sued, arguing that the state fines violated the federal government's constitutional role to regulate international commerce. The Supreme Court ruled in *New York v. Miln* that the state-level restrictions were legal, stating, "The law is not a commercial regulation, in the sense contemplated in the constitution; but a police regulation. It is a part of the system of poor laws, and intended to prevent the introduction of foreign paupers."[17] For the time being, states were free to impose immigration limits if there was a policing purpose.

In 1849, several similar objections to taxes on passengers in New York and Massachusetts again reached the US Supreme Court in what came to be known as the Passenger Cases. The Supreme Court overturned their previous precedent in a split 5–4 decision with eight different concurring or dissenting opinions from the justices. The majority decided that according to the US Constitution, the federal government alone had the right to regulate interstate commerce, including immigration issues. Therefore, the state-level limits were unconstitutional.

ANTI-CHINESE LAWS IN CALIFORNIA

The ambiguous result of the Passenger Cases, with so many different concurring and dissenting opinions, came in the same year that James McClatchy and the other 49ers were racing across the continent in search of gold in California. After California became a state in 1850, local authorities tried a series of measures to discourage arrivals from China (see table 1). The California law that locked up Chy Lung in 1874 was only the latest attempt by the state to prevent the arrival of the Chinese. In 1854, the California Supreme Court ruled that Chinese people were ineligible to testify against whites.[18] In 1855, California passed "An Act to Discourage the Immigration to This State of Persons Who Cannot Become Citizens" that imposed a fifty-dollar tax on people who arrived by ship but were not eligible for naturalization. The California Supreme Court ruled in 1857 that these rules were unconstitutional based on the Passenger Cases decision.[19] In 1858, California passed another act "To Prevent the Further Immigration of Chinese or Mongolians to This State," but it was also ruled unconstitutional in 1862. In 1860, a fishing tax was placed on Chinese people, but it was ruled to violate the commerce clause of the Constitution. San Francisco banned Chinese children in public schools, and Chinese people were not allowed to go to the city hospital. In 1862, California passed an Anti-Coolie Act, and the state legislature passed the California Police Tax, which required Chinese people working in industries other than rice, sugar, tea, or coffee production to pay $2.50 per month.[20] The California Supreme Court also ruled that these statutes violated the commerce clause of the US Constitution.[21]

The Burlingame Treaty of 1868, which established diplomatic relations between the United States and China, further limited the ability of western states to prevent Chinese immigration. In Washington, DC, the focus was primarily on strengthening trade with China. The Chinese

TABLE 1: *Anti-Chinese laws in California*

YEAR	NAME	PURPOSE
1850	Foreign Miners Tax, California	$20 per month tax, repealed 1851
1852	Foreign Miners License Tax, California	$3 per month, unconstitutional in 1870
1854	California Supreme Court ruled Chinese people cannot testify against whites	Reversed by state law in 1873
1855	Act to Discourage the Immigration to This State of Persons Who Cannot Become Citizens	Unconstitutional 1857
1855	Capitation Tax Ordinance	$50 tax at dock for individuals not eligible for naturalization, San Francisco, unconstitutional 1856
1858	An Act to Prevent the Further Immigration of Chinese or Mongolians to This State, California	Unconstitutional 1858
1860	Fishing tax, California	$4 monthly on Chinese, repealed 1864
1860	San Francisco City Ordinance	No Chinese children in public schools, San Francisco
1860	San Francisco City Ordinance	No Chinese in city hospital, San Francisco
1862	An Act to Protect Free White Labor against Competition with Chinese Coolie Labor, California	$2.50 per month on Chinese people not involved in rice, sugar, tea, or coffee production. Unconstitutional California constitution, 1863
1870	An Act to Prevent Kidnapping and Importing of Mongolian, Chinese, and Japanese Females for Criminal Purposes	Precursor to the Page Act of 1875
1870	An Act to Stop Hiring Chinese	No Chinese employees, San Francisco municipality
1870	San Francisco Sidewalk Ordinance	Ban on carrying vegetables on poles, San Francisco

(continues)

TABLE 1: *Anti-Chinese laws in California* (continued)

YEAR	NAME	PURPOSE
1870	San Francisco Cubic Air Ordinance	Ordinance requiring 500 ft³ of air in rooms, San Francisco
1873	San Francisco Laundry Tax	Tax on laundries without a vehicle
1873	San Francisco Gong Ordinance	Ban on gongs at ceremonies, San Francisco
1875	San Francisco Ceremony Ordinance	Ban on firecrackers at ceremonies, San Francisco
1875	San Francisco Fishing Ordinance	Law to limit shrimp net size, San Francisco
1875	Anti-queue law, San Francisco	Cut men's hair if arrested, ruled unconstitutional
1879	Changes to California state constitution	Banned municipal governments from hiring Chinese, imposed limits on people who could not be naturalized as citizens, unconstitutional 1880
1880	Fishing Act, California	Ban on Chinese in fishing industry, unconstitutional 1880
1880	Act to Prevent Issuance of Licenses to Aliens	Ban on business licenses for Chinese
1880	Anti-ironing ordinance, San Francisco	Attempt to shut Chinese laundries

immigration issue that was roiling western politics was not yet a national issue. In fact, the fifth article of the treaty recognized the "inalienable right" of free movement: "The United States of America and the Emperor of China cordially recognize the inherent and inalienable right of man to change his home and allegiance, and also the mutual advantage of the free migration and emigration of their citizens and subjects respectively from the one country to the other for purposes of curiosity, of trade, or as permanent residents."[22] Prior to this, it was against Chinese law to emigrate, and those who traveled to the United States were from the restive southern provinces around Hong Kong, far from the center of power in Beijing. In the fourteen years between the signing of the Burlingame Treaty and the

Chinese Exclusion Act, the treaty would be cited to overturn or veto multiple laws to prevent Chinese immigration into the United States.

From 1870 to 1875, San Francisco banned hiring Chinese for city contracts, using poles to carry vegetables, setting off firecrackers, and using gongs in ceremonies. The city also put in place ordinances that required 500 ft³ of air within buildings to try to reduce density in Chinatown and a tax on laundries that used horse-drawn carts. These regulations were meant to prevent Chinese people from immigrating to California while also making their lives difficult if they did come in order to encourage them to leave.

The Chinese were frequently accused of being the vanguard of an invasion force that would turn the West into a Chinese colony, a claim perhaps fueled by some uncritical introspection on the part of white settlers who were themselves an invasion force that defeated Mexico and displaced Native Americans to claim the territory. The physical appearance of Chinese men was often held up as an example of their continued loyalty to the emperor of China. At the time, the emperor required all Chinese men to wear a "queue," a haircut that involved shaving their heads except for a long braid down their backs. White settlers noted that Chinese men continued to wear their hair in this way in America, which to them was a signal of their true loyalties to China. For many Chinese, however, it was a pragmatic choice. If they ever wanted to travel back to China to visit their families, they would be arrested if they cut their queue, so many kept it just in case. Nevertheless, San Francisco passed a law banning the haircut for prisoners in 1876, requiring men to cut their hair within one inch of their scalp. There were many Chinese men already in jail for violating other anti-Chinese ordinances who had refused, on principle, to pay the fines. One of the prisoners, Ho Ah Kow, challenged the jail's haircut rule; it was ruled to violate the equal protection clause of the Fourteenth Amendment of the Constitution.[23]

Despite the effort by politicians from California and other western states to raise the issue, the arrival of the Chinese did not register in the eastern United States until 1869. The completion of the transcontinental railroad that year opened up the Pacific Coast and made it possible to imagine people from China making the trip east. That summer a number of business owners met in Memphis, Tennessee, to discuss importing Chinese workers to replace lost slave labor. The Chinese were described like a commodity: hardworking, compliant, and cheap. The event, along with a marketing effort by import agents in San Francisco, generated lurid newspaper headlines, but no Chinese workers were actually moved across the country in 1869.[24] The following year, a factory owner in North Adams, Massachusetts, was the first to bring contract labor from China to work in his factory in order to break a strike by unionized workers. Few others followed suit, although some used the specter of Chinese contract workers to elicit concessions from workers. This was an era of increasing immigration from Europe and population growth in the United States. The reality was that there were plenty of workers already and no real need to resort to what was perceived as a more risky option of bringing Chinese workers. In 1870, the California delegation in Congress led an effort to ban the importation of Chinese laborers, but it failed.

The issue faded, as very few people from China actually left California and other western states and territories. However, in December 1874, while Chy Lung remained in the San Francisco jail as her case made its way through the courts, President Ulysses S. Grant spoke publicly against contract labor from China and linked it to the fear of prostitutes being brought into the country. In his annual address to Congress, Grant said,

> I call the attention of Congress to a generally conceded fact that the great proportion of the Chinese immigrants who come to our shores do not come voluntarily to make their homes with us and their labor productive of general prosperity, but come under contracts with head-men who own them almost absolutely. In a worse form does this apply to Chinese women. Hardly a perceptible percentage of them perform any honorable labor, but they are brought for shameful purposes, to the disgrace of communities where settled and to the great demoralization of the youth of these localities. If this evil practice is legislated against, it will be my pleasure as well as duty to enforce any regulations to secure a desirable end.[25]

The legacy of slavery is evident in Grant's position, which he framed as protecting the poor from the exploitation of unscrupulous employers who would use their debts to force them into work in conditions akin to slavery. However, rather than focusing on the employers, the enforcement fell squarely on the Chinese.

THE FIRST NATIONAL IMMIGRATION LAW

Back in San Francisco, Chy Lung probably knew nothing of President Grant's speech and the growing support for restrictions on Chinese immigration. Her case moved through the courts, reaching the US Supreme Court in 1875. It was a significant moment because it was the first time that a case involving anyone of Asian ancestry was heard before the court, but it was a one-sided affair because no one from the state of California showed up to defend the ordinance. The opinion was delivered on October 1, 1875, by Associate Justice Samuel Freeman Miller, who was appointed to the US Supreme Court by Abraham Lincoln in 1862. From today's vantage point of highly politicized and contentious nomination fights over Supreme Court justices, it is difficult to believe, but Miller was confirmed by the Senate to the lifetime appointment on the court only thirty minutes after his nomination was delivered to the Senate. He served until his death in 1890.

Justice Miller found the California ordinance inadequate because it violated the rights of liberty guaranteed in the Constitution. He cited many examples of people who would fall afoul of the ordinance but who would be valuable members of society, including

> the blind, or the deaf, or the dumb passenger is subject to contribution, whether he be a rich man or a pauper. The patriot, seeking out shores after an unsuccessful struggle against despotism in Europe or Asia, may be kept out because there his resistance has been adjudged a crime. The woman whose error has been repaired by a happy marriage and numerous children, and whose loving husband brings her with his wealth to a new home, may be told she must pay a round sum before she can land, because it is alleged that she was debauched by her husband before marriage. Whether a young woman's manners are such as to justify the commissioner in calling her lewd may be made to depend on the sum she will pay for the privilege of landing in San Francisco.[26]

The ruling presages the concept of a refugee that would be developed in the twentieth century.

After laying out the flaws in the law, Miller concluded, "In any view which we can take of this statute, it is in conflict with the Constitution of the United States, and therefore void." Chy Lung and the other women were freed, and in conjunction with another decision in *Henderson v. Mayor of the City of New York* on the same day, the Supreme Court definitively ruled that immigration regulation was the domain of the federal government.

The ruling in Chy Lung's case confirmed that any restriction on the entry of the Chinese had to be passed at the national level. By that point, the anti-Chinese legislators in Congress had already proposed "An Act Supplementary to the Acts in Relation to Immigration" to do exactly that. The act came to be known as the Page Act of 1875, after its primary author in the House of Representatives, Horace F. Page, a Republican from California.[27] Page was born in New York but moved to California in 1854 during the gold rush, where he worked in a sawmill and stables before practicing law. He lost a race for the California State House in 1869 but was elected to the US House in 1872, filling the seat of Aaron Sargent, another anti-Chinese campaigner who had moved to the US Senate. Page remained in the House until 1882, where he would also be the sponsor of the Chinese Exclusion Act, but he lost his reelection campaign later that year.

The Page Act of 1875 targets people from Asia, specifically "any subject of China, Japan, or an Oriental country" that has "a contract or agreement for a term of service within the United States." The act prohibits the coolie trade, as Asian contract laborers were called at the time, but is primarily focused on women who are contracted "for lewd and immoral purposes" and "prostitution." It also put in place a ban on people with felony convictions, "persons who are undergoing a sentence for conviction in their own country of felonious crimes other than political." The act required people from Asia to have a certificate declaring they are moving freely before they depart and subjected them to an inspection when they arrived, if the customs inspector "shall have reason to believe that any such obnoxious persons are on board." The Page Act was not focused on protecting women from human trafficking or the dangers of prostitution. Instead, the focus was on protecting the purity of white men.[28] The Chinese women were described as vectors of disease, as agents of moral decline, and of literally diluting the white race through pregnancy and mixed-race children. The Page Act was completely uncontroversial and passed by voice votes in the House and Senate. It was signed into law by Ulysses S. Grant, officially becoming the first US law restricting immigration.

The Page Act effectively banned the entry of women from China. Even though the majority of Chinese women were not prostitutes, they had to prove that fact. The intrusive interviews and embarrassing medical examinations deterred many women from even trying. In 1870, 7.2 percent of the Chinese population in the United States were women, but by 1882, only 0.3 percent of the people who were admitted to the United States from China were women.[29] However, the Page Act had no impact on the migration of Chinese men. Labor recruiters simply changed what were previously labor contracts into loans to pay for the travel of the Chinese, a loophole that allowed for their continued arrival across the West. In the years that followed, politicians from the Pacific Slope, as the West Coast was commonly called at the time, redoubled their efforts to achieve something that the country never had before: a national policy on immigration that specifically limited the entry of a particular group of people.

— CHAPTER 3 —

WHATEVER HAPPENS, THE CHINESE MUST GO

The overflowing crowd at Faneuil Hall in Boston arrived early and waited anxiously to hear the famous orator. The heavily male and working-class gathering rippled with excitement and impatience in anticipation of finally seeing their man. As he bounded up on the stage, the crowd whooped and hollered, chanting his name and cheering his arrival: "Here he is!" and "That's him!" He looked the part of Irish American provocateur with a medium build, a generous mustache, and a thin face accentuated by hair that resembled a wave cresting on the top of his head. He smiled and clapped a few times before holding his hand low in front of him, signaling it was time to settle down. Sweat formed on his brow as the poorly ventilated and tightly packed hall thickened the spring air. "It is getting hot, Mr. Chairman," he said, and he threw off his coat and unbuttoned his collar, signaling to the audience he was one of them. They ate it up.

He knew how to read a crowd and always started with a few lines to string along the initial excitement that surged through the audience at the beginning of a rally. He smiled slightly and nodded toward the back of the room with his surefire applause lines. The reporters gathered there with pen and paper in hand, who learned to expect the taunts, girded themselves for the onslaught. "First and foremost, I will pay my respects to the newspapers." The crowd erupted into cheers and laughter. He let them wallow in the anticipation before calming them again. He went on: "For the villainous serpents, the shiny imps of hell that own these newspapers,

I have the utmost contempt." More laughter and applause. He read off some newspaper reports from the *San Francisco Chronicle* and the Associated Press, mocking what he said were lies about him. "I mention these facts to show and impress upon your minds the necessity of ignoring all newspaper reports, and principally reports sent by the Associated Press—a band of pirates." The audience roared, an equal part applause and guffaws at the chastened reporters in the back.[1]

During a speech a few weeks later at a park in Chicago, there was a commotion at the back of the crowd as he launched into his ice-breaking routine of haranguing the press. As he stood on a makeshift dais of two dry goods boxes pushed together, a crowd of eight thousand people pulsed in front of him. The following day's newspaper account called those gathered a "fetid, unkempt, boisterous mob" of "general idlers" who "surged and swore, elbowed and wrangled, and made the night hideous with cat calls, profanity, and indecent exclamations." He knew exactly how to rile them up. "In the first place, I propose to pay my respects to the thieving, dirty contemptable lickspittles that run newspapers in Chicago." A voice from the crowd: "Give it to them heavy!" He continued, "They take exception to my denouncing newspapers." Knowing laughter from the crowd. "I have never denounced a newspaper in my life, but I have and will continue to denounce slimy sheets, dirty sheets." He broke off as crashes and screams grew in the back near the press. The heads of the eight thousand people craned their necks in unison to see what was going on. Confusion reigned and the crowd was in an uproar. Finally, a man yelled out, "That is a reporter getting slugged!"[2]

On his second night in Boston, he paced across the length of the stage, pausing briefly to emphasize a point by raising his hand and then seemingly lobbing the thought like a bomb at the audience. After his demonization of the press was finished, he continued into the second recurring theme of his stump speech as he railed against capitalists who were exploiting the poor, a familiar riff for the working-class crowd and an easy target given the lack of any sort of worker protections or regulations on capital in the Gilded Age. Then he got to the conclusion, the red meat part of his speech they were all there to hear. He slowly built toward it. "The air is filled with the mutterings of thunder that precedes the coming storm. . . . Will you adopt my battle cry?"—"We will," the crowd responded. "It is in California," he tells them, before finally saying it: "The

Chinese must go!" The audience broke into prolonged applause. "Are Chinese to occupy this country?" "No!" the audience responded. "They are filthy, they spit on clothes, and if they have any disease it is transmitted to men and women through such washed clothing. Do you want leprosy here?" "No!" the audience roared. He looked out at the audience, satisfied he had made his point. "In conclusion, fellow workingmen. Awake! Arise! . . . We will do it with bullets if our ballots fail. We will drive these moon-eyed lepers back by steamship or sail!" The audience rose in sustained applause as he left the stage.[3]

Denis Kearney, a rabble-rousing thirty-one-year-old union leader from California, toured the eastern US in the summer of 1878, drawing crowds curious to see if his reputation as a vulgar provocateur was true. Kearney was born in Cork County, Ireland, in 1847 at the height of the Great Potato Famine. His father died when he was eleven, and his family sent him to the docks to be a cabin boy on a ship. He settled in the United States in 1868, moving to San Francisco in 1873, the same year he became a citizen. In 1877, he began giving speeches to the poor in the city, which quickly led to the creation of the Workingman's Party. The Page Act was three years old in 1878, and its impact on Chinese immigration was becoming clear. Chinese women almost completely stopped attempting to migrate to the US, turned away by the embarrassing questions about their sexual history and the demeaning medical tests that were required to prove they were not prostitutes. However, the ban on coolies in the Page Act had little effect on the immigration of Chinese men. Kearney was fed up and believed that the hardworking Chinese were undercutting his white union men's wages by working for much less and doing a better job.

He was criticized by the press and the establishment in San Francisco, but that seemed to only increase his popularity. Crowds grew at the Sandlot, an open-air gathering place in the city, topping two thousand people on occasion. His speeches often included calls for violence and he was arrested several times, but the charges were dropped because no one stepped forward to testify against him. His reputation growing, he decided to travel to the eastern United States to spread his anti-Chinese message, hoping to create alliances with more prominent East Coast politicians.

On his summer tour, Kearney lived up to the hype with his crass and rambling approach, sometimes appearing to simply do free associations of ideas as he went along. At the same time, his method was evident through

his careful demonization of the media and immigrants, which he calculated would appeal to his audience and ensure coverage by the press at
every stop. In Chicago, a reporter summed up his speech as "a conglom-
eration of vituperation, bravado, profanity, and ready use of compound
adjectives of a low plane of intellectuality, broken, and fairly incoherent
in argument."[4]

At first, the press and the public found that they could not look away.
Nevertheless, the public and media attention to the Chinese issue was
stymied by a lack of a visible Chinese presence in the still vastly more pop-
ulous eastern United States and by the Burlingame Treaty, which guaranteed free movement for the Chinese. As the summer heat faded into
cooler autumn nights, Kearney's white-hot rise to national fame cooled,
and so did attention to the issue of immigration, at least on the East Coast.

"AN EVIL OF GREAT MAGNITUDE"

In the West, politics continued to revolve around Chinese immigration.
In 1879, both California and Nevada held referendums on the Chinese
Question, as it was known, and the votes were decidedly against allowing
Chinese immigration. In California, the total was 154,683 votes for exclusion to 883 against. In Nevada, it was 17,259 to 183.[5] That same year,
the state of California amended its constitution and added several anti-
Chinese elements. The Second Amendment, which establishes the rules
for suffrage in the state, was changed to include the provision: "No native of China, no idiot, insane person, or person convicted of any infa-
mous crime, and no person hereafter convicted of the embezzlement
or misappropriation of public money, shall ever exercise the privileges
of an elector in this State." The Nineteenth Amendment, titled simply
"Chinese," dealt further with Chinese immigration. Section 1 allows the
state to enact laws to protect "from the burdens and evils arising from the
presence of aliens who are or may become vagrants, paupers, mendicants,
criminals, or invalids afflicted with contagious or infectious diseases, and
from aliens otherwise dangerous or detrimental to the well-being or
peace of the State." It also allows the removal of those who pose threats.
Section 2 bans corporations from employing "Chinese or Mongolians,"
and section 3 bans the state, counties, and municipalities from employing
Chinese, except as a punishment for a crime. Section 4 declares that

foreigners who cannot become citizens are "dangerous to the well-being of the state." These provisions were all ruled unconstitutional in 1880 by a US federal court.

In Washington, DC, the California congressional delegation continued to push for a stronger bill on Chinese immigration, proposing to limit the number of Chinese on any one boat to fifteen people rather than the hundreds that would typically arrive on the Pacific Mail Steamship Company ships from Hong Kong. The national discussion on Chinese immigration shifted when the Fifteen Passenger Bill found a surprising and prominent supporter in Maine Republican senator James G. Blaine. Prior to Blaine's support, northeastern Republicans, politicians whose views would be associated with "the Left" today, were uniformly against Chinese exclusion, seeing it through the lens of the radical republicanism that supported the abolition of slavery and the reconstruction policies after the Civil War.

Blaine was the most famous politician of his era who did not quite become president. It was not for a lack of trying. He ran for the Republican nomination in 1876 and 1880 and was the Republican nominee in the 1884 election, which he lost to Grover Cleveland. Blaine was elected to the US House of Representatives from Maine in 1863 and served as the Speaker of the House from 1869 to 1875. He was then elected to the Senate in 1876 where he served until 1881, when he became secretary of state under President James Garfield. Blaine and Garfield were talking together at the Washington, DC, train station on July 2, 1881, when Garfield was shot in an assassination attempt. Garfield died from his wounds two months later. Blaine became secretary of state again from 1889 to 1892 under President Benjamin Harrison.

Blaine played a significant role in the eventual passage of the Chinese Exclusion Act by becoming the first mainstream eastern politician to speak out against the Chinese. He took his position publicly in the debates on the Fifteen Passenger Bill in the Senate on February 14, 1879, and he also sent a letter to the *New York Tribune* outlining his position. Blaine asked, "Ought we to exclude them? The question lies in my mind thus: either the Anglo-Saxon race will possess the Pacific Slope or the Mongolians will possess it." "Mongolian" is a reference to race theories of the time, to mean inferior Asians. He stoked the fear that Americans could be replaced by an invasion from China. "We have this day to choose . . . whether our legislation shall be in the interest of the American free laborer or for the servile laborer from China. . . . You cannot work a man who must have beef and bread, and who would prefer beer alongside a man who can live on rice. It cannot be done." He concluded, "I am opposed to the Chinese coming here; I am opposed to making them citizens; I am opposed to making them voters."[6]

The Fifteen Passenger Bill was passed by Congress but was vetoed by President Rutherford B. Hayes because it violated the 1868 Burlingame Treaty with China. Hayes made it clear that he was fine with the exclusion of the Chinese, but he was worried about the impact on trade and on companies who did business in China. He dispatched an envoy to China to renegotiate the Burlingame Treaty in what came to be known as the Angell Treaty of 1880, which voluntarily limited Chinese migration and set the stage for the coming exclusions.

Blaine's defection to the anti-Chinese cause is best explained by political expedience. He was plainly focused on his presidential election prospects, and the country was very evenly split between Democrats and Republicans in all of the elections between 1876 and 1896. Consequently, the tiny West Coast states possessed enough Electoral College votes to swing the election. For Blaine, the Chinese question was almost a no-brainer because it was an issue that was not significant to East Coast voters and would not hurt him there, but it was crucial to winning the West Coast votes. In 1880, both political parties included anti-Chinese planks in their platform in order to pander to the West Coast. The Democrats stated, "No more Chinese immigration except for travel, education, and foreign commerce and therein carefully guarded," while the Republican platform said, "The Republican Party, regarding the unrestricted immigration of the Chinese as an evil of great magnitude, invokes the exercise of these powers to restrain and limit the immigration by the enactment of such just, humane, and reasonable provisions that will produce that result."[7]

In the end, Blaine did not win the Republican nomination in 1880. At the Republican National Convention, Blaine and Ulysses S. Grant received the most votes on the first round of the ballot, with 285 and 304 votes, respectively. After multiple ballots without a winner, James Garfield emerged as a compromise candidate and won the nomination. Garfield and the Democratic nominee Winfield Scott Hancock both won nineteen states in the November 1880 election, but Garfield eked out a win in the popular vote (by only two thousand votes) with a more comfortable 214 to 155 margin in the Electoral College. After Garfield died from his wounds from the assassination attempt on September 19, 1881, his vice president, Chester A. Arthur, became president.

"ANY WHITE PEOPLE UNDER THE SUN"

"An Act to Execute Certain Treaty Stipulations in Relation to Chinese" was introduced into the Senate by John Miller, a Republican from California, in February 1882. Miller had been trying to bring up the bill for weeks, but it was put off for other business. When Miller finally got his chance on the afternoon of February 28, 1882, he gave a long speech outlining why the act was necessary. He began by reminding the chamber that both political parties included Chinese exclusion in their election platforms in 1880 and that the Fifteen Passenger Bill had already passed both houses of Congress in 1879, but was vetoed due to the treaty obligations of the president. Now that those obligations had been renegotiated in 1880 with the Angell Treaty, it was time to pass restrictions on Chinese immigration: "It would seem the question of Chinese restriction has passed the stage of argument."[8]

Miller laid out four reasons for why Chinese exclusion was necessary. The first was that what might seem like an innocent migration was really an invasion. The population of China was large and could overrun the West Coast as the Chinese had already done throughout Asia. Miller argued that despite the limitations in the Page Act, Chinese men were quickly arriving in the West, reporting 18,561 arrivals in San Francisco in 1881 and four thousand more in the first two months of 1882. His second argument was that the Chinese were different from other immigrant groups because they did not assimilate, which he said was demonstrated by Chinese immigration to other parts of the world. "They remain Chinese always and everywhere," and unfortunately, Chinese and American culture were "like the mixing of oil and water, neither will absorb the other."[9]

In a somewhat confusing twist, after stating the two cultures could not mix, his third argument was that the Chinese culture was changing the behavior of white people in the West. He reported that white workers were starting to be itinerant migrant laborers like Chinese peasants and that the lack of jobs for young whites—caused by the Chinese willingness to work hard for low wages—was forcing the young to become "hoodlums." Furthermore, the Chinese were making whites sick with "strange and incurable maladies, loathsome and infectious diseases," and that "the stupefying, destructive opium habit is steadily increasing among our people." These are all examples of the "demoralizing influence of Chinese civilization."

Miller's final argument was that the history of race relations showed that different races were incompatible. The Chinese "are now a people as different from all other peoples in their characteristics, habits, methods, and physical appearance as if they were the inhabitants of another planet." He recounted all of the negative qualities of the Chinese as "rot," "spies," "thieves," "vagabonds," "ignorant," "contamination," who live in "hovels," "like swine in the sty," "eat imported rice," "disloyal," "a people destitute of conscience or moral sense." He compared the people of the United States to a body and emphasized the need to "let us keep pure the blood which circulates through our political system" and not allow "the debasement of our civilization through the injection into the body-politics of a poisonous, indigestible mass of alien humanity, or the admixture of antagonistic races."[10]

Miller concluded with a summation of the law. "We of the Pacific coast have tried all varieties of men as 'immigrants,' and our experience suggests a warm and generous welcome to our shore of the German, the Irishman, the Scandinavian, the Italian, and all who come from beyond the Atlantic; but of Chinese, we have enough and would be glad to exchange those we have for any white people under the sun."[11] When he finished, the Senate adjourned for the day.

The next day, February 29—1882 was a leap year—George Frisbie Hoar of Massachusetts rose to speak against Chinese exclusion. Senator Hoar listened to Miller's speech the day before, even asking a few questions about details as it went along. Hoar was a member of the House of Representatives from 1869 to 1877, when he took up the Senate seat that he would hold until his death twenty-seven years later. As was standard for the Republican Party at the time, Hoar held mostly liberal views, arguing for women's suffrage and against American imperialism. Hoar began by making the case that the founding documents of the United States were "intended as an explicit affirmation that the right of every human being who obeys equal laws to go everywhere on the surface of the earth that his welfare might require is beyond the rightful control of government." Therefore, he was against any law that restricts the free movement of people. He said, "I will not consent to a denial by the United States of the right of every man who desires to improve his condition by honest labor—his labor being no man's property but his own—to go anywhere on the face of the earth that he pleases." For Hoar, freedom of movement is not simply a law of the United States but a natural law and a fundamental right of all people. He concluded that if the exclusion act was passed, it would mark a dark day in the history of the United States: "As surely as the path on which our fathers entered a hundred years ago led to safety, to strength, to glory, so surely will the path on which we now propose to enter bring us to shame, to weakness, and to peril."[12]

Hoar's moralistic attack on the bill resulted in many of the bill's supporters rising to defend it and to question Hoar about what exactly he envisioned. Surely, they asked, he was not advocating for citizenship for other races, which was an implication of his remarks but was not directly stated. Did he really mean citizenship for everyone? Hoar replied, "I am in favor of admitting to the privileges of American Citizenship, under proper limitations in case of foreigners who have been educated in attachment to other governments, every human being—white, black, red, yellow, copper-colored, or whatever color nature may have seen fit to use in painting men's skins."[13] For Hoar, the primary question was whether an individual was loyal to the United States; their skin color was irrelevant. Presaging Martin Luther King Jr.'s famous formulation in his "I Have a Dream" speech some seventy-five years later, Hoar concluded, "I would have that ascertained by an inquiry into the character of the individual applicant, and not by looking at the color of his skin."

Hoar was eloquent but also out of touch with his nineteenth-century contemporaries. As speaker after speaker rose to debate the issue, it became clear that the vast majority of senators supported Chinese exclusion. Senator La Fayette Grover, the former governor of Oregon who gave the first speech at a legislature against Chinese immigration in 1870, rose to speak. He scoffed at the claim that the Constitution and the Declaration of Independence really meant that all men were equal. He pointed out that the founders' actions with Native Americans and African slaves demonstrated that they only had white Europeans in mind. He said, "Our ancestors . . .

proceeded forthwith to drive out the aborigines from the land with fire and sword, and to occupy it for themselves and their posterity." For Grover, given that the United States was already burdened with former slaves as citizens and the remnants of the Native Americans, "it is of the gravest importance to future peace and well-being of this country to that we do not voluntarily create other relations with colored foreign peoples."[14]

Other senators continued to make racial arguments for Chinese exclusion and foreshadowed much of the anti-immigrant language of the present day. Senator James George of Mississippi, whose predecessor in his seat was Blanche Bruce, the last Black senator of the Reconstruction era, explained,

> The constitution was ordained and established by white men, as they themselves declared in its preamble, "to secure the blessings of liberty to themselves (ourselves) and their (our) posterity," and I cannot doubt that this great pledge thus solemnly given will be as fully redeemed in favor of the white people of the South, should occasion for action arise, as I intend on my part and on their behalf to redeem it this day in favor of the white people of the Pacific States, by my vote to protect them against a degrading and destructive association with the inferior race now threatening to overrun them.[15]

The first version of the Chinese Exclusion Act passed by a vote of 29 to 15, with 32 not voting.[16] After the bill passed, Senator Hoar of Massachusetts rose once again to express his displeasure with it by attempting to change the title of the bill to "A bill to *violate* certain treaty stipulations relating to Chinese," but he was shouted down and overruled.[17] The House of Representatives approved the bill on March 23, by a vote of 167–66. President Chester Arthur vetoed the act but specified two changes to make in order for him to sign it: he thought a twenty-year ban was too long, and he was worried that the passport requirement was too stringent. The bill was quickly revised to expire in ten years, and the document requirement was changed to a certificate, not a passport.

During the brief second debate about the act, Senator Joseph Hawley, a Republican from Connecticut, rose to join Senator Hoar in opposition to Chinese exclusion. He acknowledged that the law was sure to pass, but he maintained his moral objection: "I leave the bill to posterity for its condemnation. I plant myself here, at this moment, on the ground of un-conditional hostility and denunciation. I will make no terms with it now or elsewhere here or hereafter, at any time."[18] Despite Hawley, Hoar, and the dozen or so other Republican senators who spoke up against the bill, the majority who voted for it proved to be more in tune with the mood of the country. The Chinese Exclusion Act again passed the US Senate on April 28, 32–15 (29 not voting) and the House by a vote of 201–37 (53 not voting). When President Arthur signed it into law on May 6, 1882, it was barely covered in the press.

Despite the fraught racial implications, the Chinese Exclusion Act proved to be extremely effective at achieving what Denis Kearney had demanded during his barnstorming across the eastern states four years earlier. In 1882, forty thousand people from China arrived in the US. By 1885, it declined to only twenty-three people.[19] In cities across the West, white people banded together to drive the Chinese out of their cities in a fit of ethnic cleansing before the term even existed.[20] The Chinese Exclusion Act continued to be renewed every ten years with fewer and fewer dissenting voices and with additional restrictions added to the limits on the Chinese and other Asian migrants. From 1880 to 1920, the US population as a whole doubled from 50 million to 106 million, but the Chinese population declined from over 100,000 in 1880 to only 62,000 in 1920. Chinese immigration stopped, and many people already in the United States opted to leave, returning to China or moving to Mexico or Canada in search of a more welcoming home.[21] The Chinese Exclusion Act was not repealed until 1943, and even then it was not for moral reasons but rather geopolitical. In World War II, China was a US ally against Japan, and it was embarrassing for the United States to ban immigration from its ally. The 1943 revision allowed 105 immigrants from China per year.

The ban on the Chinese in 1882 was not an end but rather a beginning that opened up the possibility of banning other groups. By the 1890s, many people from other parts of the world began to arrive on the shores of America. As people came from Japan, Italy, and Eastern Europe, a completely new debate emerged about the definition of "white." Congress had limited naturalization to free white persons in 1790 and added freed slaves in 1870. What Congress had not done was define what, exactly, it meant by "white."

CHAPTER 4

THE WHITE MAN, PAR EXCELLENCE

Takao Ozawa was born in Kanagawa, Japan, on June 15, 1875. He moved to San Francisco when he was nineteen, graduated from Berkeley High School, and enrolled at the University of California at Berkeley. In 1906, he moved to Honolulu and married a woman of Japanese descent who was also educated in the United States. They had two children who became American citizens at birth. The Kingdom of Hawai'i had been overthrown by a cabal of American colonists in 1893 and then annexed through a legally suspect process in 1898. In 1900, Congress extended birthright citizenship to the territory of Hawai'i.[1] Ozawa practiced Christianity, spoke English fluently, and worked for an American company. Consequently, he felt like he should be eligible for American citizenship and applied for naturalization. The petition was rejected so he took his case to the courts, but he continued to lose at the Federal District Court in Honolulu and in the Ninth Circuit Court of Appeals in San Francisco.

At that point, his case came to the attention of the Pacific Coast Japanese Association, which was looking for a test case to press for citizenship rights for people of Japanese origin. Ozawa's sterling personal history and light-skinned appearance made him a perfect vessel for their argument. In addition to his local lawyer from Honolulu, David Withington, the association paid for a top-tier New York lawyer, George Wickersham, to take the case. Wickersham was the US attorney general from 1909 to 1913 during the administration of William Howard Taft, and he had a reputation for progressive racial views. In 1912, he caused a stir when he backed William Lewis, a Black lawyer, who had petitioned to join the American Bar Association. Wickersham's stature added gravitas to the case and made it much more likely that the Supreme Court would hear it. However, it took some time. Ozawa began the legal process during World War I, which slowed things down. After the war, there were delicate negotiations with Japan at the Paris Conference about the role of racial equality in the League of Nations charter that further delayed the consideration of the case.

The Supreme Court finally heard oral arguments in the case on October 3 and 4, 1922. By then, William Howard Taft, the president Wickersham had served as attorney general, was now the chief justice of the Supreme Court, the only person to serve in both roles. The Ozawa team hoped Taft might be persuaded by his old friend. Ozawa's petition made two primary arguments for why he qualified for citizenship in the United States. The first was that many people from Japan have very light skin colors, often lighter than Europeans. If skin color was the determining factor, then people from Japan could be thought of as white. The second argument was that the character of the individual should also play a role in citizenship decisions, as Senator Hoar suggested during the 1882 Chinese Exclusion Act debates. Ozawa's petition stated, "My honesty and industriousness are well known among my Japanese and American friends. In name Benedict Arnold was an American, but at heart he was a traitor. In name I am not an American, but at heart I am a true American."[2]

Despite his upstanding behavior, Ozawa was living in a moment in which race was increasingly significant in American life. In the early years of the country, the distinction between a white person from England and Western Europe and a Black slave was clear. The United States was created by white colonists for their white progeny. However, although citizenship was limited to a "free white person" and there was widespread racialized talk in the United States, the definition of the racial category "white" was still not settled in the early twentieth century. The seemingly straightforward language of "free white person" in the naturalization law became ambiguous as different shades of human beings were born inside or made their way to the country. One of the first challenges to whiteness came from the mixed-race offspring that kept showing up in slave households as white male owners raped their female slaves. What of someone who is half white or whose skin is so light they can pass as white? As people from other parts of the world arrived in the country, a flurry of other questions about whiteness emerged. Population growth in Eastern and Southern Europe, combined with a stabilizing population in England and Northern Europe, meant that the people arriving in the US began to differ from previous immigrants. Additionally, the US expanded its colonial ambitions throughout the Pacific and Caribbean with the annexation of Cuba, Guam, Hawai'i, the Philippines, Puerto Rico, and Samoa at the end of the Spanish-American War in 1898. These acquisitions created new migration routes into the country and provoked questions about how to handle these people who were subject to the laws of the United States in colonial territories. Finally, in the years leading up to Takao Ozawa's hearing before the Supreme Court, a completely new set of scientific arguments began to lay the foundation for a very limited and exclusive definition of who was white.

RACE PSEUDOSCIENCE AND EUGENICS

Scientific research today has demonstrated that race is a socially constructed system for classifying people, not a genetic fact. Recent studies have found that the diversity within the genetic code of particular racial groups is much wider than the differences between them.[3] Similarly, large-scale genetic studies have found that migration and mixture were the norm and that "the assumption that present-day people are directly descended from the people who always lived in that same area . . . is wrong almost everywhere."[4] Genetic research has shown that there is no such thing as homogeneous races of people tied to a particular place. Even the Nordic blood revered by the white supremacists of the past and the alt-right of today does not exist. A DNA study of the Viking town Sigutuna, in modern-day Sweden, found that half the residents had migrated there from as far away as Southern and Eastern Europe.[5]

Even if race is not a legitimate scientific category, racism and exclusion based on common ideas of race still exist. Indeed, race is fundamentally a system of socially constructed hierarchy and exclusion that develops through a set of norms in a particular place, not based on universal values or facts. In the US, the "one-drop rule" was the underlying assumption of racial classification, and the idea that any Black blood makes someone Black is still prevalent today. Barack Obama is known as the first Black president even though he is equally as white as he is Black. The comedian Trevor Noah, who also has one white and one Black parent, writes in his autobiography that as a child growing up in a South African township, he was the white kid and often treated preferentially. However, when he went to white neighborhoods, he was unambiguously Black and looked down on.[6]

In the nineteenth and early twentieth centuries, science was deployed to legitimize the racial exclusion that was rampant in society, often coining new categories to justify white supremacy. The term "Caucasian" is the clearest example of this. Today "Caucasian" is ubiquitous on legal forms, driver's licenses, and the census as a stand-in for white, but its origin is completely arbitrary. Johan Friedrich Blumenbach (1752–1840) was a German anthropologist at the Georg-August University at Göttingen, in modern-day Germany. Blumenbach was a leading thinker of his day and taught English princes as well as the geographer Alexander von Humboldt, who became the most famous public intellectual of his era. After his studies with Blumenbach, Humboldt would go on to make an array of scientific discoveries during a five-year expedition in the Americas from 1799 to 1804, ranging from identifying isotherms to documenting human-induced environmental change. Humboldt published his results in his book *Cosmos*, which was widely read and lauded around the world. The book influenced generations of scholars and politicians including Simón Bolívar, who credited his friend Humboldt with inspiring him to return to South America in pursuit of revolution, and Charles Darwin, who said, "My admiration of his famous personal narrative (part of which I know almost by heart) determined me to travel to distant countries and led me to volunteer as naturalist on her majesty's ship Beagle." On Darwin's voyage, his daily diary entries were a conversation between himself and Humboldt. From the Humboldt Current to Humboldt, California, there are more features on earth named after Alexander von Humboldt than any other human being.[7]

In addition to teaching Humboldt, Blumenbach was an early proponent of what would come to be known as phrenology, the study of the shape of the head to ascertain other attributes of the individual. In the 1790s, Blumenbach came into possession of a skull of a woman from the Caucasus region, the area today that runs through Armenia, Azerbaijan, Georgia, and Russian regions such as Chechnya, Dagestan, and

Ingushetia. To Blumenbach, the skull represented the pinnacle of beauty, with clean lines and symmetry. Since he already knew that white Europeans were the most beautiful in the world, he deduced that this skull from the Caucasus Mountains represented an ancestor of Europeans. Consequently, he unilaterally decided that Europeans were originally from the Caucasus Mountains and the term "Caucasian" was born. The term is based on one German man's view that a skull was beautiful and must have been from a white person.[8]

The publication of Charles Darwin's *On the Origin of Species* in 1859 opened a whole new way of thinking about human civilizations. Darwin's careful observations on his trip through the Pacific and then his slow methodical consideration of the data resulted in a new model for understanding the diversity of traits in nature. It was soon accepted that organisms were not static and permanent; rather, they evolved through time as the better-adapted individuals survived and reproduced at greater numbers while the less well adapted died and their genes ended with them.

Within a few years, the idea of species adaption was overlaid onto human societies in what came to be known as social Darwinism.[9] Social Darwinism posited that just as the fittest species survived, there was also a survival of the fittest human societies. Darwin's theory was both a vindication and a threat to race thinking. It vindicated the idea that one group was superior to another group through its evolution, but it also suggested that the group needed to be hypervigilant and continue competing in order to avoid becoming unfit in the future.[10]

Sir Francis Galton, an English biologist and Charles Darwin's cousin, launched the eugenics movement, which applied the agricultural method of selective breeding for desirable characteristics to humanity. Before he delved into race science, Galton had already made significant scientific contributions, including the discovery that everyone has a unique fingerprint and proof of the statistical law of regression to the mean.[11] Galton was a prolific author who wrote twenty books and more than two hundred journal articles over his lifetime. In the 1870s, he coined the phrase "nature versus nurture," and he proposed the term "eugenics" in 1883, taking it from the German for "good in stock." His work on eugenics culminated with his 1889 book *Natural Inheritance*, which used statistics to trace how traits would be passed down through generations of humans.[12] Galton's research noted that the children of successful people tended to also be successful, which he attributed to superior genetics. He apparently did not consider that children of successful people were born into wealth and a system of quality education, social connections, and structural power, which play a decisive role in predicting the success of children. Eugenicists say that if horrific diseases are known to be hereditary, society should select against those to remove them from the human genome. However, the argument goes further to suggest that more intelligent or athletic people should be selected for as well.

Eugenics migrated from Europe into mainstream American thought at the end of the nineteenth century as scholars at eminent institutions such as MIT and Harvard began to look at the science of the race question. The first significant text in the US was written by Francis Walker, the president of MIT, who introduced the idea that lesser races breed more. As the idea percolated, it came to stand in as a justification for not only closing borders at home to prevent overbreeding races from entering the US but also pursuing imperial adventures abroad to bring civilization to the lesser races and control them.[13] By the early twentieth century, Walker's idea was boiled down to the slogan of "race suicide," which was trumpeted by President Theodore Roosevelt. He argued that the US would be foolish to let in too many people from lower races that breed more quickly than whites.

For the white supremacists of the era, there was little doubt that the white race was superior to the African and Asian "savages" they were in the process of conquering around the world through colonialism. The real question for the scientists was whether and where to draw the line between Northern Europeans and the Southern and Eastern Europeans who had begun to migrate to the United States. Francis Walker asked one of his former students, William Ripley, to write a book classifying the races of Europe. Ripley, who was an economics professor at MIT and also affiliated with Columbia University, later said he needed money at the time to pay for his child's school, so he took on the task. *The Races of Europe* was published in 1899 and had all the trappings of an authoritative scientific study. It was 624 pages long, contained over three hundred pictures, maps, and charts and more than two thousand citations at the end. Ripley argued that the population of Europe was not a single white people but rather was composed of three distinct groups that were identifiable regionally by their complexion and facial structure.[14]

Ripley's three races in Europe were the Teutonic, the Alpine, and the Mediterranean. The Teutonic had blond, lighter complexions and long, thin heads. During World War I, the term "Nordic" replaced "Teutonic" to emphasize Scandinavia and England rather than Germany. The Alpine were found in the middle parts of Europe and were characterized by a shorter stature and a round head. The Mediterranean race was found in Southern Europe and had a slender build with dark complexion and a long head. *The Races of Europe* made Ripley famous, and he secured a coveted professorship at Harvard where Franklin Delano Roosevelt was one of his students. Like his advisor, Francis Walker, Ripley also served as the president of the prestigious American Economic Association.[15]

The confluence of race science and genetics research led to extensive coverage in the press. From 1910 to 1914, major US magazines carried more studies on eugenics than "slums, tenements, and living standards combined."[16] The eugenics turn was not just happening in the United States. In Australia, Keith Murdoch, the father of right-wing media baron Rupert Murdoch, was a staunch believer in eugenics, which played a role in the white Australia policy to prevent the mixture of races.[17] It was also growing in popularity in Germany, where eugenics would eventually become state policy in the Nazi regime.

In 1916, Madison Grant published *The Passing of the Great Race*, which would become the most significant book on race science by combining Ripley's race classification of Europe with Walker's idea of race suicide. Like almost all of the white supremacist writers of the era, Grant was born of the patrician class in New York and was a denizen of high society, summering on his family's estate in Long Island. He graduated from Yale then earned a law degree at Columbia, and he was integral to the founding of the Bronx Zoo. He was a trustee of the American Museum of Natural History, where he socialized with much of high-society New York and became close friends with Presidents Herbert Hoover and Theodore Roosevelt, another conservationist. Grant used his wealth and connections to promote conservation causes including wildlife management and species protection. He realized that some species were not able to reproduce at a rate sufficient to allow them to survive under the current pressure from hunting and development. Consequently, he argued for protected areas to allow species like the American bison to survive. As he became familiar with race science, he grew alarmed with what he saw as a threat to his race that was similar to the threats faced by other endangered species. He realized that just as endangered species needed protected areas to prevent aggressive invasive species from taking over, so did human races, particularly the genetically superior but numerically inferior Nordic race.

The Passing of the Great Race was influential because Grant was not a scholar and consequently dispensed with the careful language of the academy. Instead, he went further than any academic had and did so in plain, easily accessible language. The book is a laundry list of shocking racial claims as he laid out the case for Nordic superiority and the inferiority of other European and global races. The tone is set in the first chapter where he explains matter-of-factly that better races use slavery to control weaker races. And, anyway, he writes, "From a material point of view slaves are often more fortunate than free men when treated with reasonable humanity and when their elemental wants of food, clothing and shelter are supplied."[18]

The bulk of Grant's book is concerned with categorizing and explaining the history of the three "subspecies," his term, of humans in Europe. While the Alpine race is subservient and "always and everywhere a race of peasants," the Mediterranean race has an inferior body. By contrast, "the Nordics are all over the world a race of soldiers, sailors, adventurers and explorers, but above all, of rulers, organizers and aristocrats." The Nordic race is the race of chivalry and knighthood, literature, scientific research, and discovery. In sum, the Nordic "is a purely European type, in the sense that it has developed its physical characteristics within the confines of that continent. It is, therefore, the Homo Europaeus, the white man par excellence."[19]

However, despite its superiority in virtually every trait, Grant sees a danger lurking for the great race. The other races of humans are coming and they are larger in number and more fertile than the great race of Nordic men. Additionally, for whatever reason, Nordic men cannot resist women of other races. He writes, "The unfortunate fact that nearly all species of men interbreed freely leaves us no choice in the matter. Races must be kept apart by artificial devices of this sort or they ultimately amalgamate and in the offspring the more generalized or lower type prevails."[20] Consequently, the only way to preserve the endangered great race is to create a protected area through immigration restrictions and guarded borders.

The Passing of the Great Race came out during World War I and was not widely read at first, but it became influential in the 1920s and sold over a million copies. Former president Teddy Roosevelt wrote the back-cover endorsement for the book: "It is the work of an American scholar and gentleman."[21] Grant's book was recommended on the Senate floor by Ellison DuRant Smith of South Carolina, known as Cotton Ed, during the debates around the 1924 national origins quotas. Smith said,

> I would like for the Members of the Senate to read that book just recently published by Madison Grant, *The Passing of a Great Race*. Thank God we have in America perhaps the largest percentage of any country in the world of the pure, unadulterated Anglo-Saxon stock; certainly the greatest of any nation in the Nordic breed. It is for the preservation of that splendid stock that has characterized us that I would make this not an asylum for the oppressed of all countries.[22]

Perhaps the clearest indication of the influence of the book is that Adolf Hitler reportedly wrote a personal note to Grant calling *The Passing of the Great Race* "my bible."[23] There was a copy of the book in Hitler's bunker in Berlin when he committed suicide in 1945.[24]

As the eugenics fervor gripped the wealthy elite of New England, a new idea of intelligence tests came into vogue. Henry Goddard, a psychologist at the Vineland Training School for the Feebleminded, decided to translate the Binet-Simon intelligence test from French into English in order to administer it to the residents, then he expanded the test to Ellis Island. Goddard found a like-minded scholar in Robert Yerkes, who was a student of eugenicist Charles Davenport at Harvard. After receiving his PhD in 1902, Yerkes began working on intelligence testing at Harvard in 1913. During World War I, he used funding from the National Academy of Sciences and the National Resource Council to expand his IQ testing to the US military. By the end of the war, they had tested 1.75 million soldiers. The army did not find the results useful and pointed out that many of the men tabbed as feebleminded by the tests turned out to be excellent soldiers. However, Yerkes was unbowed and published his results in academic venues. He realized there was a broader public interest in the work and asked another scholar named Carl Brigham to produce an accessible version. Brigham was a recent PhD graduate from Princeton who a few years later would develop the Scholastic Aptitude Test (SAT), which continues to be used for college admissions through the present day. Brigham received funding from Madison Grant to produce *A Study of American Intelligence* in 1923 with Princeton University Press.[25] The book was powerful because it used bar graphs to demonstrate the superior intelligence of the white race, even if the source of the data was not really explained. In chart after chart, English and Nordic people were on top, Eastern and Southern Europeans in the middle, and Black Americans at the bottom.

Eugenics thinking and intelligence testing resulted in laws in many US states allowing sterilization for people of lower mental acuity. The Supreme Court upheld these laws in 1927 in the case of *Buck v. Bell* in an 8–1 ruling, and from 1907 to 1956, 60,166 people were sterilized in the US. California accounted for one-third of the total, with 19,998 sterilizations. Virginia was second with 6,811.[26]

In the early 1920s, a series of other similar books were published arguing that the winding down of colonialism and the growing population around the world signaled the end of white domination. The most influential of these was Lothrop Stoddard's *The Rising Tide of Color Against White World-Supremacy*, which included an introduction by Madison Grant. Stoddard used demographic data to argue that Europe had been the location of rapid population expansion throughout the eighteenth and nineteenth centuries, but that wave was cresting and the twentieth century would be marked by growth in Asia and Africa. Like Grant, Stoddard took these trends and shaped them into a white supremacist narrative of the eminent demise of the genetically superior but numerically inferior white race.[27] Both Grant's and Stoddard's work was regularly republished in the influential *Saturday Evening Post*, where the danger that the white race could be replaced by other inferior races became part of the mainstream media diet of everyday Americans in the early 1920s.

WHO IS WHITE?

Takao Ozawa's case was finally taken up by the US Supreme Court in 1922, the same year that Warren Harding, the sitting president of the United States, recommended Stoddard's book *The Rising Tide of Color Against White World-Supremacy* in a speech.[28] Although it was the first time the Supreme Court considered how to interpret the phrase "free white person" in the naturalization law, there had been a series of previous federal district and appellate court rulings, often with contradictory or seemingly arbitrary results, reflecting the illusory nature of the category "white."

In 1878, a court found that Chinese people were not white. In 1889, Hawaiians were not white. In 1894, Burmese were not white. In 1894, 1902, 1908, and 1910, Japanese were not white, which did not bode well for Takao Ozawa's case. In 1897, Mexicans were white. In 1900, Native Americans were not white. In 1905, Armenians were white. In 1909 and 1917, South Asians were not white. In 1910, 1913, 1919, and 1920, South Asians were white. In 1909, 1910, and 1915, Syrians were white, but in 1913 and 1914, Syrians were not white. In 1916 and 1917, Filipinos were not white. In 1921, Koreans were not white.[29] There were also cases that considered whether someone was white if one parent was white and another was Native American (1880), Chinese (1909), Japanese (1912), or Filipino (1912 and 1916).[30] In every case, the courts decided people of mixed heritage were not white.

Since there was no scientific basis to whiteness and others who had once been on the outside eventually were incorporated into it, such as the Irish, Syrians, Armenians, Mexicans, and, to some extent, South Asians, it was not outrageous for Takao Ozawa to think that a well-behaved and light-skinned Japanese person could also plausibly be redefined as white.

The Supreme Court only took a month to reach a unanimous decision in the case, which Associate Justice George Sutherland announced on November 13, 1922. Sutherland was born in England in 1862; his family moved to Utah, where he was elected to both the House of Representatives and the Senate. He had just joined the court in 1922 but went on to be one of the "Four Horsemen," the conservative block of justices that would impede Franklin Delano Roosevelt's New Deal legislations in the 1930s.

The ruling in the *Ozawa* case begins by explaining that the basic role of the Supreme Court is to ensure that Congress's laws are being executed faithfully, not to create laws itself. Then it describes the history of the terminology in the naturalization law, which limited citizenship to "free white persons" from 1790 and was expanded to include "aliens of African nativity" and "persons of African descent" in 1870.[31] Sutherland says that it is not enough to point out that the framers of the law did not think of a particular case, but that it is also necessary to consider what they would have done. For Sutherland, it is clear that the framers meant to exclude

Black slaves and Native Americans. Furthermore, the terminology in the law is not meant to gauge individuals but rather groups. Although the law says "free white person," Sutherland writes that it does not mean simply white skin:

> Manifestly the test afforded by the mere color of the skin of each individual is impracticable, as that differs greatly among persons of the same race, even among Anglo-Saxons, ranging by imperceptible gradations from the fair blond to the swarthy brunette, the latter being darker than many of the lighter hued persons of the brown or yellow races. Hence to adopt the color test alone would result in a confused overlapping of races and a gradual merging of one into the other, without any practical line of separation.

Rather than relying on an individual test, Sutherland turned to the term Blumenbach made up after examining a beautiful skull: "The words 'white person' were meant to indicate only a person of what is popularly known as the Caucasian race." Sutherland then writes that there are, of course, borderline cases and those should be individually adjudicated, but Ozawa's is not one of them. "The appellant, in the case now under consideration, however, is clearly of a race which is not Caucasian and therefore belongs entirely outside the zone on the negative side." Ozawa lost his case, but since the ruling pointed to Blumenbach's fantastical idea of a Caucasian race as the defining characteristic of a "white person," it opened up other avenues for plaintiffs to argue they were white.

Early in 1923, the US Supreme Court heard the case of Bhagat Singh Thind, whose lawyers "expected a favorable decision" because the court decided in *Ozawa* that white meant Caucasian and the people of North India were predominantly Aryan and Caucasian.[32] Like Takao Ozawa, Bhagat Singh Thind performed the role of model American citizen. He was born in a village near Amritsar in the Punjab district of British India on October 3, 1892. In 1913, he came to the United States to attend the University of California at Berkeley for a theology PhD. As World War I raged, he joined the US Army, rising to the rank of acting sergeant before his honorable discharge at the end of the war. He applied for citizenship in 1920 and was initially given it by a US district court. However, the Bureau of Naturalization appealed to the Supreme Court, which heard the case on January 11 and 12, 1923, only two months after the *Ozawa* decision.

The Thind brief goes farther than Ozawa did in arguing that he shared a kinship with white America. In addition to citing linguistic studies that showed the connections between Hindi and European languages, Thind argued that like white Europeans who conquered and colonized other people, his Aryan ancestors conquered and subjugated the lesser races of India "The high-class Hindu regards the aboriginal Indian Mongoloid in the same manner as the American regards the Negro, speaking from a matrimonial standpoint."[33]

As with the *Ozawa* case, the court quickly reached a unanimous decision in about a month, again written by Associate Justice Sutherland, overturning the lower court's ruling and denying Thind citizenship. Sutherland argued that the law is based on a common understanding of terms, not an academic one. The verdict went further to suggest that language is not the same as race: "The term Aryan has to do with linguistic, and not at all with physical, characteristics, and it would seem reasonably clear that mere resemblance in language, indicating a common linguistic root buried in remotely ancient soil, is altogether inadequate to prove common racial origin." Finally, the court suggested that there was substantial mixing between groups in India, producing darker skin, so even if North Indians were once white, they no longer were.

The result of the decision was calamitous for other South Asian people who had previously received US citizenship and then had it rescinded. Many appealed the loss of citizenship but without success. In the years that followed, lower courts followed the precedent set by the Supreme Court in *Ozawa* and *Thind*, understanding "free white person" narrowly as a person with white skin with European ancestry. In 1923, 1925, 1928, 1939, and 1942, courts reconfirmed that South Asians were not white. Filipinos were again ruled not white in 1927, 1935, and 1941. People from Afghanistan were not white in 1928. People from the Arabian Peninsula were not white in 1942 and 1944.[34]

Baghat Singh Thind finally become a US citizen in 1936 after a new law gave citizenship to all foreign veterans from World War I, but the "free white person" provision in citizenship law remained in place all the way until 1952. Consequently, for the first 162 years of the United States, citizenship was formally limited to whites only and, after 1870, former African slaves and their descendants.

Despite these restrictions on citizenship, by the first decades of the twentieth century, it became clear that it was not just Chinese immigrants who wanted to come to the United States to work. People from across Asia and from Eastern and Southern Europe began to make the journey. With a growing scientific consensus about the racial superiority of the Nordic race, Congress would soon turn its eye to these other immigrant groups who were arriving in increasingly large numbers at the ports of the United States.

CHAPTER 5

THE VERY FABRIC
OF OUR RACE

V. S. McClatchy strolled down Market Street in San Francisco on a cool February day in 1924 when, unexpectedly, his brother C.K. appeared on the sidewalk ahead. The McClatchy brothers, only a year apart in age, were the sons of James McClatchy, the journalist who made the harrowing journey to California during the gold rush in 1849. After James's death in 1883, the brothers took over his *Sacramento Bee* and were longtime business partners, but they had not seen each other for several months before the chance encounter on Market Street. By 1924, the devastation of the 1906 earthquake was a distant memory in San Francisco. Market Street cut a diagonal through the orderly grid of the city and was the place to be seen in the Roaring Twenties with modern streetcars, upscale cafes, and luxurious shops lining the sidewalk. Both men were tall and impeccably dressed, but the older V.S. retained his athletic build and looked younger and fitter than his heavy-drinking brother. C.K. smiled and approached his brother with his hand extended. V.S. looked at the gesture of reconciliation incredulously, gave a deep sigh, and stormed off. The next day he wrote C.K. a letter to express his displeasure: "I marvel that you should have offered me your hand on Market Street yesterday, apparently assuming I would take it."[1]

James McClatchy's two sons toiled for decades to transform the *Sacramento Bee*, the fledgling newspaper founded in the haze of the gold rush, into a leading voice of news and commentary in the capital of California, which had grown to become the dominant state in the West. Today's

McClatchy Company operates thirty-eight weekly papers across the United States as well as twenty-nine dailies, including the *Charlotte Observer*, the *Kansas City Star*, the *Miami Herald*, the *Raleigh News and Observer*, and of course the *Sacramento Bee*. McClatchy newspapers have won five Pulitzer Prizes.

Although close in age and business partners for decades, the two brothers were often at odds. Valentine Stuart, who went by V.S. professionally but was called Val or Vallie by his family, was outgoing, athletic, and studious. He was a strong rower and would later in life be a baritone in a local singing group he organized. Charles Kenny, who went by C.K. professionally but was Charlie to his family, was introverted and did poorly in school. Both brothers went to Santa Clara for college. V.S. wrote for the student newspaper and graduated in 1877 with honors. C.K. dropped out but finally got a degree in 1901 at the age of forty-three.[2]

By the beginning of the twentieth century, the two brothers settled into different roles at the paper. V.S. was the hard-nosed publisher who handled sales, accounting, circulation, and marketing, while C.K. ran the day-to-day operations of the paper as the editor. The role of publisher gave V.S. time to engage in other activities, including serving on the California Land Reclamation Board and in the prestigious position of president of the Associated Press. V.S. also managed vast real estate holdings across the Central Valley. The majority of his personal correspondence, which is held at the Sacramento Historical Society, is about land sales and business transactions, not about the paper itself. However, when it came to protecting the *Sacramento Bee*, V.S. was ruthless and repeatedly pressured advertisers not to support competing papers. The editor of the rival *Sunday News*, John Sheehan, expressed his displeasure in an editorial in 1897. "The scoundrelly McClatchys," he wrote, were "malevolent rascals" and "ghouls of the press," while V.S.'s "nose has acquired an edge like a cimitar [*sic*] from sharp and incessant pursuit of the nimble dollar."[3]

Cracks eventually began to appear in the relationship between the brothers. While V.S. was a disciplined workaholic, C.K. was a gifted writer and provocateur who did not abide by schedules. He also became an alcoholic. At one point, V.S. sent letters to all the local bars around Sacramento informing them that "Charles K. McClatchy is a person addicted to an inordinate use of intoxicating liquors" and cited a new law he had pursued at the state legislature that would fine establishments that served a known alcoholic. C.K. regularly took off on long trips, often to get sobered up, which meant that V.S. had to cover for him at the paper. V.S. would use those opportunities to intervene in the editorial direction by writing anti-Asian editorials, which angered C.K.

The brothers had a massive falling out in 1923, a few months before the awkward meeting on Market Street. Their company had acquired the *Fresno Bee* paper, and the brothers agreed that their sons would run it. While V.S. was the more competent of the brothers, his sons were not and constantly caused problems at the *Fresno Bee*. C.K.'s son Carlos wanted them removed, but V.S. insisted on them staying on. The dispute escalated to the point that the brothers agreed that one of them had to leave the company. V.S. ran the business for years as his brother drank and traveled, so he was sure he was destined to retain control. However, when they held the auction that would determine which brother ran the business, C.K. secured additional outside investments and made the highest bid. V.S. was furious and the brothers did not speak for years. Even when V.S. attempted some reconciliation of his own by sending a wedding gift to C.K.'s daughter Eleanor, she returned it unopened. Her note said, "As you refuse to have friendly relations with my father, you can, of course, understand my not wishing to accept your gift, no matter how kindly intended."[4]

HYPHENATED AMERICANS

One of the areas where the brothers' editorial views diverged was on the issue of immigration, which the *Sacramento Union* paper cited at the time as the primary dispute in their messy falling-out.[5] While C.K. was ambivalent, V.S. grew ever more concerned with the arrival of Japanese immigrants in California. By the early twentieth century, the impact of the Chinese Exclusion Act was clear. People from China were no longer able to migrate to the United States, and the number of Chinese people residing in the country was declining. However, an unintended consequence was an increase in migration from other Asian countries to fill the labor gap left by the Chinese. In 1870, there were only fifty-six people of Japanese origin in the United States, but by 1900, it was over 24,000, mostly in California.[6] V.S. made it his mission in life to reverse that trend and used his perch in the media as the president of the Associated Press to write many anti-Asian editorials and to testify before Congress as the issue was debated in 1923 and 1924.

At the national level, the issue of Japanese immigration was complicated by diplomatic relations with Japan. Japan was seen as a rival in the Pacific after its defeat of Russia in the 1904–5 Russo-Japanese War. Afterward, Japan sought to be treated as an equal power on the global stage. V. S. McClatchy saw the Japanese in the United States as an invasion force preparing to replace the white population. He pushed for a Japanese exclusion act akin to the Chinese version, but President Theodore Roosevelt was worried about the impact that would have on relations with Japan. Instead, Roosevelt worked with the Japanese government on what came to be known as the Gentleman's Agreement of 1907. In the agreement, the government of Japan would stop issuing passports for Japanese citizens to go to the United States in exchange for a promise from the US not to legislate the exclusion of the Japanese. The agreement also applied to people from Korea, which was colonized by Japan at the time.

The Gentleman's Agreement was a victory for anti-Japanese campaigners like V. S. McClatchy as arrivals from Japan were cut by 90 percent from 1907 to 1909, but it became clear there were some major loopholes.[7] The first was that Japan could continue to issue passports for spouses of Japanese people who already lived in the United States. As a result, the "picture bride" phenomenon emerged in which Japanese men in the US would marry Japanese women in Japan, having only seen their photograph, in order to get them a passport to come to the US. Additionally, the agreement did not cover the territory of Hawai'i, which the US occupied and then annexed in the 1890s. Many Japanese workers went there first before making the unencumbered trip to the mainland. Members of Congress were also unhappy with the deal because it was not an official treaty ratified by Congress but a private agreement between the executive branches of the governments.

In addition to the Chinese Exclusion Act and the Gentleman's Agreement, from 1882 until the start of World War I in 1914, Congress passed a series of other acts to restrict different groups of people from entering the US. In August 1882, only a few months after Chinese exclusion, Congress passed an immigration law similar to Massachusetts's limits on the poor. It directed immigration commissioners to deny entry to "any convict, lunatic, idiot, or any person unable to take care of himself or herself without becoming a public charge."[8] Over the years, Congress extended the bans to people with particular political beliefs (communist and anarchist), people who had committed crimes, people with illnesses such as tuberculosis or epilepsy, people with a history of insanity, people who were morally questionable (polygamists, for example), and particularly the very poor, whether paupers or beggars (see table 2).

TABLE 2: *Major US immigration acts and agreements*

YEAR	TITLE	PURPOSE
1790	Naturalization Act of 1790	Citizenship limited to "free white persons"
1870	Naturalization Act of 1870	Citizenship extended to "aliens of African nativity" and "persons of African descent"
1875	Page Act	Banned Chinese labor contracts and prostitutes
1882	Chinese Exclusion Act	Banned all Chinese immigration
1882	Immigration Act of 1882	Banned criminals, the insane, the sick, and those likely to become a public charge
1891	Immigration Act of 1891	Created Bureau of Immigration in the Treasury Department
1892	Geary Act	Renewed the Chinese Exclusion Act (continued to be renewed every ten years until 1943) and tightened restrictions on the Chinese
1903	Anarchist Exclusion Act	Banned anarchists, polygamists, beggars, and epileptic people
1907	Immigration Act of 1907	Banned new groups of disabled and diseased people
1907	Gentleman's Agreement	Stopped Japanese immigration
1917	Immigration Act of 1917	Added a literacy test, created an Asiatic Barred Zone
1921	Emergency Quota Act	Imposed a temporary quota of 3 percent of that country's immigrant population in the US as of 1910
1924	Johnson-Reed Immigration Act	Banned Asian immigration, created strict national origins quotas for everywhere else except the Western Hemisphere

(continues)

TABLE 2: *Major US immigration acts and agreements* (continued)

YEAR	TITLE	PURPOSE
1952	McCarron-Walter Immigration Act	Removed "free white person" requirement for citizenship, removed ban on Asian immigration, added bans on communists and totalitarians
1965	Hart-Celler Immigration Act	Ended national origins quotas, shifted immigration visas toward family reunification
1980	Refugee Act	Created a yearly quota for refugee resettlement
1986	Immigration Reform and Control Act	Gave amnesty to undocumented in US, made it a crime to hire undocumented workers
1996	Illegal Immigration Reform and Immigrant Responsibility Act	Added penalties for undocumented people who commit crimes or overstay visas, strengthened enforcement at border
2002	Homeland Security Act	Moved all immigration-related agencies to DHS
2005	REAL ID Act	Prohibited driver's licenses for undocumented people, provided waivers for border wall, restricted habeas corpus for immigrants
2006	Secure Fence Act	Authorized construction of 700 miles of border wall
2012	Executive order, Deferred Action for Childhood Arrivals	Deferred immigration actions against people brought to the US as children without documents

Despite the expanded list of excluded categories, only 1 percent of the 25 million people from Europe who arrived between 1880 and 1915 were denied entry.[9] Additionally, many of these immigrants were coming from completely new places. In the 1870s, 2.7 million people migrated to the United States, and 74 percent of them were from Northern Europe. From 1901 to 1910, 8.6 million people arrived, but only 21 percent were from Northern Europe. Cities like Chicago were settled by immigrants from these new places. In 1850, the city had only 5,000 people, but in 1900, it was 1.69 million. In 1920, New York was 44 percent immigrant,

Cleveland was 41 percent, and most northern cities were over 20 percent.[10] These new migrants were derisively referred to as hyphenated Americans, implying that their allegiances were to their homelands and they could not be trusted as true Americans.

THE NATIVIST ALLIANCE

As these different groups of immigrants began to arrive in America, V. S. McClatchy and the West Coast anti-Asian organizations settled into an odd coalition with other regional groups that wanted to restrict immigration.[11] In the Northeast, Massachusetts senator Henry Cabot Lodge and his wealthy elite friends at MIT and Harvard were worried about diluting the racial stock of America. In the Midwest, labor organizers like Samuel Gompers feared that the new immigrants were a threat to the wages and jobs of American workers. In the Jim Crow South, the Ku Klux Klan was reborn as an anti-Black and anti-immigrant organization.

The original Ku Klux Klan was founded in Tennessee by former confederate soldiers in December 1865 in the aftermath of the Civil War. The name is derived from the Greek word for circle or cycle, *kyklos*. The secret fraternal society for former Confederates spread quickly across the South as an "invisible empire" that targeted African Americans and sympathetic whites in order to resist Reconstruction. By the early 1870s, President Ulysses S. Grant cracked down on the clandestine militias and the first Klan collapsed.

The second Klan's meteoric rise to prominence in American politics was begun by D. W. Griffith's 1915 film *The Birth of a Nation*. The film captured the zeitgeist of the era as the post–Civil War Reconstruction was seen as a mistake in the white community. The film recast the original Klan not as cowardly separatists but as brave patriots standing up for the white race in the face of inferior African Americans who were violent rapists. The film was based on the book *The Clansman* written by Thomas Dixon Jr., who happened to have been a classmate of the president of the United States, Woodrow Wilson. Dixon was able to set up a screening of *The Birth of a Nation* in the White House, which is thought to be the first film ever shown there.

In Atlanta, a preacher named William Simmons followed the success of the film through the news as he recovered from an automobile accident.

Simmons had previous experience with fraternal organizations. He was a member of the Knights Templar, and his father was in the original Klan. On Thanksgiving Day in November 1915, Simmons held what the *Atlanta Constitution* called "impressive services" on the top of Stone Mountain to reestablish the Klan.[12] They burned a cross and initiated fifteen members into the "invisible empire, Knights of the Ku Klux Klan" with Simmons as the first imperial wizard. He based his Klan on the movie version, introducing white robes, burning crosses, and public parades, which were all cinematic flourishes, not things done by the original Klan. In addition to terrorizing Black people, he also planned it as a scheme to sell insurance.[13]

Simmons was disorganized and not good at managing money. Additionally, World War I was in full swing, which pulled attention away from race relations and immigration. By 1920, the Klan had only five thousand members, so Simmons brought in two professional publicists, Edward Young Clarke and Elizabeth Tyler, to run the Klan's membership campaign. The end of the war brought more poor refugees from Europe and an economic downturn in the US, providing an audience for the reactionary rhetoric of the Klan. By focusing on newspapers and Masonic temples, Clarke and Tyler grew the membership to over ninety thousand people in eighteen months, with the majority of the new members outside the South.

By 1922, immigration was a key tenant of the Klan's activism under the slogan of "100% American," and the Klan positioned itself as the protectors of "the interest of those whose forefathers established the nation."[14] While the first Klan was white supremacist through and through, it was fundamentally a separatist organization that venerated the Confederacy rather than American nationalism. The new Klan retained the white supremacy but combined it with patriotic nationalism, anti-Catholic religious bigotry, and anti-radicalism, particularly against communists in the aftermath of the Bolshevik Revolution in Russia in 1917. Even though membership in the new Klan was restricted to native-born protestant whites, it grew exponentially. In 1923, the Klan had 3 million members and could turn out 75,000 people at events. In Indiana, one-fifth of the state's white male population was a member of the Klan.[15]

In addition to the Klan and the West Coast anti-Asian activists like V. S. McClatchy, the political arm of the anti-immigrant coalition was led by Massachusetts senator Henry Cabot Lodge. At the time of the debates around the 1921 Emergency Quota and the 1924 Immigration Act, Lodge was the Senate majority leader, the chair of the Republican Conference, and the chair of the Senate Foreign Relations Committee. In contrast to other liberal Republican Massachusetts senators, Lodge's views were deeply shaped by the academic theories about eugenics and race science. He grew up in a blue-blooded Boston family among the elites of MIT and Harvard who were pushing race science. His best friend was Teddy Roosevelt. Lodge attended Harvard and received the first PhD in political science from the university, writing about the history of Anglo-Saxon law at the same time that his professors were beginning to theorize the racial superiority of Anglo-Saxons. He was elected to the US House of Representatives in 1887 and then was selected in 1893 to replace Senator Henry Dawes, one of the handful of senators who had spoken and voted against the Chinese Exclusion Act. Lodge was a progressive, but his policy positions were colored by his desire to protect his well-heeled family and position. He feared the potential unrest that could be unleashed by the masses if they were allowed to coalesce into a mob.[16]

In 1896, Lodge first rose in the Senate to propose a literacy test for immigrants. In his speech, he echoed the racial views of his Boston clique of friends and the emerging eugenics race science of the era. He began by laying out the "great change" in immigrants since 1875. Since then "other races of totally different race origin, with whom the English-speaking people have never hitherto been assimilated or brought in contact, have suddenly begun to immigrate to the United States in large numbers. Russians, Hungarians, Poles, Bohemians, Italians, Greeks, and even Asiatics." For Lodge, there might be other pressing political issues of the day, but nothing else rose to the threat immigration posed to the white character of the United States. "It involves, in a word, nothing less than the possibility of a great and perilous change in the very fabric of our race."

In the middle of his speech, Lodge recounted the state of eugenics and race science at the time, clearly influenced by his elite Boston circle of MIT and Harvard professors. He stated as fact that "the men of each race possess an indestructible stock of ideas, traditions, sentiments, modes of thought, an unconscious inheritance from their ancestors, upon which argument has no effect. What makes a race are their mental and, above all, their moral characteristics, the slow growth and accumulation of centuries of toil and conflict." However, the indestructible stock of white men apparently was in fact very easily destroyed. "There is only one way in which you can lower those qualities or weaken those characteristics, and that is by breeding them out. If a lower race mixes with a higher in sufficient numbers, history teaches us that the lower race will prevail." Although he did not use the term "race suicide" that his best friend Teddy Roosevelt would soon popularize, it is the core of his argument. He ended by suggesting that immigration restrictions are the only option to prevent the replacement of the white race: "The danger has begun. . . . The time has certainly come, if not to stop, at least to check, to sift, and to restrict those immigrants."[17]

Congress passed the literacy test in 1896 but President Grover Cleveland vetoed it. Congress again passed it in 1912 and 1915, but it was vetoed by Presidents William Howard Taft and Woodrow Wilson. In 1915, Woodrow Wilson explained his position: "If the people of this country have made up their mind to limit the number of immigrants by arbitrary tests and so reverse the policy of all the generations of Americans that have gone before them, it is their right to do so. . . . But I do not believe they have."[18] In each instance, the House of Representatives voted to override the veto, but Lodge came up just short of the two-thirds majority in the Senate that was necessary to enact the law. He continued to push for it and would soon succeed.

THE COMING RESTRICTIONS

In 1917, after overriding another veto by Woodrow Wilson, the US Congress passed a sweeping immigration law that presaged the broad changes coming in the early 1920s. Lodge finally got his literacy test, which banned anyone over sixteen who could not read thirty to forty words in their own language. In practice, it turned out to have little effect because most immigrants were able to do that, particularly after a little coaching during the long sea journey to America. The law also created an Asiatic barred zone that extended from Saudi Arabia and Afghanistan to the Pacific Islands. The only exceptions were Japan, with which immigration was still governed by the Gentleman's Agreement, and the Philippines, which was a US territory. At the time, there were not a substantial number of migrants from these parts of Asia, but it did represent the extreme step of banning over half the world's population from entering the United States. The law also raised the head tax at the border to $8 (AFI $162) and expanded the tax to Mexican citizens. The result was the emergence of smuggling networks, which would take people across the border for half that amount, saving the laborers money. These smuggling networks on the US-Mexico border would expand further with the prohibition of alcohol in the US in 1920, and they have remained in place ever since.

The 1917 law still did not completely prohibit Japanese immigration, and V. S. McClatchy redoubled his efforts to get a full ban. In 1920, he formed the Japanese Exclusion League of California and became a leading voice in the country for more restrictive immigration policies. The league was supported by a range of different civic organizations including the American Legion, American Federation of Labor, and Federation of Farm Bureaus of California. McClatchy used the *Sacramento Bee* as a platform and parlayed his newspaper contacts developed through his term as president of the Associated Press to roll out a powerful campaign against immigration.

V. S. McClatchy and the Japanese Exclusion League prepared a brief titled "Japanese Immigration and Colonization" for the State Department in 1921 explaining the threat. In the aftermath of World War I, McClatchy made the case that "Japan is the Germany of Asia" and that it, too, had expansionist designs on the Pacific Ocean, including the West Coast of the United States. Immigrants from Japan, the brief warned, were not a benign group of people looking to find work and a home in America. The document promised "conclusive evidence of the grave and imminent danger, not only to California and the Pacific Coast States, but to the Nation itself." As with the Chinese, and every other demonized immigrant group before or since, the report emphasized that the Japanese are simply unable to assimilate. Instead, "their many advantages enable them to drive the whites out of industries and out of communities. . . . They thus displace white mechanics, store keepers, and small business men." McClatchy's strategy was to focus on the dangerous threat that Japan represented, hiding his exclusionary views behind his supposed deep respect for the Japanese. He wrote, "There is no claim or belief as to racial inferiority involved in this issue. There is, on the contrary, a frank admission that because of conditions fully explained herein, the white race may not hope to survive in this country if compelled to meet the

Japanese in competition for economic advantage and racial existence."[19] The real problem was race suicide through replacement. Even if Japanese immigrants did intermix with white Americans, "American whites would have been swallowed up by the Japanese race before this biological change could have taken place."[20]

V. S. McClatchy's timing was auspicious. In the post–World War I era, the elite circles of Boston, New York, and Washington, DC, discovered Madison Grant's *The Passing of the Great Race* just as the Ku Klux Klan's membership drive was exploding across the South and the Midwest. In Congress, Lodge was the Senate majority leader, and Republican Albert Johnson of Washington state, who campaigned for Congress on a platform of immigration restriction, became the chair of the House Immigration Committee. The stage was set for a massive crackdown on immigration to the United States.

CHAPTER 6

KEEP AMERICA AMERICAN

With curly hair parted down the middle and pince-nez spectacles balanced on his nose, Albert Johnson looked the part for his original career as a peripatetic journalist. Johnson was born in Springfield, Illinois, in 1869 and grew up in Kansas. He got his first job at the *St. Joseph Herald* in Missouri before moving on to the *St. Louis Globe-Democrat* and the *New Haven Register* in Connecticut, where he became managing editor in 1896. In 1898, at the age of twenty-nine, he was named the news editor at the *Washington Post* before moving that same year to Tacoma, Washington, to take the position of managing editor of the *Tacoma News*. In Washington State, he became alarmed about the issue of Asian immigration, which continued to roil the West. The dangers of Eastern European immigration also became clear to him after he reported on the impact of Russian immigrants who brought Marxist theories of communism to the local labor unions in Washington. He ran for Congress in 1913 on a platform of strict immigration controls to protect the white people and capitalist culture of the United States. He won the election and remained in Congress for the next twenty years. As a legislator, he was rumored to take bribes, and he was a public drinker, even after Congress passed Prohibition. After serving as a captain in the Chemical Warfare Service during World War I, he became chair of the House Committee on Immigration and Naturalization in 1919.[1]

As the chair of the committee, Albert Johnson invited many of the advocates of eugenics and race science to testify before Congress. In 1920, Harry Laughlin, the director of the Eugenics Records Office, testified about the dangers of race mixing. Johnson said that Laughlin had convinced him that "factors of this nature are the basis upon which the American people must develop their permanent immigration policy."[2] Johnson then named Laughlin as the "Expert Eugenics Agent" for the committee. Johnson began a regular correspondence with Madison Grant, the author of *The Passing of the Great Race*. Lothrop Stoddard, the author of *The Rising Tide of Color Against White World-Supremacy*, testified before the committee. Johnson ordered the Government Printing Office to publish several of V. S. McClatchy's pamphlets on the danger of a Japanese invasion of the West Coast, and McClatchy also gave testimony before the committee.

The foundation for what would become the 1924 Immigration Act was laid with the 1921 Emergency Act to limit the arrival of refugees from Europe after World War I. Albert Johnson's initial draft of the 1921 Emergency Act called for a complete ban on all immigration to the United States for one year. The Senate version, written by Republican William Dillingham of Vermont, who had chaired the Dillingham Commission that studied immigration from 1907 to 1911, instead created quotas based on national origin in which 3 percent of the foreign-born population in the 1910 census would be admitted each year. The Emergency Quota Bill passed both houses of Congress in early 1921 but was vetoed by President Woodrow Wilson in the final days of his term. After Warren Harding was inaugurated as president in March, Johnson brought the bill up again. It passed the House with a voice vote, signifying how broadly it was supported. The vote in the Senate was 90–2, with three present votes. Harding signed it into law on May 19, 1921.

The emergency quotas went into effect two weeks after the bill was signed, which meant that some ships that set sail before it was passed were still at sea when it went into effect, resulting in chaotic races to reach port before the quotas were filled. For Italians and Greeks, the new quotas represented a 99 percent reduction in the number of spots available. Consequently, the monthly quotas would often be filled immediately by a single ship on the first day of the month. As a result, ships would position themselves off the port on the last day of the month, then race into harbor the next morning to unload passengers. On August 31, the *King Alexander* and the *Acropolis*, two ships filled with Greek passengers, eyed each other warily off New York Harbor. After midnight on September 1, they raced for the port; the *King Alexander* won by two minutes. Its passengers filled the Greek quota for the entire month, and the *Acropolis* was forced to sail back to Europe.[3] At the other end of the spectrum, the vast British quota of 77,342 went only half filled in 1921.

THE NATIONAL ORIGINS QUOTAS

When Calvin Coolidge ascended to the presidency after the sudden death of Warren Harding in August 1923, it was clear that Johnson's House committee was going to formulate a permanent restriction bill. Coolidge had written an article about race in 1921 titled "Whose Country Is This?" and said in his December 1923 annual message to Congress that "America must be kept American. For this purpose, it is necessary to continue a policy of restricted immigration."[4] Coolidge used the campaign slogan "Keep America American."

With the winds at their backs, Albert Johnson and the eugenics movement pushed for a final and definitive immigration law. Johnson found a new ally in John B. Trevor Sr., who took up the baton and got the law across the finish line. Trevor was born into old money in New York and was educated at Harvard for his BA (1901) and MA (1903) and then Columbia for law school (1906). Trevor moved in the same elite circles of the Northeast as those promoting race science and eugenics. As with seemingly all of the other eugenics advocates, Trevor was a trustee of Henry Fairfield Osborn's American Museum of Natural History, which at the time was the center of the eugenics movement. Trevor's office in New York was next door to Madison Grant's. Trevor's wife was friends with Eleanor Roosevelt, and John D. Rockefeller Jr. was Trevor's close friend and lifetime benefactor. In World War I, Trevor served as a commander in military intelligence and was tasked with monitoring for subversives in New York, where he focused on Jewish anarchists and communists. As part of his work, he created ethnic maps of New York and became concerned about the stock of the new immigrants. After the war, he became assistant attorney general of New York before moving to Washington, DC, to consult on the planned immigration law.[5] Trevor hit it off immediately with Representative Johnson, who in addition to chairing the House Committee on Immigration and Naturalization had become the president of the Eugenics Research Association at Cold Spring Harbor in 1923.

Johnson made Trevor an informal advisor for the committee where as an unpaid volunteer he wrote reports, sat in on meetings, and developed restriction schemes.[6]

The problem that Johnson and other legislators were stuck on was how to ensure the new law shifted the immigration flow back to the Nordic population at the expense of Eastern and Southern Europeans but did so without being obviously discriminatory to Italians, who were a growing political constituency in the United States. Trevor solved the puzzle with a statistical model that showed that the 1921 emergency quotas, despite their harsh reductions in Southern and Eastern European numbers, were actually still tilted in the new immigrants' favor. His argument was that because the quotas were based only on data of recent immigrant arrivals, the origins of native-born Americans were not considered and thus their immigrant heritage was devalued. Consequently, Trevor suggested that the only fair option was to base the quotas on the national origins of all Americans, not just the national origins of recent immigrants. The Senate majority leader, Henry Cabot Lodge, called Trevor to his office and congratulated him on a scheme that finally provided "an answer to the charges of discrimination" with impartial data.[7] The final decision was to use data from the 1890 census as the baseline for the quotas, to ensure the vast majority of immigration slots went to Northern Europeans.

The push for restrictions in Congress was met with support from the labor movement, the Ku Klux Klan, and even the editorial board of the *New York Times*. For many years, labor unions were divided on the issue of immigration. Most of their members were immigrants themselves and tended to have solidarity with other immigrants to the country, but there was the persistent fear that new immigrants were willing to work for less than unionized workers, undercutting their job security and wages. Samuel Gompers, who headed the American Federation of Labor, supported Lodge's literacy test in the 1890s and wrote publicly in favor of immigration restrictions in 1924. He published an article titled "America Must Not Be Overwhelmed" that emphasized the importance of controls for "the persistence of racial characteristics."[8] The grand dragon of the South Carolina Ku Klux Klan wrote an article titled "The Regulation of Immigration" that argued it was time to "do a bit of house cleaning" to avoid being the "dumping ground of the world from millions of heterogeneous elements." The grand dragon argued there would no longer be an

"America for Americans" if the country continued to allow the "influx" of "Anarchism and Bolshevism," "undesirables," "Jews," "paupers, diseased, and criminals," and "hyphenated-Americans" who "do not deserve the respect of any decent, loyal, patriotic, red-blooded, pure and unadulterated American citizen."[9] What is striking is how closely the KKK position matched the mainstream at the time. The *New York Times* editorial page endorsed the proposed law in an editorial on April 5, 1924, titled "Preserving the American Race."[10]

At first, it appeared that the Japanese Exclusion League and its founder, V. S. McClatchy, the newspaper publisher who pushed for a complete ban on Japanese immigration, would have to settle for a continuation of the Gentleman's Agreement.[11] Several senators, including Henry Cabot Lodge, were uncomfortable with the secret contents of the Gentlemen's Agreement and asked the US secretary of state, Charles Hughes, to clarify it with the Japanese ambassador, Masanao Hanihara. Hanihara responded with a letter laying out the terms as the Japanese government understood them, which amounted to a ban on Japanese immigration. However, Hanihara ended the letter by saying, "Relying on the confidence you have been good enough to show me at all times, I have stated or rather repeated all this to you very candidly and in a most friendly spirit, for I realize, as I believe you do, the grave consequences which the enactment of the measure retaining that particular provision would inevitably bring upon the otherwise happy and mutually advantageous relations between our two countries."[12]

Opponents of Japanese immigration pounced. What did the phrase "grave consequences" mean? they asked. Were the Japanese making a threat against the United States? Whether the ambassador meant it as such or not, the sentiment in the Senate quickly shifted, and Lodge convinced his colleagues that the complete exclusion of the Japanese was the only reasonable response. V. S. McClatchy was elated.

In the final debate in the Senate, the need for restrictions was a given, and speakers mostly rose to argue for more or less extreme versions. While the debates about Chinese exclusion in the 1880s had a strong minority who opposed it, by the early 1920s the idea that the country could and should limit migration had taken hold, and the speeches were more explicitly about race. Senator Oscar Underwood of Alabama began by focusing on labor, but after a question, he seemed to drop his talking points and dove into race: "There was never a race in the world that did not desire to maintain its own racial integrity." He continued, "Racial integrity will be maintained always by every race of people and we cannot permit the yellow and brown races to come to this country in large numbers without destroying racial integrity."[13]

Then the other senator from Alabama, James Thomas Heflin, rose to speak. Heflin has the honor of being the author of the bill that created the Mother's Day holiday, but he was also a consistent voice for white supremacy in his native Alabama and in the US Senate. In 1901, he helped write the Alabama constitution that prevented African Americans from voting, and he was said to be a member of the KKK. While he was in the House of Representatives, he introduced a bill to enforce segregated streetcars in Washington, DC. As it was under consideration, he rode a streetcar and attempted to kick a Black man out of a section for white riders. When the man resisted, Heflin pulled out a pistol and accidentally shot a tourist from New York in the leg. Heflin claimed he was defending a white woman, and the charges were dropped after he paid the tourist's medical bills.[14]

On the Senate floor, Heflin recounted a loose history of the 1813 Fort Mims massacre in his home state of Alabama. He said that the leaders of the fort felt that the defeated Creek Nation was of no threat to them, so they left the gate of the fort open. A young girl, Lucy Dean, asked, "Who left the gate open?" and said, "Close the gate," but no one did. When the Creek warriors arrived, everyone screamed, "Close the gate!" Unfortunately, Heflin shouted to his colleagues, "it was too late!" He paused for effect, then he added more quietly, "Too late." The "whole white population" was massacred. For Heflin, the implications were clear, and he ended by appealing to the Senate to close the gate to nonwhite immigrants before it was too late.[15]

There were a few senators who spoke against the restrictions. David Walsh of Massachusetts railed against the amendment that switched the baseline of the law to the 1890 census, in which 87 percent were from Western and Northern Europe. If they used the most recent census from 1910, it would have been 56 percent. "It simply amounts to reducing and practically eliminating all emigration from southern and eastern Europe. Whatever may be the surface reason for the change in date, it must be insisted that the true reason is racial discrimination."[16]

However, the voices against restrictions were in the distinct minority. The mood of the country had turned against immigration, a reality reflected in the Johnson-Reed bill. The bill passed in the US House by a vote of 308–62 and the Senate 69–9 on May 15 and was signed by President Calvin Coolidge on May 24.[17] The reaction in the press was unequivocal. The *Los Angeles Times* headline cheered, "A Nordic Victory!" Henry Cabot Lodge called the law "one of the most important, if not the most important, Congress has ever passed."[18] It would also be one of Lodge's last acts as Senate majority leader. He died six months later.

V. S. McClatchy celebrated his victory but then turned to what he saw as a third wave of the Asian invasion of the United States, Filipinos who were able to move to the mainland because the Philippines was a US colony. He reconstituted the Japanese Exclusion League as the California Joint Immigration Committee and pressed for legislation to limit Filipino migration and to restrict return migration from people living in Japan who possessed US citizenship. McClatchy never reconciled with his brother and died of a heart attack on May 15, 1938. His son H. J. McClatchy took over as the executive secretary of the California Joint Immigration Committee and was a vocal supporter of the internment of Japanese Americans during World War II, arguing, "It was impossible to separate the loyal from the disloyal. While the loyal might therefore suffer in mass treatment, this was preferable to endangering the welfare of the nation."[19]

In March 1929, the quota board released the finalized quotas for the Johnson-Reed Immigration Act, which reduced the total immigration cap further to 153,700.[20] Descendants of former African slaves were not counted as immigrants, so their native countries did not get higher quotas. Asian residents, even those with birthright citizenship, were not counted because new migrants from those countries could not be naturalized. Territories like Hawai'i and Puerto Rico, which had large nonwhite citizen populations, were also excluded. The result was an even whiter data set for an already mostly white country. The largest share went to Great Britain with 65,721 slots per year. Germany was second with 25,957, and Ireland was third with 17,853. The German quota would play a role in the lead-up to World War II, as Jews fleeing the Nazi regime were nevertheless turned away when the yearly quota was met. Most other countries received the minimum quota of 100. Some countries, like Palestine,

Ruanda [Rwanda], Nauru, and Muscat [Oman], got quotas but with the caveat that the immigrant needed to be eligible for naturalization, which meant that these quotas were only open to white European colonists who were residing there.[21]

The impact of the Johnson-Reed Immigration Act was immediate. While in 1914, the last year of open migration before World War I, 1.2 million people arrived in the United States, in 1924 that was reduced to 164,700. While in 1920–21, only 25.7 percent of immigrants were from Northern and Western Europe, by 1925 it was back up to 75.6 percent.[22] The impact on particular countries was even more dramatic. Italians and Greeks were the most affected. Italian arrivals went from 222,260 in 1921 to 2,662 in 1925. Greek immigration to the US was nonexistent in 1890, so the quota was set at the minimum of 100 people per year, down from over 20,000 arrivals in 1921.[23] From 1880 to 1920, 23.5 million people immigrated to the US. From 1921 to 1965, only 6 million more would come.[24]

— CHAPTER 7 —

THE ETHNIC MIX OF THIS
COUNTRY WILL NOT BE UPSET

On April 20, 1924, as the US Congress debated the Johnson-Reed Immigration Act, Adolf Hitler celebrated his thirty-fifth birthday in a cell in Landsberg Prison in Germany. After his discharge from the German military in 1920, Hitler began to develop his fascist political views and hone his speaking skills at beer halls in Bavaria. He felt the sting from what he saw as Germany's humiliating and unwarranted defeat in World War I, and, in his speeches, he explained away Germany's economic troubles by scapegoating immigrants and Jews. By 1923, he was a leader of the National Socialist Party, and he looked to Benito Mussolini's rise in Italy as a model for how his Nazi Party could grab power in Germany. On November 8, 1923, Hitler led an attempted coup in what came to be known as the Beer Hall Putsch. He barged into a Bavarian government meeting with his storm troopers in tow. After a few hours of uncertainty, the coup failed. Hitler was arrested for high treason on November 11 and sentenced to five years in prison on April 1, 1924.

From his prison cell, Hitler followed the debates around the Johnson-Reed Immigration Act in the US and found a lot to like. He used the time in prison to dictate *Mein Kampf* (My struggle), which was published in two volumes in 1925 and 1926, after he was pardoned and released from prison. The first volume, titled *A Reckoning*, was autobiographical and traced his life in concert with the plight of Germany in World War I. The second volume, titled *The National Socialist Movement*, focused on his ultranationalist vision for Germany in which immigrants and Jews were singled out as the cause of Germany's problems. Hitler criticized birthright citizenship and Germany's willingness to naturalize people born elsewhere, whom he referred to as a poison in the body of the nation. He wrote, "And so every year these formations, called states, take into themselves poison elements which they can scarcely overcome."

Hitler, however, saw reasons for hope in the example of America. In *Mein Kampf*, he wrote, "There is today one state in which at least weak beginnings toward a better conception are noticeable. Of course, it is not our model German Republic, but the American Union, in which an effort is made to consult reason at least partially. By refusing immigration on principle to elements in poor health, by simply excluding certain races from naturalization, it professes in slow beginnings a view which is peculiar to the folkish state concept."[1]

There were also those in the United States who saw hope in the rise of the Nazis. Hitler was cheered on by the leading figures in the eugenics movement in America. Madison Grant, whose book *The Passing of the Great Race* deeply influenced Americans in the lead-up to the 1924 Immigration Act and which would be found in Hitler's bunker after his suicide, supported the goals of the early Nazi movement. Madison Grant wrote another book in 1933 titled *The Conquest of the Continent*. Scribner's, the venerated publishing house, promoted it by explaining, "National problems today are, at bottom, race problems. Herr Hitler has stated that problem for Germany—and is working out his own solution. We in America have our own problem."[2] Harry Laughlin, who was the director of the Eugenics Records Office and the "expert eugenics agent" for Albert Johnson's House Committee on Immigration and Naturalization, used his publication, the *Eugenical News*, to publish Nazi propaganda. He also extolled the regime's use of eugenics: "Germany is the first of all the great nations of the world to make direct practical use of eugenics."[3] He was close with German doctor Carl Schneider, who carried out a euthanasia program for the Nazis and who hanged himself in 1946 while awaiting trial for war crimes. Laughlin accepted an honorary degree from Schneider at the University of Heidelberg in 1934. Laughlin even mused about making Hitler an honorary member of his Eugenics Research Organization.[4]

THE PIONEER FUND

In 1937, Laughlin became the first president of the Pioneer Fund, which was founded by a wealthy New Yorker named Wickliffe Draper. The Pioneer Fund was a mechanism to funnel money to politicians, researchers, and journalists who continued to support eugenics and white supremacy and, in the early years, to cheer on the Nazi Party's concrete steps in these directions. Draper's father was a general, a US congressional representative from Kentucky, and the creator of a successful textile business. Wickliffe Draper, bespectacled and unassuming, graduated summa cum laude from Harvard in 1913. He was impatient because the United States was slow to enter World War I, so he joined the British Army before transferring to the US Army once it finally stepped in. After the war, he continued to wear his uniform but never worked another day in his life and never married. Instead, he was a recluse who lived on the top three floors of an expensive condominium on East Fifty-Seventh Street in Manhattan, where he decorated the walls with hunting trophies and dabbled in race science. Despite his desire for privacy, he occasionally made the rounds of New York high society, where he was known as "the Colonel" and was an acquaintance of eugenicists Charles Davenport and Madison Grant. Draper quietly sent money to various white supremacist groups for years and paid for a thousand copies of the book *White America* to be sent to all the members of Congress in the mid-1930s. The book, by Earnest Sevier Cox, argued for the repatriation of all African Americans back to Africa to preserve the white character of the country. The mailing resulted in support from Mississippi senator Theodore Gilmore Bilbo, who even read the text of *White America* into the *Congressional Record* during his filibuster of the Anti-lynching Act. In 1939, Bilbo also introduced the Greater Liberia Act into the Senate, which, if it had passed, would have attempted to repatriate all Black Americans to Liberia within a generation.[5]

Having seen the impact his money could have, Draper established the Pioneer Fund to continue these efforts.[6] The founding board of the Pioneer Fund included many of the regulars of the eugenics movement. In addition to Harry Laughlin, who served as president, Frederick Henry Osborn, the nephew of Henry Fairfield Osborn (the president of the American Museum of Natural History who hosted many eugenics meetings), was on the board along with Malcolm Donald, who was Draper's lawyer. The one surprising member was John Marshall Harlan, who was the grandson of the Supreme Court justice who bore the same name and who had served from 1877 until 1911. The younger Harlan was a New York lawyer who was involved in many nonprofits when he became one of the founding members of the Pioneer Fund in 1937. He remained on the board until 1954, just a few months before he himself was nominated to the US Supreme Court in January 1955 by Dwight D. Eisenhower. The younger Harlan went on to serve on the court until September 1971.

The charter of the Pioneer Fund was not subtle about its racial purpose. It explained that it would support "research into the problems of heredity and eugenics in the human race," and "consideration shall especially be given to children who are deemed to be descended predominantly from white persons who settled in the original thirteen states prior the adoption of the constitution . . . and/or from related stocks." The Pioneer Fund's first project was to pay for the US distribution of the Nazi film *The Hereditary Defective*, which was produced by the German Office of Racial Politics.[7]

Outside the most fervent true believers, however, eugenics and race science were falling out of favor in scholarly and popular circles in the United States. By the 1930s, scholars refuted the pseudoscience of Madison Grant's and William Ripley's theories of Nordic racial superiority and poked holes in the eugenics-based intelligence testing of Henry Goddard and Robert Yerkes. Goddard, who pioneered IQ testing on immigrants at Ellis Island, explained to his former friends in the eugenics movement that "I think I have gone over to the enemy side," at least on some of the most extreme claims.[8] Carl Brigham, who developed the SAT test and received funding from Madison Grant to write *A Study of American Intelligence* in 1923 with Princeton University Press, also changed his mind. He decided his book was wrong and wrote that his findings, which had presented chart after chart showing Nordic peoples as having superior intelligence compared to immigrants and African Americans, were "without foundation."[9] As younger, more scientifically rigorous scholars entered the academy, there were fewer and fewer voices supporting the racial sciences of the past.

In Germany, the Nazis took eugenics to its grisly conclusion with Hitler's Final Solution and the murder of 6 million Jews and other minorities, which forced a national reckoning with the consequences of racial pseudoscience. In the US, there was never a full reckoning but rather a modest reconsideration of the worst aspects. Although the underlying pseudoscience was disproved, the policies that were created based on eugenics have persisted through the present day. The bias inherent in the eugenics-derived IQ and SAT tests, which measure affluence as much as ability, have been known since the 1930s, but society continues to use them all the same.[10]

The same goes for immigration laws. As the 1924 Immigration Law was passed, cosponsor David Reed of Pennsylvania took a victory lap in the pages of the *New York Times* explaining that the fear of the great replacement of the Nordic race was the reason for the law. He wrote, "There has come about a general realization of the fact that the races of men who have been coming to us in recent years are wholly dissimilar to the native-born Americans." For Reed, "unless immigration is numerically restrained she will be overwhelmed by a vast migration of peoples." However, rather than allow the "Nordic race" to be overwhelmed, his immigration law ensured that "the racial composition of America at the present time is thus made permanent."[11] The fallacy of pseudoscience theories of Nordic racial superiority were known since the 1930s, but the immigration laws they spawned continue to exist through the present day. In the years since, rather than reconsider a law that was created based on pseudoscience and was hailed by Adolf Hitler in *Mein Kampf*, the United States has instead built a substantial border security infrastructure to enforce it.

In the aftermath of World War II, as the horrific atrocities of the Nazi extermination programs became clear, eugenics and race science lost almost all legitimacy and support in the United States. Prior to the war, many millions of Americans supported Nazism, but after the Holocaust, almost none would admit it. In the post–World War II period, there was a broader reconsideration of the role of race in American society as more people began to question the racial order of the Jim Crow South and the Euro-American colonization of the rest of the world. Both of these unjust systems began to unravel through the civil rights movement in the United States and independence movements around the world.

Some of this critical attention to race shone a negative light on the racial quotas that were still in place in the United States in both naturalization and immigration law. The US naturalization law still included the requirement to be a descendant of a freed slave or a "free white person," a phrase that remained unchanged since the law was first written in 1790. After Harry Truman's unexpected election victory in 1948, his administration pursued changes to both the 1790 free white person requirement for naturalization and the 1924 national origins quotas, but he faced opposition. The bill that emerged, the 1952 McCarren-Walter Act, did not go as far as Truman wanted and he vetoed it, writing, "The greatest vice of the present quota system is that it discriminates, deliberately and intentionally, against many peoples of the world." He continued, "The idea behind the discriminatory policy was, to put it boldly, that Americans with English or Irish names were better people and better citizens than Americans with Italian or Greek or Polish names. . . . Such a concept is utterly unworthy of our traditions and our ideals."[12]

Congress overrode Truman's veto and the McCarren-Walter Immigration Act of 1952 became law. There were some positive steps in the bill, which finally removed "free white person" from the naturalization requirement, 162 years after it was originally written. The new law said instead, "The right of a person to become a naturalized citizen of the United States shall not be denied or abridged because of race or sex or because such a person is married." However, shaped by the start of the Cold War, the law denies naturalization to people based on their political beliefs, including communists, anarchists, and totalitarians. It also banned people who published the writings of these ideologies. The bill kept the national origins quotas, but it did remove the complete ban on Asian immigration, replacing it with very small quotas for each country. Truman was not satisfied with the law and formed a presidential commission to review immigration policy. The commission's report recommended a more liberal system, but by that point Truman's term had ended and Dwight D. Eisenhower was the president. Any further changes to the immigration law were put on hold.

Even after the atrocities of the Nazi movement were exposed and the civil rights movement began to undo the legal regime of segregation in the United States, Wickliffe Draper and the Pioneer Fund did not reconsider their support for eugenics and white supremacy. Instead, seeing their worldview under threat, they expanded their giving in an effort to counter the civil rights movement in the United States. In 1958, Harry F. Weyher Jr., a Manhattan-based, Harvard-educated lawyer originally from North Carolina, become the president of the Pioneer Fund, a position he would hold until his death in 2002. Weyher and Draper became key supporters for southern white supremacists, often as their only source of funds. In the 1960s, the Pioneer Fund paid for the publication of arch-segregationist Carleton Putnam's books, lawsuits to overturn *Brown v. Board of Education*, citizen committees to establish alternatives to desegregated schools, and politicians like Francis Walker of the House Un-American Activities Committee.[13]

Wickliffe Draper died in 1972 and angered his relatives by leaving them only $10,000 each while giving $2.6 million (AFI $16.7 million) to what they called his "Hitlerite" Pioneer Fund.[14] Harry Weyher remained the president and began to work closely with John Trevor Jr., the son of John Trevor Sr., who was the primary behind-the-scenes architect of the 1924 Immigration Act. Over the decades, Weyher, Trevor, and the Pioneer Fund board grew the endowment while giving millions of dollars to a who's who of the increasingly fringe white supremacist movement. They also funded dozens of academics looking at the connections between race and intelligence. Some of the major recipients were Stanford professor William Shockley, who among other things challenged successful Black intellectuals to provide him with blood samples so he could test if their intellect was actually due to white genes, and Roger Pearson, a professor who ran the publications *Mankind Quarterly* and the *Journal of Social, Political, and Economic Studies*, which were the two primary outlets for the publication of eugenics and race science in the last decades of the twentieth century.

THE CIVIL RIGHTS MOVEMENT

While the Pioneer Fund worked behind the scenes to maintain white supremacy in the United States, the civil rights movement was upending the most visible aspects of it. Through sit-ins, peaceful marches, and civil disobedience, the civil rights movement had begun to deconstruct the system of segregation and Jim Crow laws that divided Black and white people and maintained the supremacy of white Americans for a century after the end of slavery. As racial discrimination was challenged in the streets, in courts, and in Congress, the foundations for a more comprehensive revision of US immigration policy were beginning to fall into place.

John F. Kennedy played a significant role in the push to amend the immigration law, drawing inspiration from Harry Truman's passionate veto statement in 1952. In the mid-1950s, Kennedy was the junior US senator from Massachusetts. His book *Profiles in Courage*, ghostwritten by his advisor and speechwriter Theodore Sorenson, won the Pulitzer Prize for Biography in 1957. Kennedy followed it up with *A Nation of Immigrants* in 1958, also likely ghostwritten, but this time by another aide, Meyer Feldman. The book tells a positive history of immigration to America, focusing on the contributions of European immigrants and glossing over the exclusion of the Chinese. The book ends with a forceful critique of the racial national origins quotas instituted in the 1924 Johnson-Reed Immigration Act and perpetuated in the 1952 revision of the immigration law. Kennedy wrote, "The national origin quota system has strong overtones of an indefensible racial preference. It is strongly weighted toward so-called Anglo-Saxons." Instead, Kennedy proposed a new vision. American "immigration policy should be generous; it should be fair; it should be flexible. With such a policy we can turn to the world, and on our own past, with clean hands and a clean conscience."[15]

Kennedy rode his intellectual reputation, good looks, and early mastery of the new medium of television to the presidency in the 1960 election against Richard Nixon. In the months before his assassination in Dallas on November 22, 1963, he and his brother, Robert F. Kennedy, the attorney general, were working on a revised version of *A Nation of Immigrants* as part of a planned push for a new immigration legislation. After he was killed, the book was rereleased in 1964 with a new foreword by Robert F. Kennedy, who left the administration to run for the Senate from New York. He won the election and took his seat in the Senate in January 1965, alongside his younger brother Ted, who was a senator from Massachusetts, and they worked together on a revision to the immigration law.

Initially, Lyndon Johnson did not focus on immigration in his push for civil rights and social programs in the extremely productive legislative years that marked the conclusion of Kennedy's term and the start of Johnson's. In addition to the Civil Rights Act of 1964, which passed after the longest filibuster in the history of the Senate, the Eighty-Eighth Congress also passed the Equal Pay Act, the Clean Air Act, the Wilderness Act, and the Food Stamp Act. The Eighty-Ninth Congress, which began in 1965, continued with the Social Security Act, the Voting Rights Act, and the creation of the National Endowment of the Arts.

The Civil Rights Act of 1964 banned discrimination based on race, color, religion, sex, or national origin. This meant that US immigration law, which excluded whole groups of people based on national origin, was in violation of the law. However, just as the Civil Rights Act faced substantial opposition in Congress and across the country, the effort to reform the immigration act faced headwinds in Congress. In addition to opposition from many southern senators and representatives, the Johnson administration had to overcome another substantial obstacle. Michael Feighan, a fellow Democrat from Ohio and the chair of the House Subcommittee on Immigration and Nationality, was also staunchly opposed to changes to the immigration law. With a square jaw and stylish wavy hair, Feighan knew his support was required to get the proposed bill out of the committee and to a vote in the House of Representatives. Feighan had voted in favor of both the Civil Rights Act in 1964 and the Voting Rights Act in 1965, but he was conservative and concerned that his rural district would not be in favor of expanded immigration to the United States. When the White House approached him with the new immigration bill that would end the racial quotas and replace them with skilled-based immigration, his response was "very cool."[16]

Feighan had two primary objections to Johnson's immigration bill. First, Feighan worried that Johnson's proposal to replace the national origins quotas with skill-based quotas might result in a dramatic shift in the demographics of the people immigrating to the United States, as the sheer numbers of people in Asia would replace the traditional immigration sources in Europe. Second, Feighan was concerned that the White House's draft continued to exempt the Western Hemisphere from any restrictions, which would mean Mexicans could continue to freely enter the United States.

Feighan found an ally in John Trevor Jr., the Pioneer Fund board member whose father was the architect of the national origins quotas. At the time, Trevor Jr. was in charge of the American Coalition of Patriotic Societies, and he used the organizations to make an all-out push to save his father's law, publishing editorials warning that any changes would "let down the bars to swarms of Asiatics and Africans." Trevor was invited by Feighan to testify before the House Subcommittee on Immigration and Naturalization, where he called his father's national origins quotas "fair" and argued that they conformed with the "composition to our own people."[17] During the Senate debates about the bill, Senator Spessard Holland of Florida explained the fear of replacement that drove their opposition to a more open immigration law. He said,

> We are going to open the gates to all people, disregarding the fact that our background is largely European. . . . I merely state that when we open our doors wide to all the oriental nations of this earth, with some 700 to 800 million in 1 country alone, and with countless other millions in other nations, and when we offer to admit them on terms of exact equality with people from our own forefather nations, we are making a radical departure of which I cannot, and do not approve. That is the point.[18]

Representative Feighan suggested an alternative to Johnson's plan by proposing that most immigration visas be reserved for family reunification. Just as the 1924 quotas were meant to favor immigration from traditional European sources, the family reunification model was meant to give preference to immigrants from the same countries as the current residents of the United States. Since 84 percent of Americans were white and of European ancestry in 1965, Feighan reasoned that the majority of people applying for family reunification visas would also be white and European. The Johnson administration adopted this position without much consideration of what it would really mean.

Feighan and his allies argued against the Western Hemisphere exemption by flipping the nondiscrimination language of the Civil Rights Act on its head, saying free movement for Mexicans and Canadians discriminated against Europeans. As the bill was debated in the House of Representatives on August 25, 1965, Republican representative Clark MacGregor of Minnesota proposed an amendment to remove the Western Hemisphere exception. He explained the logic: "We will be perpetuating and even increasing a new form of discrimination—discrimination based not upon race, which we eliminate in this bill and rightly so—but discrimination based on national origin and the location of one's birth."[19] MacGregor's amendment did not pass the House, but as the bill moved over to the Senate, different provisions including the Western Hemisphere ban continued to be debated.

THE HART-CELLER IMMIGRATION ACT

The US Senate convened on Wednesday, September 22, 1965, to consider the bill to end the national origins quotas. Heads of state from around the world were gathered in New York at the United Nations General Assembly where the topics of discussion were the growing conflict in Vietnam and efforts to broker a cease-fire in the month-long war in Kashmir between India and Pakistan. Washington was a balmy 88 degrees, well above the norm for late September. However, air-conditioning was installed in the Capitol Building in the late 1950s, making what had been an unbearable place to be in Washington's humid summers much more pleasant. In the Senate chamber, Carl Hayden of Arizona, the president pro tempore as the most senior member of the majority Democratic Party, called the body to order at the stroke of noon. As senators milled about the cloakroom and made their way to their desks, the clerks read the business of the day, announcing the bills passed by the House of Representatives and reading statements from the president and a series of nominations from the secretary of state. Then the Senate went through a series of bills ranging from an amendment to the Lead-Zinc Small Producers Stabilization Act to a proposal to honor "Father Flanagan and Boys Town, Nebraska."

A few hours later, the Senate turned to the immigration legislation. The bill was introduced to the Senate by Phillip Hart of Michigan, but it was shepherded through the debates by the two Kennedy brothers. Early in the debates, Senator Ted Kennedy tried to quell fears that it would lead to more immigration from Asia or Africa, reassuring critics that "our cities will not be flooded with a million immigrants annually. . . . The ethnic mix of this country will not be upset."[20] The bill faced opposition from southern senators, but a compromise with conservative North Carolina senator Sam Ervin reinstated the Western Hemisphere cap that Clark MacGregor proposed in the House. With Ervin's support, the immigration bill was virtually certain to pass with a large majority.

Several senators still rose to express their concern about the threat of replacement that the immigration law posed to the white character of the United States. Senator Allen Ellender of Louisiana gave extended remarks about his reservations. Ellender was elected to the Senate in 1937 and was a staunch segregationist who had voted against the Civil Rights Act and the Voting Rights Act. The senator from Louisiana began his comments with a quite thoughtful history of the emergence of the state system in Europe and the history of immigration laws in the United States. As with other white supremacists, he did not deny that the early history of the country was oriented to the white population. His argument was simply that the inclusive language of the civil rights movement of the 1960s was an abandonment of the white foundations of the country. He continued, "Those who wish to denounce me as a bigot may do so, but I for one want this Nation to remain Christian, and civilized in the Western European and American sense of the word." For Ellender, allowing more immigrants from Asia or Africa would be an enormous mistake. In his view, immigrants from those places would not assimilate or contribute to the United States. Instead, the country would be "swamped by the Asians and Africans coming into the United States." "They are going to install themselves in the Harlems, the Watts, the South Bostons and other over-crowded areas, plagued by poverty, ignorance and disease." Ellender concluded that if they wanted his vote, there should be a five-year ban on all immigration to the United States.[21]

The Kennedy brothers worked with other progressive senators to rebut the arguments of Ellender, Holland, and their fellow southern segregationists. Joseph Tydings, a first-term Democratic senator from Maryland, responded that the white supremacist view of American history did not live up to the promise of the country's founding documents. He argued, "It is sheer hypocrisy to extol the virtues of the Declaration of Independence and the Constitution, and at the same time uphold an immigration system which is based on the principle of racial superiority." As the vote neared, Ted Kennedy of Massachusetts summed up the consensus that the racial national origins quotas had to be replaced: "As many senators have pointed out, this is a historic occasion. The bill we will pass today will be considered, in the light of history, as one of the most important accomplishments of this Congress."[22]

Despite the opposition from southern segregationists, the bill easily passed the House by a vote of 318–95 and the Senate 76–18. Lyndon Johnson signed it into law on October 3, 1965, at the Statue of Liberty with the Kennedy brothers standing behind him. For Johnson, it was the culmination of the effort to undo the history of racial discrimination in the country. Nevertheless, the president emphasized that it was not meant to be a significant change to immigration policy.

He said,

This bill that we will sign today is not a revolutionary bill. It does not affect the lives of millions. It will not reshape the structure of our daily lives. . . . Yet, it is still one of the most important acts of this Congress and of this administration. For it does repair a very deep and painful flaw in the fabric of American justice. It corrects a cruel and enduring wrong in the conduct of the American Nation. . . . And today we can all believe that the lamp of this grand old lady is brighter today—and the golden door that she guards gleams more brilliantly the light of an increased liberty for people from all countries of the globe.[23]

Although President Johnson and the Kennedy brothers said repeatedly that the Hart-Celler Immigration Act of 1965 was primarily about correcting an unjust law and would not have substantial material impacts on the "ethnic mix of this country," they turned out to be wrong. Both of the compromises they made, with Representative Feighan to focus on family reunification and with Senator Ervin to end the Western Hemisphere exemption, have had profound and long-lasting impacts on the United States. In the years after the law went into effect, demand for labor in the American agricultural and construction sectors remained high and laborers from Mexico continued to come to work. However, the US Border Patrol used the new law to make many more arrests in the vast border zone. While in 1965, the Border Patrol apprehended 52,422 people, by 1974 it soared to 596,796.[24] At the same time, the switch to family reunification visas allowed for an increasing number of people to enter the United States. While in 1965, the country welcomed 297,000 immigrants, by the late 1970s it was over 600,000 per year. In the 1970 census, 4.7 percent of the US population was foreign born. By 2010, it was 12.9 percent, a comparable rate to the 1890s.

Just as the immigrants of the 1890s were met with an anti-immigrant backlash, since the passage of the 1965 Immigration Act a new anti-immigrant movement has grown in the United States. Although it would eventually convulse national politics and lead to the election of Donald Trump, the latest effort to close America's borders to nonwhite immigrants began in a seemingly unlikely place: the grassroots environmental movement that arose in the 1960s to protect wilderness, endangered species, and the natural beauty of the United States.

— CHAPTER 8 —

PEOPLE, PEOPLE, PEOPLE, PEOPLE

Johnny Carson wore a light-green jacket, a brown tie, and his mischievous grin as he hosted the *Tonight Show* on Monday, February 9, 1970. Carson had already been introduced by Ed McMahon with his trademark "Heeeeeere's Johnny," and they were talking about the guests that night. He sat behind his signature desk with a gauzy fake nature scene in the background, like they used to have in every photography studio in the 1970s. Carson told his jokes before a scene of blue mountains and a white sky framing a misty lake. The comedian Bob Newhart was there, as well as the actors Robert Lansing and Leslie Uggams, but they were preparing to bring out a more unusual guest, a Stanford professor named Paul Ehrlich. Carson found that most professors were too serious and pedantic for his millions of viewers who wanted to laugh and be entertained as they fell asleep, so he rarely booked them.

As Ehrlich strode out in a blue suit and confidently shook Carson's hand, the worry that he would be boring subsided. It turned out that the thirty-seven-year-old was a natural for television. He spoke clearly and authoritatively, leaning in toward Carson as his closely cropped beard and smile exuded a disarming confidence. The story he told, however, was anything but comforting. He laid out the horrors of population growth that could lead to a total breakdown of the ability of the earth to support the human population. He also provided a simple solution. "You have to get the death rate and the birth rate in balance," he explained as Carson nodded with his hands folded in front of him, "and there's only two ways to do it. One is to bring the birth rate down, the other is to push the death rate up."[1] Since increasing the death rate is unpalatable, for Ehrlich the only option was population control. In the weeks after Ehrlich's appearance, the *Tonight Show* got hundreds of letters from viewers, indicating Ehrlich had struck a nerve. Carson invited him back on April 16, just days before the first Earth Day on April 22, 1970.

The 1960s were a decade of many monumental changes in American society, including the awakening to the damage humanity could inflict on the earth. Rachel Carson (no relation to Johnny) initiated the movement in 1962 with her book *Silent Spring*, which told of the potential for catastrophic harm to the environment through the wanton use of pesticides.[2] In 1968, Garrett Hardin, a professor of human ecology at the University of California at Santa Barbara, published "The Tragedy of the Commons" in *Science* magazine. The Tragedy of the Commons posits that if a group of people have unrestricted access to a common resource, say, a grove of trees for firewood, they will follow their own self-interest to cut down as much as they need without considering the impact on others or on the stability of the forest as a whole. Although the Tragedy of the Commons has been discredited by other scholars, including in the work of the Nobel Prize–winning economist Elinor Ostrom, the idea that humanity was destroying the remaining natural areas of the world resonated. Stalwarts like the Sierra Club and the Audubon Society had been around for decades, but a series of new environmental groups were formed to push for more protections, including the World Wildlife Fund in 1961, the Environmental Defense Fund in 1967, Friends of the Earth in 1969, the Natural Resources Defense Council in 1970, and Greenpeace in 1975. This groundswell of support was followed by a series of legislation in the United States, including the creation of the Environmental Protection Agency in 1970, the Clean Water Act of 1972, and the Endangered Species Act of 1973.

Ehrlich's book *The Population Bomb* added the specter of unchecked population growth to the equation. Ehrlich's vision of a world threatened by rapid population growth was shaped by a trip he took to India in 1966. The first page of *The Population Bomb* vividly described the experience of riding a taxi back to his hotel in Delhi:

> The seats were hopping with fleas. . . . The streets seemed alive with people. People eating, people washing, people sleeping. People visiting, arguing, and screaming. People thrusting their hands through the taxi

window, begging. People defecating and urinating. People clinging to buses. People herding animals. People, people, people, people. As we moved slowly through the mob, hand horn squawking, the dust, noise, heat, and cooking fires gave the scene a hellish aspect. Would we ever get to our hotel? All three of us were, frankly, frightened.[3]

Shaken, Ehrlich and his wife, Ann, worked together to write *The Population Bomb* to draw attention to the issue. The book used hyperbole, predicting dire consequences within a decade, but it also presented the issue as a neutral, global imperative to protect the environment. Nevertheless, Ehrlich's alarm was tinged with racial views from the beginning. His moment of clarity was produced in Delhi, which in 1966 had a population of fewer than 3 million people, where he saw "people, people, people, people" everywhere. Somehow, he did not have the same reaction closer to home in New York City, which at the time was home to 8 million.

The Population Bomb was published in 1968, but Ehrlich struggled to bring attention to it and to the new advocacy group he founded, Zero Population Growth. Before Ehrlich went on *The Tonight Show*, Zero Population Growth had six chapters and six hundred members. In the months after his appearance, it grew to six hundred chapters and sixty thousand members.[4] *The Population Bomb* became a best seller, and Ehrlich would be invited back on *The Tonight Show* twenty times.

Among the millions of Americans shocked by *The Population Bomb*'s dire predictions, Ehrlich found a particularly devoted reader in John Tanton. At the time, Tanton was a thirty-five-year-old ophthalmologist just getting his practice started in the remote upper reaches of Michigan. However, Tanton was already active in the local conservation movement and was a key organizer of Earth Day activities in Michigan. He gave thirty lectures on the connection between population growth and environmental damage in the weeks leading up to the first Earth Day in 1970. The paths of Tanton, Ehrlich, and Garrett Hardin would cross only a few months later at a conference in Chicago, and their lives would become deeply intertwined, serving on boards together, corresponding regularly, and becoming close collaborators in a series of environmental, population control, and anti-immigration groups. Tanton's boundless energy and superb organizing skills, along with good looks that could have landed him a job as a television doctor, would vault him into the leadership of the environmental conservation and population control movements in the United States. By 1975, Tanton would be elevated to the position of president of Zero Population Growth. Eventually, prominent scientists like Ehrlich and Hardin would find themselves rubbing elbows with white supremacists as their ties with John Tanton led them deeper and deeper into extreme views about immigrants. In 1970, however, the mainstreaming of anti-immigrant politics was not yet visible on the horizon. Instead, the three men's concerns were squarely on the environment as population growth and rapacious capitalist development threatened the natural world they knew and loved. The idea that immigrants specifically were the biggest threat still lingered unsaid in the background. John Tanton would ensure that it once again became the defining issue in American politics.

TANTON'S FORMATIVE YEARS

John Tanton's early life as a hardworking conservationist did not foretell his future alliances with white supremacists. He was born at the height of the Great Depression on February 23, 1934, in Detroit, Michigan.[5] His family left Detroit for a rural home, at the front of the wave of white flight from urban areas that would occur after World War II. Tanton's childhood in the Depression and then the World War II years instilled in him a firm belief in conservation. He saw firsthand that resources can be limited, and in his daily life he worked to reuse and conserve what was around him.

Tanton was a good athlete in high school, playing football, basketball, and baseball. He was the second-leading scorer on his basketball team and class president of his small school. He attended Michigan State University where he got a BS in chemistry in 1956. Tanton was the president of the Delta Upsilon fraternity, and one of his fraternity brothers was Paul Stookey, who would go on to fame in the 1960s singing songs like "Puff the Magic Dragon" and "Leaving on a Jet Plane" as the baritone in Peter, Paul, and Mary. During the last semester of his senior year, Tanton met his wife and co-organizer on many of his projects, Mary Lou Brown, at a fraternity mixer at which Stookey was the featured singer. At the mixer, John and Mary Lou hit it off as they sensed each other's shared disdain for the awkward social outing. In Mary Lou, John found someone who shared his passion for nature and who was even more successful than he was. She

was born in 1935 in Hillsdale, Michigan, and was her high school vale-
dictorian. She graduated magna cum laude from Michigan State in 1957
with a BA in elementary education. She was her senior class secretary and
voted one of "fifty outstanding college senior women."

Tragedy shaped Tanton's outlook on life. In 1958, his younger brother
Tom died from a blood disease while he was a student at Michigan State.
Tom's death was hard on Tanton, but it also taught him that life was precious and that every day could be your last. This ethos motivated him
not to waste time but rather to take action to achieve his goals. In an oral
history in 1989, he explained, "If you want to get something done, you'd
better realize that the clock is running and get on with it."[6]

Tanton was nominated for a Rhodes scholarship and made it to the final round but was not selected. Disappointed, he decided to go to medical
school at the University of Michigan in Ann Arbor, where he graduated in
1960, seventh in his class. Tanton did his internship at the first birth control clinic in the United States at Denver General Hospital before returning to the University of Michigan for his residency in ophthalmology.[7]
Mary Lou got her MA in 1963 in special education from Michigan State.
In 1964, the couple moved to Petoskey in northern Michigan, where they
resided for the rest of their lives. Tanton joined the Burns Clinic and
Mary Lou raised their two daughters, born in 1961 and 1965, while also
volunteering in the local community.

Petoskey was a small tourist town of about five thousand people and
was over 95 percent white. In the winter, when the tourists were gone, the
cold wind from the Little Traverse Bay swept through the sleepy main
street with cute cafés and quaint shops. In the summer, the tourists frol-
icked in the lake and the countryside exploded with greenery. The Tantons used the land around their home to plant gardens, and John took
up beekeeping. Later in life, his personal stationery had a beehive in the
corner. In 1988, his bees produced literally over a ton of honey.

In Petoskey, the Tantons' interests in health care and environmental
conservation found many outlets in the local community. Mary Lou became a leading advocate for family planning and abortion rights in the
years before the Supreme Court legalized abortion in *Roe v. Wade*. She
founded the Northern Michigan Planned Parenthood office in 1967 and
the Michigan Women for Medical Control of Abortion. John was the
president of the local Planned Parenthood office from 1970 to 1975.

The Tantons also saw the need for environmental conservation in the emerging consumer culture of the 1960s as the development of cheaper disposable products exploded in an era that lacked environmental regulations. The wasteful consumerism clashed with their upbringing in the war years when everything was precious and needed to be conserved. There was also self-interest in their efforts to prevent development that would allow others to move in and spoil their rural idyll. Their first target was the filthy Bear River in Petoskey, which was polluted by trash, old tires, and debris. They founded the Bear River Commission in 1966 to clean up the river. They founded the Petoskey Regional Audubon Society in 1967, the Hartwick Pines Natural History Association in 1969, and the League of Conservation Voters for the Eleventh Congressional District in 1970.

By the late 1960s, their family planning and population control work merged with their environmental conservation, spurred by Paul Ehrlich's book *The Population Bomb*. The Tantons were enthralled. Tanton would later explain, "I was very much taken with this book. I bought many copies of it to distribute, and read it many times myself."[8] They saw the light and realized that to protect the environment meant that they needed to address the problem at the source rather than the effect. To them, the effect was environmental degradation, but the source was overpopulation. The solution was simple: the world needed population control. In the late 1960s, the Tantons joined Ehrlich's Zero Population Growth and worked to spread the literature from the group.

Tanton got his chance to meet his idols in the environmental movement only two months after the first Earth Day. In June 1970, he traveled to Chicago for the Congress on Optimum Population and Environment, which was attended by a who's who of the population control and environmental conservation movement. Speakers included Paul Ehrlich; Garrett Hardin, the author of "The Tragedy of the Commons"; Willard Wirtz, the labor secretary under Presidents Kennedy and Johnson; Stewart Udall, a former US representative from Arizona and the secretary of the interior from 1961 to 1969; and Hubert Humphrey, who had just concluded his term as vice president after losing the 1968 election in a landslide to Richard Nixon. Humphrey caused a stir at the conservation event by wearing alligator leather shoes for his speech. At lunch, Tanton found himself seated next to the author Bill Paddock, whose book *Famine,*

1975! America's Decision, Who Will Survive? had been published the year
before Ehrlich's *The Population Bomb*.

In a single weekend, Tanton managed to meet all of the major players
in the environmental and population movements. Tanton was relentless
in working his contacts and parlaying each as a building block onto another. He developed a friendship with Paddock, who then opened doors
for Tanton in the larger movement. He used his new connections from
the conference to be nominated to the Sierra Club's National Population Committee. He was elevated to the chair of the committee in 1971.
When he became chair, Tanton noted that Garrett Hardin was a member
of the committee, so he wrote him to solicit ideas. Hardin apparently did
not know he had been appointed to the role and promptly wrote back to
resign. Tanton was caught off guard, but the two men became friends and
longtime correspondents, trading hundreds of letters over their lifetimes,
finding a venue to share their increasingly extreme ideas privately with
each other.

In 1972, Tanton somehow found time during his busy schedule as
a full-time ophthalmologist at his clinic to establish or join a series of
additional environmental organizations. He was appointed by Michigan's
governor William Milliken to the Wilderness and Natural Areas Advi-
sory Board within the Department of Natural Resources, he founded the
Little Traverse Conservancy, and he formed a population committee for
the Michigan branch of the Sierra Club. At a meeting of the Sierra Club
in 1972, he met a geography professor from San Francisco State University named Georg Treichel. Treichel was on the Zero Population Growth
board and nominated Tanton for it. Tanton joined the ZPG board in 1973
and became the president of Ehrlich's group in 1975. In 1978, Tanton
testified before the Select Committee on Population at the invitation of
Representative James Scheuer of New York on behalf of ZPG.

THE MITCHELL PRIZE ESSAY

In the lore of John Tanton, his followers often point to his Mitchell Prize
essay in 1975 as the moment of departure for the anti-immigrant movement. In later correspondence, Tanton would call the piece his "Mag-
num Opus."[9] Tanton and his supporters always refer to it as "the Mitchell
Prize Essay," which implies that he won it. It turns out that the essay

actually came in third place in an essay contest at a small conference held in Woodlands, Texas, organized by the oil executive George Mitchell. Nevertheless, the essay marks the turning point in which Tanton shifted from focusing on population reduction to protect the global environment to immigration restrictions to protect the American environment.

The argument of the essay is that anyone who is serious about population control within a particular country has to consider immigration restrictions. Using data from the 1970s, Tanton argued that immigration, legal and undocumented combined, accounted for over half of the natural increase of the population in the United States. Additionally, Tanton noted that globally almost all population growth was in poorer countries, suggesting they will also want to leave, whether Mexico, Central America, or farther afield. He wrote, "These promise large increases in migration pressures in the future if conditions continue to deteriorate in the less developed countries."[10] Tanton acknowledged that past immigration restrictions were about race, but he insisted that for him only the environmental concerns drove the need to restrict immigrants. Nevertheless, the essay goes on to list a range of social impacts of immigration that echo the language of the racial discrimination from generations before. Tanton lamented that immigrants do not speak English, they are poor and thus do not contribute to the economic growth of the country, and they are drawn to poor urban slums in American cities. Tanton wrote, "Migrants tend to concentrate in urban areas where jobs and their relatives are found. . . . They thus add to already massive urban problems." This echoes the words of segregationist Louisiana senator Allen Ellender's speech on the Senate floor a decade earlier: "They are going to install themselves in the Harlems, the Watts, the South Bostons and other over-crowded areas, plagued by poverty, ignorance and disease."[11]

The focus on immigration made sense at that moment. By the late 1970s, the US baby boom was winding down and domestic population growth was stabilizing, but globally population was surging. Additionally, immigration to the United States was also surging. In 1978, the Border Patrol apprehended 900,000 people at the border, the largest number since Operation Wetback in 1954. At the same time, the family reunification system in the 1965 Immigration Act allowed 600,000 legal immigrants to the United States in 1978, the largest number since 1920, the last year of relatively free immigration before the Emergency Quota

Act and the subsequent national origins quotas. Tanton had tried to use his position as the president of Zero Population Growth from 1975 to 1977 to move the organization toward taking a stronger position on immigration, but he faced resistance. As his biographer, John Rohe, frames it, most of the other members were too "politically correct" to follow Tanton's lead. Tanton explained in his oral history, "We produced two monographs on the role of immigration in the population growth of the United States—one that detailed the numbers, a second that made policy suggestions. For instance, such things as better control of the borders and better control of visas. We questioned whether or not family unification was a proper basis for an immigration policy."[12] However, the rest of the board did not think these areas should be the focus of ZPG.

Frustrated, Tanton left the presidency of Ehrlich's ZPG in 1977 but remained on the board until the end of 1978. He realized that if he was going to achieve his vision of limiting immigration to protect the American environment, he would have to do it himself. Tanton explained, "I found virtually no one was willing to talk about this! It was a forbidden topic. I tried to get some others to think about it and write about it, but I did not succeed. I finally concluded that if anything was going to happen, I would have to do it myself," which he did.[13]

On January 2, 1979, John Tanton founded the Federation for American Immigration Reform (FAIR) to push for more restrictions on immigration to the United States. The FAIR mission statement said, "We don't want to project an image of racism, jingoism, xenophobia, chauvinism, or isolationism. . . . We plan to make the restriction of immigration a legitimate position for thinking people, and to have FAIR identified in the minds of leaders in the media, academia and government as speaking for a consensus of American thought and opinion." Although Tanton found "virtually no one" willing to talk about what he saw as the dangers of immigration, he was not completely alone. There was one other movement that shared his singular focus on reducing immigration to the United States: the white supremacist movement.

— CHAPTER 9 —

ON OUR SAME SIDE

The eggs started flying immediately, but David Duke brushed the sticky cracked shells off his jacket and made his statement.[1] Duke, only twenty-seven years old in October 1977, was the self-proclaimed grand wizard of the Ku Klux Klan. He would go on to serve as an elected member of the Louisiana House of Representatives, and he ran for president in 1992, receiving 119,115 votes (1 percent) in the Republican primaries.[2] In 2016, Duke endorsed Donald Trump for president, saying on his radio show, "Voting against Donald Trump, at this point, is really treason to your heritage." Trump's reaction to the news followed his pattern of delaying any condemnation for a few days to signal his support. On CNN, Trump said, "I don't know anything about what you're even talking about with white supremacy or white supremacists. So I don't know. I don't know—did he endorse me, or what's going on? Because I know nothing about David Duke; I know nothing about white supremacists." A full five days later Trump said, "I disavow."[3]

Back in 1977, David Duke and a handful of other men had traveled from his home in Metairie, Louisiana, to the San Ysidro Port of Entry between San Diego and Tijuana. At his news conference, held at night in the dark along a rugged area near the border, there were more reporters and protesters with eggs than Klan members, but Duke was used to that. He explained that the United States was facing a catastrophe as the open and unguarded border with Mexico was allowing for an influx of illegal crossings. Echoing the language of many nationalist politicians, Duke claimed that "the support of the American people" was behind him and that he was coordinating with the Border Patrol and the Department of Justice, both of which denied any connection to his group.[4] Duke announced there would be 230 Klan members patrolling in California, 150 in Texas, and "60–75" in New Mexico. However, on this night, there were only a few men in cars with hand-drawn "Klan Border Watch" posters taped to the side doors. Duke and his men posed with their guns by the signs but apparently did little else. The event was treated as an amusing side story by the media, essentially a photo op for the Ku Klux Klan that reinforced their position on the extreme fringe of American politics.

From today's vantage point, the Klan Border Watch looks much more significant. It was an early indicator of the importance of the border as a symbol for white nationalism in the United States as David Duke blazed the path for future, more polished politicians to appeal to the simmering resentments of white Americans. In the decades since, dozens of other militias followed Duke's lead and set up their own vigilante border patrols and crowdfunded private border walls, including a group called American Border Patrol, which developed close ties to the Tanton Network.[5] By 2015, what had been fringe ideas demonizing immigrants and building a wall became the campaign slogan of a major political party, but that is getting ahead of ourselves.

In the 1970s and 1980s, systemic racism persisted as segregation was replaced by policing and mass incarceration for Black communities in the United States.[6] However, overt white supremacy was well outside the mainstream.[7] The aftermath of Nazism and World War II, followed by the ugliness of massive resistance to the civil rights movement, banished racial speech from acceptable public discourse in the United States. Although many people retained racial ideas, it was no longer something that could be voiced in public. Those who still spoke openly about their racist worldview found themselves marginalized and isolated. They persisted in smoky back rooms in New York through the Pioneer Fund, in rural pockets of the South where the KKK remained active, and in the remote backwoods of Idaho and Montana where groups such as the Aryan Nation built compounds.

A wide range of ideologies could be grouped under white supremacy, including neo-Nazis, neo-Confederates, and the KKK. These groups each had their own focus, but they shared an opposition to many of the same things ranging from gay rights and abortion to feminism and immigration. They also shared a veneration of a threatened Western civilization and a connection to the Vietnam War, where many of them served and learned to hate a racialized other. In the 1980s, there were only 25,000 hard-core members of these groups, but an additional 150,000 people attended an event, and 450,000 more were on mailing lists that allowed the dissemination of racist materials.[8]

The disaffected white men and women in these compounds shared a belief that Jews, minorities, and immigrants were replacing them in their own country.[9] The slogan known as "the Fourteen Words" became a pledge for white supremacist groups: "We must secure the existence of our people and a future for white children." The idea of race suicide, which was popularized by President Teddy Roosevelt during the push for more immigration restrictions at the turn of the twentieth century, morphed into the great replacement theory of white genocide. They bided their time by training with assault weapons, learning to build bombs, and reading books that foretold of a future race war to reassert white dominance.

The foundational texts for white supremacists included Hitler's *Mein Kampf* and Madison Grant's *The Passing of the Great Race* as well as some newer volumes such as *The Turner Diaries* and *The Camp of the Saints*. *The Turner Diaries*, written in 1978 by Andrew MacDonald, the pseudonym of William Pierce, the head of the neo-Nazi National Alliance, foretells a future race war in which white supremacists take over the United States while massacring Jews, African Americans, and collaborators. The book has sold 500,000 copies and was distributed by Timothy McVeigh in the years before he carried out the bombing of the Murrah Federal Building in Oklahoma City in 1995. *The Camp of the Saints* was written originally in French by Jean Raspail in 1973, and its first run was published in English in 1975 by Scribner's. It begins with an invasion of Europe by boats, "caked with rust, unfit for the sea" but full of refugees from India led by a man known as the "shit eater." The immigrants, refusing to assimilate to European culture, flood the continent, resulting in the collapse of Western civilization. *The Camp of the Saints* would eventually be a favorite book of Steve Bannon, the chief executive of Donald Trump's 2016 campaign and later a senior White House advisor.[10]

In the 1980s and 1990s, the white supremacists who were republishing and reading these then-obscure books could never have dreamed that a senior White House advisor would also admire them, and even say so publicly. At the time, they were marginalized and, after the assault on their fellow white supremacist compound at Ruby Ridge in 1992, living under the fear that the US government was going to wipe out the remaining reactionaries. White supremacists persisted at the edges of society, waiting for the future moment when the public would again be more receptive to their arguments. To most Americans, they were a fringe movement pushing laughable, discredited ideas, but not to John Tanton. He managed to know and correspond regularly with many of them. In the 1990s, Tanton himself became the primary American publisher of *The Camp of the Saints*, one of the bibles of the movement, after the Scribner's version went out of print.[11]

THE FEDERATION FOR AMERICAN IMMIGRATION REFORM

John Tanton, his wife, Mary Lou, and their younger daughter Jane were excited, and nervous, for their road trip to Washington, DC, in 1981. Two years earlier, Tanton had founded FAIR to advocate for more immigration restrictions in the United States, but they grew frustrated that their home in Petoskey, Michigan, kept them far from the action in the capital. In 1981, an opportunity came up. Tanton's clinic had just hired a new ophthalmologist that summer, and Tanton offered to take a leave for a year to give the new doctor the chance to build a patient base using his rotation. The clinic agreed and the Tantons packed a rental van and set off for Washington on September 1. However, their departure proved inauspicious. Moments after leaving Petoskey, the van broke down and they were stranded on the side of the road, suddenly stuck at the beginning of their migration. Tanton worried it was an ominous sign, but after renting a new van and repacking all of their stuff, they finally made it to Washington, DC.

FAIR had already gotten off to a successful start. Tanton's skills at networking and fundraising allowed him to tap into like-minded Zero Population Growth supporters for the initial staff, board of directors, and funding for the organization. Tanton invited a fellow ZPG board member, Roger Conner, to be the first executive director of FAIR. Tanton and Conner met in 1970 while working on Earth Day in Michigan, and Tanton had suggested Conner for the ZPG board. At FAIR, Tanton handled everything behind the scenes in terms of organizing and fund-raising, while Conner was the public face who talked with the media and politicians. While Tanton was still in Petoskey, they would hold weekly phone meetings on Mondays, Tanton's day off from his ophthalmology work, to discuss progress and make plans for the coming week. They initially had trouble staffing the new organization because "immigration reform was a new and disquieting subject . . . and no prospective employees experienced in the field were readily available." Their solution was to focus on college campuses and hire recent graduates who were inexperienced and impressionable. For their headquarters, they rented a cramped, crevice-like basement office with seven-foot ceilings on New Hampshire Avenue in Washington, DC. The awkward space became "ground zero in the immigration reform movement."[12]

The first board of directors for FAIR consisted of Tanton; two colleagues from ZPG, Sherry Barnes and Bill Paddock, the author of *Famine, 1975!* whom Tanton had happened to sit beside at the 1970 environmental conference; Otis L. Graham Jr., a professor at UC Santa Barbara; and Sidney Swensrud, the former chair of Gulf Oil. Swensrud and another ZPG colleague, Jay Harris, provided the crucial early funding to get the group off the ground. Swensrud donated to FAIR every year, and even after his death in 1996 from pancreatic cancer, his foundation has continued to lavish money on the Tanton Network through the present day. The second initial supporter, Jay Harris, was an heir to the fortune of Henry Flagler, the founder of Standard Oil. Tanton and Harris had met on the board of ZPG, and Harris agreed to give FAIR $100,000 (AFI $350,000) over the initial five years. Tanton explained, "He knew that we needed more than just one year's funding, but he also knew that he should not support it forever. He gave us the money to get started—and lots of encouragement—but said that we'd eventually have to go elsewhere to find other funds."[13] Tanton also received $50,000 (AFI $175,000) from another extremely wealthy donor with ties to both Standard and Gulf Oil who wanted to remain anonymous, but her identity was later revealed.

FAIR hit the ground running in 1979, immediately diving into the debate about the Refugee Act of 1980. As Tanton would later recall, they were the only ones in the game at the time even though they did not really know what they were doing. They lobbied for a lower cap on the number of refugees, but exactly how much influence they had is unclear. The early trial by fire gave them a sense of what worked and what did not. As Roger Conner, the new executive director, and the other new employees at FAIR set to work building connections in Congress, Tanton started to look for more donors to fill the coffers after Jay Harris's pledge ran out.

Tanton pleasantly, but relentlessly, worked his contacts to build a larger network of funders and supporters. A key early conduit to other politicians was Richard Lamm, who was the governor of Colorado for three consecutive terms from 1975 to 1987. With a round face and winning smile, Lamm shared Tanton's environmental and population focus and was a regular correspondent of Tanton's. Lamm was a Democrat, which helped with Tanton's desire to make FAIR appear moderate and bipartisan. Lamm also attended most of Tanton's anti-immigrant gatherings in the 1980s, even hosting one in Denver while he was the governor. Lamm's stature allowed him to contact people that would have been unreachable for an ophthalmologist from upstate Michigan, even one that had been the chair of a national organization like ZPG. Lamm knew Jimmy Carter, a fellow former Democratic governor, and was friendly with Gerald Ford. He had all of the US senators in his contacts as well as important donors like the financier Warren Buffett. Tanton convinced Lamm to schedule meetings and introductions with Buffett, who would become a key donor for Tanton and FAIR in the mid-1980s and even served on the FAIR board of directors.

TANTON AND THE PIONEER FUND

Even as Tanton courted mainstream politicians and publicly professed a desire to distance FAIR from racist groups, he began a long-term collaboration with the Pioneer Fund, Wickliffe Draper's foundation that bankrolled Nazi propaganda films and the White Citizens' Councils in the South during the era of segregation. The charter of the Pioneer Fund, which said it was meant to support "children who are deemed to be descended predominantly from white persons who settled in the original thirteen states prior to the adoption of the constitution . . . and/or from related stocks," presaged the message of the Fourteen Words of the white supremacist movement. Pioneer also served as a crucial supporter for eugenics and race science for decades after these theories were completely discredited. By the 1980s, Pioneer Fund founder Wickliffe Draper had passed away and the fund was being run by Harry Weyher and John Trevor Jr. Trevor's father, John Trevor Sr., was the behind-the-scenes architect of the 1924 national origins quotas. John Trevor Jr. had testified before Representative Michael Feighan's House Sub-Committee on Immigration and Naturalization in 1964 in a failed bid to save his father's national origins quotas. In John Tanton, Weyher and Trevor found a man who shared their concerns about how immigration could change the character of America. Tanton and his network received over $1.3 million (AFI ~$2.7 million) of funding from Pioneer between 1982 and 1995.

John Tanton became a regular correspondent with Weyher and Trevor. Their letters display a familiarity that highlights a personal closeness and a common cause, with Tanton clearly admiring the work of the Trevor family over the decades. He also admired Wickliffe Draper, the founder of the Pioneer Fund, once writing, "The haunting question: Where would we be today if it were not for Col. Draper's foresight and financial arrangements?"[14] Tanton took it upon himself to ensure that both of the Trevors' papers were archived at the Bentley Historical Library at the University of Michigan alongside his own. Tanton wrote to Trevor Jr. that his father's archive "demonstrates the good and commendable ideas of those who led the movement to restrict immigration in the early years of this century, and then defend it afterwards."[15] In 2001, Tanton sent Trevor Sr.'s unpublished autobiography to a group of correspondents, including FAIR board member Donald Collins, saying it was "a guidepost to which we must follow again this time."[16] In addition to serving on the FAIR board, Donald Collins also served on the board of Roger Pearson's white supremacist publication, the *Journal of Social, Political and Economic Studies*.[17] Like FAIR, the journal was also supported by the Pioneer Fund.

Tanton's letters with Weyher and Trevor Jr. make clear that he had no illusions about the Pioneer Fund's eugenics focus. In 1988, he wrote to Weyher, "I continue to be very interested in genetics and I hope you will keep me abreast of developments there."[18] On February 28, 1991, he wrote to Weyher, which was copied to Professor Garrett Hardin, who was also a recipient of Pioneer Fund support, "There certainly are a lot of good things coming out on the genetics front these days. It must be harder for the opposition to deny that there must be some connection between our genes and ourselves, both mental and physical."[19] Tanton's interest in eugenics continued to grow. In 1995, he wrote a letter to

Robert K. Graham, the wealthy inventor of shatterproof glasses, that he and his colleague Wayne Lutton "will have some serious conversations about what might be done to breath [*sic*] some life back into the eugenics movement, whether through restarting the American Eugenics Society, or some other means." He mused, however, that they might "need to try a new name—some euphemism," since eugenics had a negative stigma.[20] In 1996, Tanton figured out what the euphemism should be and started his own pro-eugenics group, the Society for Genetic Education.

GROWING TIES TO WHITE SUPREMACISTS

Beyond his connections to the Pioneer Fund and his support for eugenics, Tanton corresponded with white supremacists, including Peter Brimelow, Sam Francis, and Roger Pearson among others. Tanton would frequently recommend Larry Auster's book *The Path to National Suicide* and Leon Bouvier's *Peaceful Invasions*, published by his own Center for Immigration Studies, both of which laid out the threat of the great replacement.[21] Most significantly, Tanton became a frequent correspondent with the white supremacist Jared Taylor.

Tanton first met Taylor, who today is among the most prominent white supremacists and a fellow recipient of Pioneer Fund support, in 1990. Taylor affects a patrician air by speaking with an accent as if he were an aristocrat. He has stately gray hair and is always dressed nicely in suits or, at the minimum, a blue blazer and starched shirt. He has used his clean-cut appearance to occasionally access mainstream news, including an interview with CNN's Fareed Zakaria in 2019. However, his primary message is white supremacy, even if he prefers to call it "race realism." For example, in 2005, Taylor published an article in his magazine *American Renaissance* that said, "The races are different. Blacks and whites are different. When blacks are left entirely to their own devices, Western civilization—any kind of civilization—disappears." In 2012, he wrote that the founders had a "clear conception of the United States as a nation ruled by and for whites," and his goal was only to adhere to that.[22]

Tanton was immediately taken with Taylor. When Taylor first reached out to Tanton in 1990, Tanton said he was glad to meet and exchange ideas. In the letter, Tanton's first reading recommendation to Taylor was a eugenics article on the topic of competitive breeding. Tanton also in-

vited Taylor to a regular salon he organized to bring like-minded people together, which he called a witan. "Witan" is a shortened version of
witenagemot, an old Anglo-Saxon term for a meeting or gathering. Tanton
ended the letter by saying, "I would hope that there might come out of
this some arrangement whereby we could work closely together."[23] After
they met, Tanton wrote a nice thank-you agreeing to stay in touch.

Later in 1990, Taylor asked Tanton for feedback on his new publication, *American Renaissance*. Taylor's opening essay said,

> In fact, blacks and Hispanics are, compared to whites, far more likely to
> be poor, illiterate, on welfare, or in jail; they are far more likely to have
> illegitimate children, be addicted to drugs, or have AIDS. By no defini-
> tion of international competitiveness can the presence of these popula-
> tions be anything but a disadvantage. Americans of European heritage,
> the cultural heirs of the people who founded and built this nation, were
> silent. The United States is unquestionably less competitive because so
> many blacks and Hispanics are in jail or on welfare, but none dares say
> so. America is an increasingly dangerous and disagreeable place because
> of growing numbers of blacks and Hispanics . . . , but none dares say
> this either.[24]

After reading the editorials and articles in the first issue, Tanton replied, "You are saying a lot of things that need to be said, but I anticipate
that it will be very tough sledding. As you note in your cover letter, this is
not material that people want to hear." Instead, he counseled Taylor to be
more "discreet" and to pick a positive message.[25]

After the first issue of *American Renaissance* was published, Tanton
spread the word, recommending it to friends and sending copies to ac-
quaintances.[26] Tanton wrote to Taylor, "I thought you were off to a good
and sufficiently controversial start with the *American Renaissance*," asking
to be added to the mailing list and providing money for a subscription.
He also provided Taylor with the home address of former Colorado governor Richard Lamm, a longtime supporter of Tanton's work, and suggested sending him a copy as well. Harry Weyher of the Pioneer Fund,
who funded the publication of *American Renaissance*, wrote to ask Tanton's
opinion of it. Tanton said he hoped it would be a useful addition to the
debate and offered to send Weyher a copy of Taylor's as-yet-unpublished

book, at the time titled *Black Failure—White Guilt* but eventually published as *Paved with Good Intentions: The Failure of Race Relations in Contemporary America*.[27] In a letter to the FAIR board in 1998, Tanton encouraged them to pay attention to what writers like Taylor were saying because "we are on the same side."[28]

When John Tanton died after a long struggle with Parkinson's disease on July 15, 2019, Jared Taylor eulogized him on the next episode of his *American Renaissance* podcast. Taylor began the show with the news of his death:

> We have to start with some sad news. The sad news has to do with John Tanton. I don't know how many of our listeners know about John Tanton. . . . He was a great American patriot because he cared about who was coming into the United States, not just how many. He was of course denounced as a racist, white supremacist, for some of his correspondence that he had with Sam Francis and even your servant has come to light and merited him a place in the crosshairs of all the people who hate the founding stock of America. . . .
>
> He was involved, also, with the establishment of the Center for Immigration Studies, which I believe is one of the most effective think tanks in the United States. Some of the material they come out with nobody else would come out with and as I often say, everything I learned about immigration I learned from CIS. Those are really great people. He took a lot of criticism for the fact that he got some of his funding from the Pioneer Fund, some of you who may not be aware of the Pioneer Fund, it started, I believe, in the 1920s and it was unabashedly in the interest of what was then called race betterment. The Pioneer Fund is no more, but any organization, no matter how outstanding it was, if it got any money from Pioneer Fund, they'd be criticized by the Southern Poverty Law Center. The Federation for American Immigration Reform, FAIR, as well as the Social Contract Press, are designated as hate groups by Southern Poverty Law Center. So you know they are doing great work.[29]

Taylor knew Tanton was a kindred spirit.

In the 1980s and 1990s, privately John Tanton was writing incendiary things about eugenics and growing closer to white supremacists, but publicly FAIR maintained a moderate veneer. FAIR's public statements studiously avoided racism, and the leaders would deny then, and continue to deny now, that race played any role in the Tanton Network's push to limit immigration. FAIR focused on their three primary questions about immigration: How many people should be admitted? How should they be selected? How should the rules be enforced?

The organization's influence grew on Capitol Hill. Tanton, with help from Governor Lamm, managed to enlist a series of ever more prominent mainstream figures to join the boards of the Tanton Network organizations. In addition to prominent professors like Garrett Hardin and Paul Ehrlich, among the many boldface names that sat on Tanton Network boards in the 1980s were the news anchor Walter Cronkite, the Minnesota senator and Democratic presidential nominee Eugene McCarthy, the authors Saul Bellow and Gore Vidal, the financier Warren Buffet, former Kentucky senator Walter Huddleston, US Representative and mayor of New York John Lindsay, the publisher of *Time* magazine Henry Luce III, former US representative (IL) Robert McClory, former governor of Illinois Richard Ogilvie, former US attorney general William French Smith, and former secretary of the army and president of Indiana University and West Virginia University Elvis Stahr.

However, the most consequential contact Tanton developed was Cordelia Scaife May, the anonymous donor that secretly gave $50,000 to help found FAIR. When she was born in 1928, newspapers in the United States put her baby pictures on the front page and speculated about whether she was the richest baby in the world. By the 1990s, Cordelia Scaife May was the richest woman in the United States.

CHAPTER 10

INVADED ON ALL FRONTS

Cordelia Scaife May was born as Cordelia Mellon Scaife in Pittsburgh, Pennsylvania, on September 24, 1928, into a family of stupendous wealth. Her maternal grandfather was Richard B. Mellon, the brother and business partner of Andrew W. Mellon. The Mellon brothers made a fortune as they used the small Pittsburgh bank their father established as a vehicle to drive industrialization across the Midwest. Mellon National Bank grew into one of the largest in the United States as it owned or founded many of the companies that would become the backbone of the twentieth-century American economy. These included the metals company Alcoa, Gulf Oil (now Chevron-Texaco), the technology company Westinghouse (now ViacomCBS), and aviation and defense firm Rockwell. Mellon Bank was also heavily involved in the early funding of Andrew Carnegie's US Steel, Heinz Foods, General Motors, and Standard Oil (now Exxon-Mobil). Both of John Tanton's key early funders, Sidney Swensrud of Gulf Oil and Jay Harris of Standard Oil, gained their fortunes from oil companies funded by Mellon Bank.

Cordelia, who went by Cordy, had an unhappy childhood. Her mother was an alcoholic whom Scaife May later described as "a gutter drunk." She and her brother, Richard Scaife, were raised by nannies at Penguin Court, the family estate in rural Ligonier, Pennsylvania, outside Pittsburgh.[1] The name referred to actual emperor penguins her eccentric mother tried to have bred to wander the grounds.[2] She recalled that the only time there was laughter in the home was when family friend and Planned Parenthood founder Margaret Sanger was visiting. Cordy was sent away to boarding school at Foxcroft in Virginia and then attended the University of Pittsburgh and the Carnegie Institute of Technology, both of which were heavily funded by her family. In 1967, the Carnegie Institute of Technology merged with the Mellon Institute of Industrial Research, which her grandfather had founded, to become Carnegie Mellon University.

At twenty, with short, prim hair and a smile that emphasized her cheeks, Cordy dropped out of college to marry Herbert A. May Jr. in 1949. The wedding announcement merited a column in the *New York Times* titled "Cordelia Scaife's Troth," but it did not last.[3] They were divorced the following year, but she retained his last name. In 1951, Scaife May established the Laurel Foundation as a vehicle to give her money to the local causes she supported in Pittsburgh. By the late 1950s, her family was the pinnacle of wealth in the United States. In the first *Fortune* magazine ranking of the wealthiest Americans in 1957, her mother Sarah Mellon Scaife, her uncle Richard King Mellon, and their cousins Alisa Mellon-Bruce and Paul Mellon made up four of the top eight positions.[4] Scaife May's mother used her wealth to donate generously to many causes, including the grant that built Jonas Salk's virology lab at the University of Pittsburgh, which produced the polio vaccine.[5]

After her divorce, Scaife May settled into a reclusive lifestyle on her own estate in Ligonier, Pennsylvania. She named it Cold Comfort, after the 1932 Stella Gibbons novel of the same name that parodies a romanticized version of rural life. Colcom, her second charitable foundation established in 1996, is also named after the novel and her estate. Scaife May lived simply but had a private plane at a nearby airport that allowed her to jet off to nature reserves around the world. Scaife May's father died in 1958 and her mother in 1965. Their massive fortune went to Scaife May and her brother Richard Scaife as well as their mother's foundation, the Sarah Scaife Foundation, which the two siblings controlled.

RICHARD MELLON SCAIFE

Like Scaife May, Richard Scaife, who sometimes went by Dickie, lived a reclusive life, rarely giving interviews to journalists despite being one of the wealthiest men in the United States and the single most significant donor to conservative causes in the 1970s and 1980s.[6] Richard inherited alcoholism from his mother and battled the disease his whole life. He was kicked out of Yale for his drunken antics, which had resulted in a class-mate breaking his leg. Richard severely injured himself and a family of five in a car crash when he was twenty-two.[7] Richard established the Carthage Foundation in 1964 with a goal of providing grants to conservative causes as a counterweight to the liberal presidency of Lyndon Johnson and the Supreme Court of Earl Warren. He also gave to Barry Goldwater's and Richard Nixon's campaigns.[8]

In 1971, Richard found his call to arms in the Powell Memorandum.[9] Lewis Powell, who only three months later would be introduced as Rich-ard Nixon's pick for the Supreme Court, was asked by the conservative, pro-business US Chamber of Commerce to write a memo about the anti-business climate in the United States and what the Chamber could do about it. The memo proposed the creation of an alternative suite of conservative institutions ranging from think tanks to media outlets to provide an intellectual counterweight to what he saw as a liberal bias in the press and universities.

Richard Scaife had the clarion call he needed, and for the remainder of his life he served as one of the primary funders of the right-wing coun-terattack proposed in the Powell Memo. In the 1970s, Richard focused on building the network of foundations and think tanks almost exactly as Powell recommended. One of his earliest efforts was with the Heri-tage Foundation, which was established in 1973. Heritage's initial grant came from the beer magnate Joseph Coors, but by 1976 Richard Scaife was the largest donor, providing 42 percent of its $1 million (AFI $4.55 million) budget that year. The joke at the time was that while Coors gave six-packs, Scaife gave cases.[10] Richard Scaife continued to fund a wide range of organizations to fulfill Powell's vision, including the Hoover Institution, the Center for Strategic and International Studies, Judicial Watch, and the American Enterprise Institute. He supported the Amer-ican Legislative Exchange Council (ALEC), which produced draft bills for state and local legislatures in order to further pro-business laws. He also bought newspapers, including the *Pittsburgh Tribune-Review*, in or-der to expand conservative voices in media.[11] In 1999, the *Washington Post* reported that his foundations had given $1.4 billion (AFI $2.8 billion) to various causes that "had a disproportionate impact on the rise of the right, perhaps the biggest story in American politics in the last quarter of the

20th century," driving the rise of Ronald Reagan in the 1980s and Newt Gingrich's Republican Revolution in 1994.[12]

Initially, Richard and Cordy worked together on their charitable giving and supported many of the same causes through their individual foundations and their mother's. Both were active in the 1972 election year, with Richard giving $1 million to Richard Nixon's reelection campaign while Cordy gave the most money of any American to congressional races across the country.[13] However, they had an irreconcilable split in 1974. In August 1973, Cordy had secretly married a childhood friend from Ligonier, the Allegheny County district attorney Robert Duggan, in a private ceremony at Zephyr Cove at Lake Tahoe, Nevada. Tragically, the marriage was destined to be even shorter than the six months of her previous marriage.[14] Duggan was already under investigation for taking payoffs to ignore illegal gambling rings, and it is thought that Cordy married him to provide cover, essentially to suggest that the unexplained money Duggan had was from her. If that was the scheme, it did not work. On March 5, 1974, Duggan was indicted on federal corruption charges. His dead body was found later that day at his estate in Ligonier. It was ruled a suicide, but there were doubts about the scene. He died from a shotgun blast, and the gun, with a long barrel, was found ten feet away from his body. Furthermore, some investigators wondered how he could have fired the gun at himself, given the long barrel. Cordy was sure that her brother Richard was involved, and the two did not speak for the next thirty years.[15]

"BREED LIKE HAMSTERS"

Scaife May became even more reclusive and eccentric, often only meeting with people if they came to her Cold Comfort Farm. Perhaps influenced by her childhood interactions with Margaret Sanger, Scaife May developed strong views about population control as an adult. Sanger is remembered today as a women's rights advocate and the founder of Planned Parenthood who established the first birth control clinic in the United States in 1916.[16] She was also part of the eugenics and race science elite of the 1920s. She wrote in 1921, "Today Eugenics is suggested by the most diverse minds as the most adequate and thorough avenue to the solution of racial, political and social problems." She continued, "The most urgent problem today is how to limit and discourage the over-fertility of the mentally and physically defective." For Sanger, "Upon this basis only may we improve the quality of the race."[17] Consequently, her push for access to abortions and family planning has a more sinister edge than most people realize.

Scaife May idolized Sanger. She had a portrait of Sanger hanging in her home and a "Stop the Stork" bumper sticker on her car.[18] She was a donor to Planned Parenthood and sat on the board of the International Planned Parenthood Foundation.[19] After Scaife May's death, her foundation would give hundreds of thousands of dollars to the Margaret Sanger Papers Project at New York University.[20] Scaife May also contributed to and joined the board of the Population Council, a group founded by John D. Rockefeller III to support family planning around the world. However, after the death of her second husband, her views seemed to grow more radical. She left the Planned Parenthood board in late 1974 and the Population Council board in 1976. Rockefeller was shocked and wrote her a letter that he "had not been aware that a difference of this seeming magnitude existed between us."[21]

Scaife May's dislike of other people and her desire to protect the environment drew her toward the population control and environmental conservation movements that were developing in the 1970s, with John Tanton increasingly at the lead. In the early 1970s, her letters brought up population control, but in measured and reasonable ways. By the 1980s, her views were hardening and included blunt language about immigrants. She told one family member that the United States was "being invaded on all fronts" by immigrants that "breed like hamsters."[22]

Cordelia Scaife May and John Tanton first met in 1978 through the Environmental Fund (now called Population-Environment Balance), another environmental and population control group that Scaife May provided the initial funding to establish. The other members of the board were the key players in the push for a more forceful integration of population control measures in the environmental movement, including the professors Paul Ehrlich and Garrett Hardin.

Tanton immediately saw that Scaife May could be the source of funds for his anti-immigration crusade. They became friends through their work on the board and would see each other four times a year at the meetings. Tanton's letters to Scaife May often flattered, for example, praising her home in Ligonier, Pennsylvania, as "attractive" and "salubrious."[23] Eventually they would even vacation together. In 1988, Scaife May took Mary Lou and John on a trip to the Swiss Alps on her private jet. Despite their friendship, Tanton's memos to the FAIR leadership indicated that he felt the need to tread carefully around her given her misanthropic tendencies and her vast wealth. On June 23, 1983, Tanton wrote that he set up his own line of communication with her about financial matters, while suggesting that FAIR director Roger Conner needed to be "somewhat more circumspect" as they "decide on just the right touch."[24] Tanton's secretary wrote a memo in 1983 that Tanton's plan was to "get close enough to Cordy to become her advisor in a decade or so" because her current close advisor, Adolph Schmidt, was "much older than [John], so he will probably die first."[25] Tanton maintained dossiers on all of his large donors, including Warren Buffett, Sidney Swensrud, and Jay Harris. In 1985, his file on Scaife May concluded, "That relationship is pretty well under control." Tanton also carefully advised the leaders of his network of foundations on how to interact with her. He wrote to Don Mann, the president of Negative Population Growth, on how to cultivate Scaife May: add her to your mailing list, then in November send her "a letter of no more than one and a half pages, very tightly worded, with a minimum of jargon" describing how the funds were used, followed by another request for funds the following March.[26] Even as he carefully groomed Scaife May in the 1980s, Tanton could not have foreseen how crucial she would be for his cause.

ESTABLISHING THE TANTON NETWORK

While Tanton was building his relationship with Cordelia Scaife May and privately flirting with white supremacists in the 1980s, he demonstrated that he was a masterful organization builder as he created an anti-immigrant network similar to the conservative network that grew out of the Powell Memo. His experience with the Sierra Club and Zero Population Growth familiarized him with what steps were crucial for a fledgling organization to get off the ground. These included producing documents that established what the organization stood for in direct language, identifying and cultivating key politicians who were sympathetic to the cause, and building a membership base to gather funds from and to demonstrate that the organization had broad support in the American public. In the pre-Internet era, the tried-and-true method for building an organization was through direct mail solicitations. Tanton already had access to some address lists from his previous activism, and he hired DC-based firms to manage the mailings. Tanton knew it was a money loser for a new fledging organization, but the need for a membership base made the cost worth it because it made FAIR appear to have broader support, when in fact well over 90 percent of its funding in the early 1980s came from four sources: the Pioneer Fund, Sidney Swensrud, Jay Harris, and Cordelia Scaife May.

FAIR decided to focus on illegal immigration because that was politically palatable, but all along they also argued that from time to time it was right for a country to also consider its legal immigration system and decide if it still fit the goals of the country.[27] They had some early success and found sympathetic ears in both the Senate and the House as they "educated," as they referred to it, the politicians on the impact of immigration on the environment.[28]

Wyoming Republican senator Alan Simpson became their strongest ally. At 6'7", Simpson towered over most people, but his grandfatherly bald head and disarming smile drew people to him. He joined the Senate in 1979 and served three consecutive terms until 1997, when he did not seek reelection and instead began to lecture in public policy at Harvard. In 2010, he was tapped to lead the National Commission on Fiscal Responsibility and Reform, along with Erskine Bowles, in the aftermath of the 2008 financial crisis. Tanton, FAIR executive director Roger Conner, and Simpson regularly traded correspondence. Simpson wrote to Tanton and Conner on March 27, 1981, that he was "ready to 'jump in and get wet all over.' Here we go!" In the same letter, he asked FAIR to draft language for an op-ed, which was published in the *Washington Post* on April 28 under Senator Simpson's name with no acknowledgment of FAIR. The FAIR board was ecstatic. Garrett Hardin commented, "Senator Simpson says substantially the same thing we said in our ad, but at greater length and in softer language." Roger Conner responded, "Especially since we wrote the first draft of this."[29] The clubby correspondence continued with Simpson writing to Conner on May 23, "We can finally make a dent in this amorphous botch of verbiage called the Immigration and Naturalization Act of 1950 [*sic*; he must mean 1965]. Hang on tight, chum. Here we go!"[30] On November 1, 1981, Senator Simpson gave a speech to a seminar sponsored by the Rockefeller Foundation and the Ford Foundation in Williamsburg, Virginia, that was heavily written by FAIR and even included their signature three questions, verbatim: "1) How many immigrants and refugees should be admitted? 2) Which applicants should be given preference? 3) How should the United States enforce the policies which are adopted?"[31] The relationship continued through the 1980s with the passage of the Immigration Reform and Control Act in 1986. In appreciation, Simpson was awarded FAIR's Franklin Society Award in 1986, and Simpson's thank-you note said, "Dear Friends, You are all a bunch of honeys!" alluding to Tanton's now famous beekeeping. He continued, "There are many reasons to be appreciative of FAIR. The principal and immediate one is my receipt of the beautiful Franklin Society Award. That is indeed very special to me."[32]

In addition to courting funders like Cordelia Scaife May and politicians like Alan Simpson and Colorado governor Richard Lamm, the final crucial decision John Tanton made in the 1980s was to continue to establish new groups and organizations as he identified different areas of need (see table 3). In July 1981, just before heading to DC for the year, the Tantons had created an organization called the Conversation Workshop. A year later, they changed the name to U.S. Inc., and it received donations of $90,000 ($225,000 AFI) per year from 1983 to 1986 from the financier Warren Buffett.[33] The purpose of U.S. Inc. was to serve as an incubator for new projects that the Tantons wanted to pursue. The benefit of U.S. Inc. was that they could use the infrastructure and mailing lists of the corporation to get a new idea off the ground and decide if it was worth spinning off into a stand-alone operation. The list of projects they began under U.S. Inc. demonstrates the breadth of their interests, ranging from Recycle North, the first recycling program in northern Michigan, to the Alcohol and Drug Awareness Hour, which they created after they learned that a friend had trouble with alcoholism. John and Mary Lou Tanton even gave up alcohol themselves in solidarity.

The Tantons also used U.S. Inc. to start groups that went on to be designated hate groups. They established the Social Contract Press, which publishes extremist books, including *The Camp of the Saints*. U.S. Inc. also published Tanton's journal, the *Social Contract*. Garrett Hardin allowed Tanton to reprint "The Tragedy of the Commons" as the very first article in the *Social Contract* in 1990 to help it get off the ground. U.S. Inc. was also the home of the Emergency Committee on Puerto Rican Statehood, which framed the issue as a threat to national unity in the United States.

TABLE 3: *Groups established or substantially funded by John Tanton and his organizations*

NAME	YEAR	PURPOSE
Bear River Commission	1966	Started to clean and protect the river in Petoskey
Northern Michigan Planned Parenthood	1967	Local branch of national group; Mary Lou Tanton played a large role
Petoskey Regional Audubon Society	1967	Local branch of national environmental group
Michigan Women for Medical Control of Abortion	1968	Local branch of national group; Mary Lou Tanton played a large role
Hartwick Pines Natural History Association	1969	Local natural history organization
League of Conservation Voters for the 11th Congressional District	1970	Local branch of national environmental group
Little Traverse Conservancy	1972	Modeled on the Nature Conservancy, buys and protects land near Petoskey
Federation for American Immigration Reform	1979	Main anti-immigrant organization in the Tanton Network
US Immigration Reform Political Action Committee	1979	Run by Mary Lou Tanton, focused on lobbying Congress
Conversation Workshop	1981	Shell company to found other companies
U.S. Inc.	1982	Shell company to found other companies
U.S. English	1983	Organization to pursue English-only laws in the US
Raptor Research	1983	For field research of an ornithologist
Recycle North	1984	The first Michigan recycling initiative in northern Michigan, later folded into the city government
Great Books Foundation	1985	Reading group in Petoskey
Center for Immigration Studies	1985	Anti-immigration think tank, one of the major Tanton Network groups

TABLE 3: *Groups established or substantially funded by John Tanton and his organizations* (continued)

NAME	YEAR	PURPOSE
Immigration Reform Law Institute	1986	Anti-immigration legal office. Independent for some years, part of FAIR other years; one of the major Tanton Network groups
Californians for Population Stabilization	1986	Immigration group for environmentalists
American Alliance for Rights and Responsibilities	1987	Now Center for Community Interest, does public education for the obligations that come with citizenship
Bringing Out the Best in Ourselves	1987	Grants for small schools
Growth and Development Forum	1980s	A local initiative to provide a venue to debate conservation in Petoskey
Regrants Program	1980s	Funding for environmental, immigration, or genetics projects
PRO English	1994	English-only group originally named English Language Advocates
Center for Genetic Research	1995	Eugenics research center
Numbers USA	1997	Anti-immigrant grassroots organizing, part of U.S. Inc. until 2002; one of the major Tanton Network groups
Conservative News Service	1999	Short-lived news wire
You Don't Speak for Me!	2006	Anti-immigrant group for Hispanic Americans, subsidiary of FAIR
Choose Black America	2006	Anti-immigrant group for Black Americans, subsidiary of FAIR
Remembrance Project	2009	Documents victims of undocumented immigrants, funded partially by U.S. Inc.
Progressives for Immigration Reform	2009	Anti-immigrant group to create new coalitions
Center for Progressive Urban Politics	2014	Subsidiary of PFIR

(continues)

TABLE 3: *Groups established or substantially funded by John Tanton and his organizations* (continued)

NAME	YEAR	PURPOSE
Tanton Family Working Reserve	2016	Nature reserve near Petoskey set up with Tantons' donation
U.S. Tech Workers	2018	Lobbies against H-1B visas for immigrants, subsidiary of PFIR
Doctors without Jobs	2018	Argues foreign doctors take jobs from American doctors, subsidiary of PFIR

U.S. Inc. was also the initial home to a series of groups promoting English-only laws around the United States. The first, in 1983, was called U.S. English; then, in the 1990s, Tanton also founded PRO English, English Language Advocates, and E Pluribus Unum. The idea for U.S. English emerged out of the 1982 FAIR board meeting. Just as had happened with Zero Population Growth in the mid-1970s, Tanton tried to push the FAIR board to expand their focus to include the cultural impacts of immigration. After three years working on the issue, Tanton thought their economic and environmental arguments against immigration were not catching on. In his travels around the country, he found that there were many people upset about Mexican immigration and protecting the English language. Tanton thought FAIR should focus more on those issues to gain supporters. The rest of the board did not agree. FAIR board member Otis Graham explained to the *Detroit News* in 2017, "I didn't feel comfortable with it. I remember thinking, this is diversionary, a mistake, taking time away from us."[34] As a result, Tanton continued his previous practice of simply starting a new group to pursue his new agenda. He used U.S. Inc. to start U.S. English in 1983, which spun off as an independent group in 1987.

Throughout the 1980s, John Tanton continued to spin off sections of FAIR's work as new areas of emphasis became clear. Cordelia Scaife May's Laurel Foundation had also recommended this strategy so that their giving appeared diversified. FAIR was focused on lobbying Congress, but they needed more research and studies to support their arguments. In 1985, Tanton established the Center for Immigration Studies for this purpose. The organization had an academic name and stood on its own as a separate entity with Otis Graham, the professor and FAIR board member, running it. However, its funding was the same as FAIR's with Cordelia Scaife May providing the bulk of CIS's budget. FAIR also found itself involved in lawsuits, writing amicus briefs for cases before the Supreme Court and finding local cases to challenge new sanctuary city laws that were emerging. Tanton realized this was also a separate task and established the Immigration Reform Law Institute in 1986. IRLI seemed like a separate group, but it was also funded primarily by Cordelia Scaife May. The final significant spinoff group was established a decade later in 1997. Numbers USA was a subsidiary of U.S. Inc. from 1997 to 2002 and focused on grassroots organizing by locating a legion of people who could be summoned to call, fax, or email their congressional representatives when needed. All the while, Tanton continued to work as a full-time ophthalmologist at the Burns Clinic in Petoskey. By the time he retired in 1998, he had completed over four thousand surgeries in his career.

From the outside, it appeared that a series of anti-immigration groups were growing around the country due to a groundswell of support for restricting immigration. Similar to the proposals in the Powell Memo, the multiple groups allowed them to cite each other's work to lend credibility. When the media did stories on immigration, there were multiple anti-immigrant groups available to interview so that a single story could mention FAIR, CIS, and Numbers USA as if they were all distinct. The separation insulated each group from any controversial actions of the others. It also allowed donors to spread their money around and not appear to be funding only a single group. However, despite the facade, all of the significant immigration restrictions and English-only groups in the United States were started primarily by a single man, John Tanton, and funded primarily by a single woman, Cordelia Scaife May.

THE COLCOM FOUNDATION

In 2005, after a diagnosis of pancreatic cancer, Cordelia Scaife May took her own life on her farm in Ligonier at the age of seventy-six. Scaife May had no children or heirs, so she gave away everything to foundations and charitable causes. She left land that she owned on Maui to the Nature Conservancy of Hawaii and her land on Kauai to the National Tropical Botanical Garden.[35] The largest chunk of her fortune, $420 million (AFI

$560 million), as well as 450 acres of property in Pennsylvania, went to the Colcom Foundation, which she had established in 1996 to handle her charitable giving.[36]

Scaife May knew that Colcom would receive criticism for its work. The statement of purpose submitted to the IRS in 1996 acknowledged that her ideas were not popular. The filing stated, "Nor do I anticipate that they will be so in the future when the Directors of the Foundation will be called upon to exercise the courage of their convictions in carrying out the program I have described in this statement. I urge the directors not to fear controversy."[37]

In 2006, John Rohe became the vice president for philanthropy at Colcom, where he has been the primary contact for grant proposals ever since. With a curly gray Caesar haircut and sharp features, Rohe looks the part of a wealthy philanthropist, but he is also a lifetime devotee of John Tanton. Prior to joining Colcom, Rohe had lived in Petoskey, Michigan, and worked closely with John Tanton at U.S. Inc. Rohe was on the board of directors of FAIR in 2004 and 2005, and he wrote an adoring biography of John and Mary Lou Tanton that was published in 2002 by FAIR. In the book's introduction, Rohe demonstrated that he was exactly the type of true believer Scaife May was looking for. He began by comparing John Tanton to Susan B. Anthony, Galileo, Thomas Jefferson, and John Locke, who "all were heretics in their time. They were mocked by the raging forces of the present. Their vision awaited the validating vision of history's long view. They became prophets only when vindicated by the future."[38] He goes on to predict that in the decades to come, John Tanton will be seen in a similar light. In the years since Scaife May's death, Rohe has become the man who ensured that her funds continued to flow to the Tanton Network of anti-immigrant groups so that Tanton's future vindication could be achieved.

CHAPTER 11

HOSTILE TAKEOVER

In April 2005, the national membership of the Sierra Club faced a choice. The venerable environmental organization had been roiled for decades by debates about whether immigration was a threat to the environment in the United States. Now the membership was asked to take a final vote on the issue. Should the Sierra Club maintain a neutral stance on immigration or change its policy to "recognize the need to adopt lower limits on migration to the United States"?[1] What seemed like a dry policy question was the result of a thirty-year tug-of-war between John Tanton and the leadership of the Sierra Club. The choice was stark: would the Sierra Club maintain its position as a celebrated environmental organization, or would it join the Tanton Network of anti-immigrant groups pushing for strict limits on immigration to the United States?

For the Tanton Network, the Sierra Club was a top prize. It was not just any environmental group; it was the oldest and largest environmental organization in the United States. The Sierra Club was founded in 1892 by John Muir, a Scottish-American naturalist with a flowing beard and a burning desire to protect the natural wonders of California. Like his contemporaries James McClatchy and Denis Kearney, Muir was an immigrant to the United States from the United Kingdom. Muir arrived as an eleven-year-old in 1849, the same year that McClatchy and the other 49ers were racing to California in search of gold. Muir grew up in Portage, Wisconsin, in an extremely devout religious family and realized his interest in the natural world through classes at the University of

Wisconsin–Madison. After briefly moving to Canada with his brother to avoid the draft in the Civil War, Muir set out on a thousand-mile walk all the way to Florida in which he observed the natural world along the way. He made his way to San Francisco in 1868 and booked a trip to Yosemite a few days after his arrival. Muir was enchanted by the natural beauty of Yosemite. His spiritual upbringing merged with his love of nature, producing a view of the natural world as a cathedral. Muir built a cabin in the valley and lived in Yosemite on and off for decades. By the 1880s, he had mapped many of the groves of giant redwoods and sequoias in California and focused on creating protected areas for them. Muir succeeded in establishing Yosemite National Park in 1890, and when he founded the Sierra Club in 1892, he envisioned it as an organization to push for more protected areas across the West.

John Muir is remembered as a visionary naturalist today, but he was also a product of his time whose views were imbued with notions of white racial superiority. In 1894, Muir described the Native Americans of Yosemite as "mostly ugly, and some of them altogether hideous." For Muir, nature was a place devoid of humans, except for humans wealthy enough to take in the serene beauty through observation and meditation. There was no place in Muir's environmentalism for people who actually lived off the land, even the Native Americans who had been part of the stable ecosystems for generations. Native Americans "seemed to have no right place in the landscape" and needed to be removed from the land in order to make it pristine.[2] The national parks that are held up today as the epitome of the natural world are decidedly unnatural places where the historical human presence was erased. They are not untouched wild places but rather heavily managed human creations protected by strict regulations.[3]

Muir was part of the elite group of eugenicists and race science advocates at the turn of the twentieth century. Madison Grant, the author of *The Passing of the Great Race*, was also a strong advocate for protected areas across the American West. Muir worked on conservation efforts with Henry Fairfield Osborn, the president of the American Museum of Natural History in New York, which served as the hub for eugenics meetings. Osborn's nephew, Frederick Osborn, was the founding president of the Pioneer Fund. Muir was also friends with Teddy Roosevelt, who popularized the phrase "race suicide" and was an avid outdoor enthusiast. From the beginning, the environmentalist movement was intertwined with racism as the creation of natural spaces for the pleasure of white elites came at the expense of Native Americans who lived in those places.

The Sierra Club began to formulate its policy position on population growth in the 1960s. In 1966, it adopted the policy that "the Sierra Club endorses the objectives of legislation to establish federal machinery to deal with the problems of rapid human population growth."[4] In 1968, the Sierra Club was the copublisher of *The Population Bomb*, Paul and Anne Ehrlich's manifesto on the dangers of population growth that deeply influenced John Tanton and helped kick off the modern environmental movement. Throughout the 1970s, the Sierra Club had a dedicated population committee, which was headed by John Tanton from 1971 to 1975. In that role, Tanton tried to push the organization to take a stronger stand on immigration, but he faced some resistance. He moved on to Ehrlich's Zero Population Growth, where he was president from 1975 to 1977 before founding FAIR in 1979. Even as the Sierra Club did not focus on immigration to the extent that John Tanton thought they should, the group included population growth among their list of threats to the environment during those years.[5] They also occasionally mentioned immigration as well. In 1980, a Sierra Club representative testified before Congress: "It is perhaps less well known the extent to which immigration policy, even more than the number of children per family, is the determinant of the future numbers of Americans."[6] In 1994, the Sierra Club even copublished a book with Tanton's Center for Immigration Studies titled *How Many Americans: Population, Immigration, and the Environment*, by Leon Bouvier, who worked at CIS, and Lindsey Grant, a State Department official.

SIERRANS FOR U.S. POPULATION STABILIZATION

Throughout the 1980s, as Tanton focused on building his anti-immigration network, he maintained strong alliances with sections of the environmental movement. Paul Ehrlich and Garrett Hardin, the author of "The Tragedy of the Commons," were close associates who worked together on the boards of several organizations, including the Environmental Fund (later Population-Environment Balance). Tanton also founded Californians for Population Stabilization (CAPS) in 1986 as an organization for former members of ZPG to focus on the immigration issue.

The founding board of CAPS included Otis Graham, who was also a founding board member of FAIR and the founding president of CIS, and a UCLA professor of astronomy named Ben Zuckerman. Zuckerman was also involved with the Diversity Alliance for a Sustainable America, an anti-immigrant group primarily funded by the Carthage Foundation, Cordelia Scaife May's brother Richard's charitable foundation.[7] In a 1986 memo, Tanton discussed the Sierra Club. He wrote, "The Sierra Club may not want to touch the immigration issue, but the immigration issue is going to touch the Sierra Club!"[8] Throughout the 1980s, Tanton mused in his correspondence about the possibility of taking over a national organization in order to pursue the anti-immigrant cause using their mainstream platform.

By the mid-1990s, the dire predictions of *The Population Bomb* had not materialized, and global population growth was stabilizing. The Sierra Club's Ethnic and Cultural Diversity Task Force raised concerns about the population and immigration policies of the organization. In 1996, the Sierra Club removed immigration from their areas of focus, instead opting for a policy of neutrality: "The board's actions reflect a desire to put the immigration debate to rest within the club and to focus on other pressing components of our population program. The board instructs all club chapters, groups, committees, and other entities to take no position on immigration policy."[9]

John Tanton and his allies were furious with the decision, which they felt was shaped more by political correctness than science about the environment. They tried to get the Sierra Club to reverse course, which led to an attempted hostile takeover of the organization from 1998 until 2005. The dissidents formed a group called Sierrans for U.S. Population Stabilization (SUSPS) in order to press the Sierra Club to focus more on immigration. The leaders of the dissident faction were Ben Zuckerman, the UCLA professor who had formed CAPS with John Tanton in 1986, and Alan Kuper, who was on the FAIR board of advisors. In 1998, they were able to get their first initiative on a ballot before the Sierra Club's 550,000 members, proposing to scrap the neutrality position and focus on immigration as a key threat to the environment. The measure was supported by Anne Ehrlich, the coauthor of *The Population Bomb*, as well as several other prominent conservationists including Earth First! founder Dave Foreman and Sea Shepherd Conservation Society founder Paul Watson.

The Tanton Network set to work recruiting its members to join the Sierra Club and then vote in favor of the initiative. Tanton financially supported the effort, writing to Kuper, "I should be able to provide you with several thousand dollars of help for the campaign. Think expansively. How much could you put to good use?"[10] Tanton set Roy Beck and his new Tanton Network group Numbers USA on the task of drumming up support for the anti-immigrant position.[11] Tanton also solicited a donation of $90,000 (AFI $145,000) from Alan Weeden, whose Weeden Foundation had long supported anti-immigrant causes, but at a smaller scale than Cordelia Scaife May.[12]

The Sierra Club's executive director, Carl Pope, denounced the effort to change the organization's mission to focus on restricting immigration as "America at its worst. And for the Sierra Club to be dragged into this kind of cesspool is very unfortunate."[13] It was later revealed that a wealthy donor named David Gelbaum had given the Sierra Club over $100 million (AFI $165 million) but had threatened to stop his support if the Sierra Club adopted an anti-immigrant stance.[14] In 1998, the Sierra Club took the issue to the membership by giving them two options in a vote. Alternative A would adopt an anti-immigrant position that advocated for reducing immigration to the United States to fewer than 200,000 people per year, down from an average of almost 1 million legal immigrants per year in the 1990s. Alternative B was to maintain the Sierra Club's policy of neutrality. The vote was close, but of those who voted, 60 percent favored maintaining the neutral policy.

The Tanton Network was disappointed but did not see the vote as a total loss. Forty percent of those who voted supported their position. They also noticed that only 13 percent of members actually voted, so they did not need that many more supporters to sway the vote to their favor. For the next hostile takeover attempt, they changed their strategy and began to run members of SUSPS for the national board of the Sierra Club. Ben Zuckerman and Alan Kuper lost in their first attempts, but in 2002, Zuckerman was elected to the board of the Sierra Club. His campaign did not emphasize immigration, but once elected he focused on it, even sharing articles from VDARE, the white supremacist website, with the rest of the board. VDARE was founded with Pioneer Fund support by Peter Brimelow, a friend and regular correspondent of John Tanton's. The name comes from Virginia Dare, the first white child born in the Americas.

In 2003, two more members of the SUSPS faction, Doug La Follette, who was at the time the secretary of state of Wisconsin, and environmentalist Paul Watson, were elected to the board without mentioning immigration as a significant issue. Watson is a celebrity in the environmental movement whose shaggy white hair and taciturn manner were beamed into houses around the world on the TV show *Whale Wars*. The show documents Watson's Sea Shepherd Conservation Society's efforts to stop Japanese whaling near Antarctica, often using extreme methods of harassment against the Japanese ships, including stink bombs and dangerous maritime maneuvers. In 2003, Watson was focused on helping the Tanton Network in the hostile takeover of the Sierra Club. After joining the board, he spoke publicly about the effort and suggested that since so few members vote in Sierra Club elections, a small minority could hijack the elections for their own purposes, as the Tanton Network was attempting to do.[15] He explained, "We're only three directors away from controlling that board."[16]

By 2003, the Southern Poverty Law Center was monitoring the activities of John Tanton and his network of organizations as potential hate groups. The previous year, SPLC researcher Heidi Beirich had pored over Tanton's papers at the University of Michigan and had published the results in a cover story for the SPLC's *Intelligence Report* magazine titled "The Puppeteer."[17] When the SPLC became aware of the takeover attempt, they sent a letter to the Sierra Club's director informing him of the threat. At a public meeting, an audience member asked Paul Watson directly, "Do you in fact intend to take over the Sierra Club?" and he answered, "Yes."[18] The goal was to take the prestige of the Sierra Club and use it to promote an anti-immigrant agenda.

In 2004, the Tanton Network and their allies in the SUSPS ran a slate of five more candidates, which if they were all elected would give them enough votes to control the board. All of these candidates were connected to the Tanton Network. The most prominent was Dick Lamm, the former governor of Colorado who was a member of the FAIR board of directors and had worked closely with John Tanton to build the Tanton Network's political and philanthropic connections. Lamm hosted one of Tanton's witan salons at the Colorado governor's mansion, and it was Lamm who introduced Tanton to Warren Buffett. The other candidates were Kim McCoy, Roy van de Hoek, David Pimentel, and Frank Morris.

Pimentel served on the board of the Diversity Alliance for Sustainable America with Zuckerman. Frank Morris, a Black man, at different times served on the boards of many of the Tanton Network groups, including FAIR, CIS, Progressives for Immigration Reform, and the Diversity Alliance for a Sustainable America.

The Tanton Network turned to their base of supporters to join the Sierra Club and then vote for the anti-immigrant candidates. On the white supremacist VDARE website, Brenda Walker, a regular contributor to Tanton's journal the *Social Contract*, wrote a post explaining how VDARE readers could join the Sierra Club. She wrote, "The prize is enormous. The Sierra Club is arguably the most influential voice of the environmental movement, one well heard by Washington and the media." However, time was short: "If you care about protecting the planet, including the American chunk of it, then *join the Sierra Club NOW and have your vote influence this debate.*"[19] She then provided a link directly to the new member registration page on the Sierra Club website. The Sierra Club identified twenty different anti-immigrant and white supremacist groups that pressed their supporters to join the Sierra Club in order to vote for the SUSPS candidates in 2004.[20]

The Southern Poverty Law Center leadership was concerned about the hostile takeover to the extent that SPLC director Morris Dees joined the Sierra Club and ran for the board himself. Dees used his candidate statement not to ask the members to vote for him but to plead with them not to vote for the anti-immigrant candidates. His statement listed the anti-immigrant candidates and their connections to hate groups and then concluded, "I am not asking that you vote for me. Instead, I am running to urge that you vote against the 'greening of hate' and against those candidates backed by SUSPS. Please save the Sierra Club from a takeover by the radical right."[21] The day after Dees announced his candidacy, the thirteen living former Sierra Club presidents signed a joint letter warning of "an organized effort to elect Directors of the Sierra Club from outside the activist ranks of Sierra Club members."[22] Former Colorado governor Lamm and the other anti-immigrant candidates were furious and sued the Sierra Club to remove fake candidates like Dees, but they eventually dropped the lawsuit.

Despite the Tanton Network's effort to have their members join the Sierra Club, the SPLC tactics to get their message directly to the membership worked. When the votes were counted, the Sierra Club's preferred five candidates were elected, all with over 110,000 votes each. Roy van de Hoek did the best out of the Tanton-supported SUSPS candidates, but he finished ninth and only received 15,700 votes.[23] Pimentel, Lamm, Mc-Coy, and Morris received even fewer. Larry Fahn, the president of Sierra Club's board, was relieved: "This is a strong mandate for the board to stick to its core agenda and mission protecting our planet. It was a clear repudiation of those wanting the club to get involved in the immigration debate."[24]

The Tanton Network's effort to hijack the Sierra Club came to a close a year later in April 2005. Van de Hoek and Kuper ran for the board again but were not elected. Zuckerman's three-year term was at an end, which closed the window of opportunity to take over the board. Zuckerman, La Follette, and Watson did use their positions on the board to put one more ballot question in front of the membership, asking again whether the Sierra Club should make population and immigration areas of policy focus. The vote was 18,898 in favor of the proposed change and 102,455 opposed. The motion failed and the anti-immigrant activists moved on.

The Tanton Network continued to produce reports and describe themselves as green environmentalists, but they turned their sustained focus elsewhere. Just as John Tanton had seen during his efforts in the 1970s to get the Sierra Club and Zero Population Growth to focus more on immigration, the majority of environmental activists were not open to his nativist message. Environmentalists were more aligned with progressive political views, and the majority were not going to be Tanton's allies in a fight to limit immigration to the United States. Instead, the Tanton Network turned their gaze to a much larger organization that had increasingly become the vehicle for white cultural grievances in the United States: the Republican Party.

— CHAPTER 12 —

OUT-TANCREDO TANCREDO

The Phoenix Park Hotel in Washington, DC, sits at a prime location on North Capitol Street across from Union Station and only a few blocks from the Capitol Building. On April 22, 2007, the warm spring air made the Capitol dome seem like a mirage on the horizon as a fifty-foot tractor trailer pulled up in front of the hotel, alongside its green awning with gold trim. The bellhops gathered on the red brick sidewalk but did not know what to make of the cargo inside. It had been shipped directly to the hotel from South Florida, up Interstate 95 all the way to Washington, DC. As the doors of the truck swung open, Joyce Kaufman, a talk radio host from West Palm Beach, Florida, was on the scene to inspect the delivery she had organized, as was a crew from Lou Dobbs's show on CNN. With long, straight brown hair and bright red lipstick, Kaufman was in DC for the second Hold Their Feet to the Fire event hosted by the Federation for American Immigration Reform. The idea for the event was to bring together like-minded talk radio hosts from around the country and broadcast together for three days from Washington, DC, in order to rally support for the anti-immigrant cause.

FAIR held its first Hold Their Feet to the Fire in April 2005 in order to pressure lawmakers to pass the REAL ID Act of 2005. A bill to add security measures to driver's licenses might not seem like a priority for an immigration restriction group, but the law included a ban on states issuing driver's licenses to undocumented immigrants, which nine states allowed at the time.[1] Tucked inside the bill was also a provision that facilitated the construction of border walls by giving the secretary of the

Department of Homeland Security the ability to waive all laws necessary to speed border wall construction. Although there was no funding for border walls in this particular bill, it paved the way for much of the border wall construction over the past fifteen years. Despite numerous lawsuits challenging the expansive authority, DHS secretaries have used it to waive over fifty different laws along over seven hundred miles of the border. These have included environmental laws such as the Endangered Species Act, the Clean Air Act, the Clean Water Act, and the National Environmental Policy Act, and social and cultural protections such as the Antiquities Act, the Archeological Resources Protection Act, and the Native American Graves Protection and Repatriation Act.[2]

Following John Tanton's playbook for creating the perception that a movement was larger than it was, FAIR set out to overwhelm lawmakers to make it seem like there was massive, grassroots support for the REAL ID bill. The first Hold Their Feet to the Fire event used all of the assets FAIR had: a handful of dedicated talk radio hosts, a small set of allies in the House of Representatives, five hundred activists from around the country, and a small army of radio listeners and FAIR members across the United States. Despite the relatively small base, they marshaled these assets very effectively. The first full day of the event, Sunday, April 24, 2005, the eighteen radio hosts broadcast all day long imploring their listeners to contact their representatives by email about the bill. That way, on Monday morning staffers would find their inboxes full of messages from constituents in favor of the REAL ID Act. On Monday, the radio hosts asked their listeners to call or fax their congressional offices. The FAIR website had a dedicated page that made it easy to send a fax to the appropriate office, and they processed fourteen thousand messages on that day alone. A FAIR member reported, "My impression is that we are jamming their switchboards and they cannot handle the volume of calls."[3] Also on Monday at Lafayette Park, just behind the White House, they held a rally with speakers that included Chris Simcox, the founder of the Minuteman Project, a civilian militia at the border, similar to David Duke's Klan Border Patrol. On Tuesday and Wednesday, FAIR set up meetings at all 535 congressional offices, and the volunteers in Washington, DC, visited every office at least twice. When they arrived, they found receptive hosts who had already received a mountain of emails, faxes, and calls from their constituents about the issue. On Tuesday, FAIR also held a press conference with their handful of allies from the immigration reform caucus: Virgil Goode of Virginia, J. D. Hayworth of Arizona, Dana Rohrabacher of California, Ed Royce of California, Lamar Smith of Texas, and Tom Tancredo of Colorado.

With graying sideburns and a wide nose, Tancredo was often confused at Congress with his doppelgänger, Steve King of Iowa. In addition to their looks, the two shared strong anti-immigrant views. Tancredo was elected to Congress in 1999 and established the Congressional Immigration Reform Caucus as a group to push for more restrictions on immigration. He regularly worked with the Tanton Network to draft bills including the Mass Immigration Reduction Act in August 2001, which would have placed a five-year moratorium on immigration to the country.[4] It never came up for a vote.

After the hotel press conference in 2005, Tancredo held a reception on Capitol Hill to push for the passage of the REAL ID Act. The pressure campaign worked, and despite criticism from social libertarians who bemoaned the implications of a national ID card, state bureaucrats who worried about logistical challenges, and immigrant activists who saw it pushing people further into the shadows, the final version of the REAL ID Act passed the House 368–58 and then the Senate 100–0. It was signed into law on May 11, 2005, by President George W. Bush. FAIR proclaimed it a great victory: "This is perhaps the most significant immigration reform victory since the reforms enacted in 1996."[5]

The 2007 event at the Phoenix Park Hotel sought to replicate the success of the first Hold Their Feet to the Fire, but it was taking place in a different atmosphere. In the 2006 midterm elections, the Democrats retook both the House of Representatives and the Senate. Additionally, although more Republicans were sympathetic to the restrictionist cause, FAIR saw Republican president George W. Bush as an adversary on the immigration issue because he had repeatedly pushed for a comprehensive immigration reform bill that would legalize the millions of undocumented people in the United States and bring them into the formal economy. Bush and his advisor Karl Rove argued that demographically the Republican Party needed to appeal to the growing Latino population in the United States. Consequently, in early 2007, with new Democratic majorities in both the House and Senate, Bush saw comprehensive immigration reform as one potential place for bipartisan legislation. FAIR was now on the defensive and focused on blocking any reform bills that might be proposed.

For the 2007 Hold Their Feet to the Fire gathering, FAIR billed it as "the biggest immigration reform event in history." They increased the number of radio personalities in attendance from eighteen to thirty-seven, and they broadcast from 5:00 a.m. to midnight each day at thirteen makeshift studios set up around the hotel dubbed "Radio Row." Joyce Kaufman realized that many of her listeners on WFTL 850 AM in South Florida felt strongly about immigration and wanted to go to DC with her to show their support. However, many were unable due to the cost, work commitments, and the difficulty of traveling so far away. So that they could be there in spirit, she came up with another idea. In the month before the FAIR event, she implored her listeners to send their souls, in the form of soles, to Washington to show their support for strong immigration restrictions. The result of her gimmick, "Send your sole to Washington," was a truckload of five thousand pairs of shoes stacked up in a ballroom of the hotel. Even after the truck left for DC, thousands more pairs arrived at the station in West Palm Beach. The FAIR newsletter declared, "Not since Imelda Marcos cleaned out her closet has anyone seen so many pairs of shoes in one place."[6] Lou Dobbs's report on CNN showed the boxes and boxes of shoes while Dobbs marveled at Radio Row with an amazed smile.[7]

Lou Dobbs was an ideal advocate for FAIR. With his guttural voice, confident demeanor, and, most importantly, a perch at 7:00 p.m. Eastern on CNN's prime-time lineup, Dobbs had the mainstream national platform that the Tanton Network craved. Dobbs got his start as a business reporter but was radicalized after the events of September 11, 2001, matching a trend across the country. Before September 11, immigration and border policy was often discussed in economic terms, but after, it entered the security domain. The wave of funding dramatically expanded the reach of the Border Patrol, and the media fanned the flames of the threat posed by terrorists entering the country. In Congress, Tom Tancredo's Immigration Reform Caucus had ten members before the attacks but swelled to fifty-nine in the months after.[8] Dobbs used his nightly show to warn of the threat of Islamic extremism and the danger posed by lax border protections, along the way drawing the ire of immigrants' rights groups and eventually CNN's management. In 2004, the Center for Immigration Studies awarded him their Eugene Katz Award for excellence in coverage of immigration. Dobbs was more extreme on his nationally syndicated radio show, which he brought to FAIR's Hold Their Feet to the Fire event the following year in 2008. In 2009, despite high ratings, Dobbs left CNN as his right-wing views, particularly his support of the birther movement that questioned Barack Obama's citizenship, clashed with the network's desire to present nonpartisan news.[9] Dobbs briefly considered a run for the presidency in 2011 but instead signed on to the Fox Business network where he continued to cover the news from an anti-immigrant perspective.

The Hold Their Feet to the Fire press conference in 2007 included several more members of Congress than it had in 2005, including two that were running for the Republican presidential nomination: Tancredo and Representative Duncan Hunter of California. The press conference was organized by Republican representative Brian Bilbray of San Diego, who was just elected to Congress after having worked as a FAIR lobbyist the previous year. Bilbray took over the leadership of the Congressional Immigration Reform Caucus, which Tancredo had founded and led since 1999, so Tancredo could focus on running for president. In addition to Dobbs's CNN coverage of Hold Their Feet to the Fire, there were stories on Fox News and MSNBC, as well as articles in the *New York Times*, *Washington Post*, and *Los Angeles Times*. The *New York Times* article was wryly titled "Bringing Fire, Shoes to Immigration Debate."[10]

"A CLUSTER OF ORGANIZATIONS"

In 1986, John Tanton's assistant had written in a memo that "John feels that we need a cluster of organizations working on this problem" because more "can be accomplished with coalition organizations each coming at this from their own viewpoint and with their own constituencies."[11] By 2007, the primary organizations in the Tanton Network had settled into their respective roles, but they continued to establish new niche groups to try to build an anti-immigrant coalition in unexpected places. These included Progressives for Immigration Reform (PFIR), a Hispanic anti-immigrant group called You Don't Speak for Me!, an African American group called Choose Black America, and the Coalition for the Future American Worker, which was a group making the case that unions were for immigration reform. The connections between the Tanton Network groups are often visible through their overlapping boards of directors, with the same core group of supporters serving on the boards of several of the groups, often at the same time. For example, Frank Morris is on the board of directors of the Center for Immigration Studies, FAIR, and PFIR, and he was the executive director of the Diversity Alliance for a Sustainable America and Choose Black America. He was also one of the candidates for the board of the Sierra Club from the Sierrans for U.S. Population Stabilization.

Many of the new groups did not bear fruit, and the Tanton Network coalesced around the work of FAIR, CIS, U.S. Inc., Immigration Reform Law Institute, and Numbers USA. Despite the jumble of different names and acronyms, the organizations shared the same founder, John Tanton, and the same primary funding source, Cordelia Scaife May.[12] FAIR, led by Dan Stein, was the flagship organization and focused on lobbying Congress and media outreach. Stein, a native of Washington, DC, with a law degree from Catholic University, joined FAIR as press secretary in 1982. Stein became executive director in 1988 when Roger Conner stepped down and took over the role of president from John Tanton in 2003. Tanton remained on the FAIR board. CIS operated like a think tank, writing policy briefs and academic papers to create the foundation for the anti-immigrant position. CIS was led by Mark Krikorian, who became the president of the organization in 1995. U.S. Inc. continued to operate out of Petoskey and served as the umbrella organization for Social Contract Press and the *Social Contract* journal. John Rohe, who had been the director, moved to Colcom after Scaife May's death, and John Tanton remained heavily involved in the daily operations. The Immigration Reform Law Institute was connected to FAIR and filed lawsuits around the country supporting local restrictions on immigrants and challenging sanctuary city laws. The newest organization in the Tanton Network, Numbers USA, was becoming one of the most significant as it benefited from the flood of funds into Colcom's coffers after the death of Cordelia Scaife May. In 2004, Numbers USA received only $110,000 from Colcom. In 2005, Colcom's donation to Numbers USA increased by a factor of ten to $1.29 million. By 2008, it got $3.51 million from Colcom.[13] Numbers USA was able to expand its membership from 50,000 in 2004 to 447,000 in 2007.[14]

Numbers USA was founded in 1997 as a subsidiary of U.S. Inc. with Roy Beck as its president and CEO from the start. Beck was born in Marshfield, Missouri, and speaks with an Ozarks-inflected southern drawl. His slicked-back thin gray hair, glasses, and genial demeanor make him seem more like an evangelical pastor than the leader of a national anti-immigrant group. Prior to beginning his work with John Tanton as an editor at Social Contract Press, Beck was a journalist for the *Cincinnati Inquirer*. Numbers USA was established to do the work of grassroots organizing for the Tanton Network. In 2002, at a conference with other anti-immigrant advocates, Beck explained what his Numbers USA was up to, counseling his colleagues that although they were all working hand in hand, it "needs to look like a grassroots effort."[15]

AN ALLY IN THE SENATE

In addition to building the grassroots network of supporters, Roy Beck recruited a political ally who would become integral to the Tanton Network. The Tanton Network worked closely with Tom Tancredo and several other collaborators in the House of Representatives, but after the retirement of Alan Simpson in 1997, it no longer had an advocate in the Senate. In 2006, Beck met with Jeff Sessions, a conservative senator from Alabama whom Beck thought could be a supporter in the effort to block the seeming bipartisan consensus to implement immigration reform.[16] With red cheeks, silver hair, and a soft-spoken southern drawl, Sessions is almost elfin in appearance. At the time, Sessions was not involved in the immigration debates, but as Beck sat down in Sessions's Senate office, he listened to what Beck had to say and was intrigued.

Jefferson Beauregard Sessions III was born in Selma, Alabama, on Christmas Eve 1946. His name is a double homage to the Confederacy. Jefferson is a nod to Jefferson Davis, the president of the Confederate States of America, and Beauregard to P. G. T. Beauregard, who was the Confederate general who presided over the Battle of Fort Sumter in Charleston, South Carolina, that started the war. Sessions was student body president at Huntingdon College in Montgomery before getting his law degree from the University of Alabama in 1973. In 1975, he was hired as an assistant US attorney for the Southern District of Alabama and was named the US attorney for the district in 1981 by President

Ronald Reagan. He remained in the position through the administration of George H. W. Bush until Bill Clinton took office in 1993.

In 1986, Sessions was nominated to a federal judgeship for the Southern District of Alabama, but his confirmation hearings became controversial after his insensitive comments about race emerged. Some of his colleagues in the US Attorney's office said that he demeaned the NAACP as "un-American," "communist inspired," and a "pinko" organization. He called a white attorney a "disgrace to his race," called a Black attorney "boy," and said the Ku Klux Klan was "OK until I found out they smoked pot."[17] Sessions said some of the lines, like about the KKK smoking pot, were jokes while he denied the others completely. Beyond the racially insensitive language, Sessions also drew criticism for a case of voter fraud he had prosecuted the previous year against African American voting rights advocates Albert Turner, Evelyn Turner, and Spencer Hogue.

Albert Turner was a close associate of Martin Luther King Jr. and a leader of the civil rights movement. On Sunday, March 7, 1965, Turner, John Lewis, and five hundred other marchers were making their way from Selma to Montgomery, Alabama, to push for voter registration for African Americans. Jim Clark, the local county sheriff, had called for the white men of the county to gather at the courthouse earlier that morning to be deputized, and the massive, untrained police force now stood arrayed against the unarmed marchers when they reached the Edmund Pettus Bridge. Albert Turner was in the second row of marchers when the white men charged, firing tear gas and beating them with batons in what came to be known as Bloody Sunday. Over eighty people were injured, and the graphic video footage shocked television viewers around the country and put pressure on President Lyndon Johnson to act, paving the way for the Voting Rights Act later that summer.

In the 1980s, the Turners were still fighting for the right for African Americans to vote. In their rural Alabama county, the polls were only open for four hours in the afternoon, which made it difficult for many older people and working people to vote.[18] Whites in the district had already been taught to vote absentee, so the Turners worked to get absentee ballots to elderly Black voters, some of whom were illiterate. The Turners helped them fill out ballots, which Sessions called voter fraud. To others, Sessions's prosecution looked like retribution for the Turners' past activism and an effort to suppress the Black vote. The case went to trial but the jury acquitted the Turners and Spencer Hogue after deliberating for only three hours. In Sessions's Senate confirmation hearings in 1986, a fellow Justice Department lawyer, Gerald Hebert, was asked if Sessions was a racist. Herbert replied, "I don't really know whether he is or he isn't. I probably ought to know, but I don't. I really can't say."

Senator Ted Kennedy of Massachusetts spoke against Sessions in the committee, saying, "Mr. Sessions is a throwback to a shameful era, which I know both Black and white Americans thought was in our past. It is inconceivable to me that a person of this attitude is qualified to be a US Attorney, let alone a United States Federal Judge."[19] Kennedy went on to call for him to resign his US attorney position. In the end, the Senate Judiciary Committee scuttled his nomination, and the decisive vote was cast against him by Sessions's home state senator, Howell Heflin. The move was only the second time in the previous fifty years that the Senate Judiciary Committee rejected a federal judicial nomination, and the rebuke was deeply embarrassing for Sessions. He found, however, that the rejection by Washington, DC, elites became a stamp of authenticity for his fellow conservative Alabamans, contributing to his political rise.

At the time, it would have been impossible to imagine that Sessions would replace Heflin in the Senate and go on to lead the entire Department of Justice as the attorney general of the United States, but it eventually happened. After the failed nomination, Sessions used the sympathy it generated in Alabama to build political alliances and was elected the attorney general of the state in 1995. When Heflin announced his retirement from the Senate in 1997, Sessions won the hotly contested race and took Heflin's seat in the Senate. He was even appointed to the Judiciary Committee, sitting beside many of the same senators that voted against his nomination only a decade before.

Sessions positioned himself on the far right of the political spectrum and developed a reputation as an ideologue. He had no interest in compromise or the political games of Washington. In his first decade in the Senate, he had not focused much on immigration, but when he sat down with Numbers USA chief Roy Beck in his Senate office in 2006, he had a revelation. Beck made the case that immigration restrictions were popular with the right-wing base, even if many senators were not yet on board, and he pointed to the economic and social changes migrants brought with them. Sessions replied, "I guess if I don't do it, nobody's going to do it."[20]

"YOUR VOICE WAS HEARD"

In the early summer of 2007, a few weeks after FAIR organized their second Hold Their Feet to the Fire event in DC, the conventional wisdom was that a comprehensive immigration reform was cruising toward passage. Congress was controlled by Democrats, and President Bush wanted to burnish his reputation as a compassionate conservative. The Tanton Network had something else in mind.[21] The Tanton Network's strategy to stop the Comprehensive Immigration Reform bill was focused on reframing the debate by establishing the boundaries of the discussion. They put together talking points that their allies in the media like Dobbs and their congressional supporters like Tancredo repeated over and over. The message was simple: (1) border security had to precede any immigration reform because otherwise more people would cross again in the future, recreating the problem; (2) there should be no amnesty for people who violated American immigration laws; and (3) guest worker programs harm American workers.

In their communications with their base, however, the Tanton Network focused more on the cultural impacts. The FAIR newsletter repeatedly called immigration "an invasion."[22] The newsletter also included a column on the "outrage of the month" that documented the great replacement in real time. In October 2006, it was that "in Texas, school children recite the pledge of allegiance . . . to the Mexican Flag."[23] In January 2007, it was the story of a family killed by a drunk driver who was an undocumented immigrant.[24] FAIR also recognized the power of framing one's opponents by adding a negative term when mentioning them. The congressional sponsors of the Comprehensive Immigration Reform bill were described as "Open Border Senators" and the immigrant rights community as "Illegal Alien," "Pro-Amnesty," or "Ethnic Interest" advocates.

The Tanton Network coined the term "angel families" to describe people who lost loved ones in crimes committed by undocumented immigrants. As with many things in the anti-immigrant movement, the angel family idea traces its roots back to John Tanton, who proposed the idea to

FAIR director Dan Stein in 1990. Tanton wrote a memo that said, "Our opposition has long had the advantage of telling the personal story, complete with photographs, of the distressed immigrant or refugee. These often pluck the heartstrings." Tanton continued, "I suggest we pull together a little publication that will tell some of these personal histories, explaining the way which immigration affects some of those already here, particularly minority groups. These could be published in a little brochure, with a picture of the affected person."[25] With funding from Tanton's U.S. Inc., the Remembrance Project focused on telling the stories of angel families. U.S. Inc. also published a book through its Social Contract Press, complete with a cover splattered with blood, titled *The Victims of Illegal Immigration: A Collection of Essays.* Lou Dobbs regularly reported on angel families on his program, and Donald Trump, as he ran for president, also latched onto this idea. He would regularly tell the stories of angel families at his campaign rallies, and after he was elected president, he even invited an angel family as his guests at his first address to a joint session of Congress.

Despite the Tanton Network's new infusion of funds from Colcom and its growing influence in Congress, it seemed like comprehensive immigration reform was on track with bipartisan mainstream support. On May 17, 2007, Senate negotiators announced they had reached a grand bargain to pass comprehensive immigration reform. The deal was a trade of stronger border security and a shift away from family reunification toward a skill-based immigration system in exchange for a guest worker program and the normalization of millions of long-term undocumented residents of the United States.

Although expanded border security and the end of family reunification were Tanton Network goals, amnesty for millions of undocumented people was not. Numbers USA, FAIR, and CIS redoubled their efforts to block the immigration reform bill. FAIR worked closely with the radio hosts who had just attended Hold Their Feet to the Fire the month before to spread their talking point that the deal amounted to "amnesty for illegals." CIS produced reports about the cost and impact on American employment. Numbers USA activated their membership base, and congressional offices were inundated. Phones were constantly ringing, email accounts were flooded, and a staggering one million faxes arrived at congressional offices via Numbers USA's website alone. That works out to over 1,860 faxed letters to each office. Roy Beck put it bluntly: "This is our citizen army."[26]

The *New York Times* reported that the senators were "under attack from the right for allowing illegal immigrants to earn citizenship and from the left for dividing families. The offices of the negotiators were under siege from critics who had the phones ringing endlessly."[27] The deluge of calls, emails, and faxes worked. Kentucky senator Mitch McConnell recalled a few years later that they "lit up the switchboard for weeks," which convinced Republicans that their base was against the bill. He continued, "To every one of them, I say today: 'your voice was heard.'"[28] On the day of a key procedural vote, the Capitol switchboard crashed because it could not handle the volume of calls. Republican senators fled the bill en masse, finally killing it on June 28, 2007, when it failed to reach the sixty-vote threshold for cloture.

The Tanton Network was ecstatic. Dan Stein, the executive director of FAIR, wrote, "Working together, we thwarted extraordinary efforts by the President of the United States, leading members of Congress, and an array of lavishly financed special interest groups who were determined to erase our borders and effectively erase our national identity." If they had not, he warned, it would have resulted in the feared replacement of Americans by immigrants. He continued, "The United States of 20 years from now would have been unrecognizable to most of us and, I believe, a far less desirable place to live."[29] FAIR credited Jeff Sessions with being a leading voice against the bill. They gave him their Franklin Society Award in 2007, and he gave the keynote address at their conference.

The defeat of comprehensive immigration reform in 2007 was the moment of arrival for John Tanton's decades-long effort to make immigration restriction a mainstream position, while simultaneously hiding his singular role in achieving it. The *New York Times* report said, "The grass roots roared," but the story included quotations from representatives of all three of the biggest players in the Tanton Network—FAIR, CIS, and Numbers USA—without realizing or acknowledging that they were all founded by one man and largely funded by the foundation established by one woman.[30]

Suddenly, the anti-immigrant crusade that John Tanton had "found no one willing to talk about" in the late 1970s became the baseline position of one of the major political parties in the United States. Tom Tancredo, who was for years a lonely voice in Congress for strict immigration controls, realized that his work was done. At the Republican presidential candidates' debate on November 28, 2007, Tancredo stood at his podium at the edge of the stage and beamed as the mainstream candidates each put forward anti-immigrant proposals that he and the Tanton Network had been raising for years. When he finally got the chance to speak, he said, "All I've heard is people trying to out-Tancredo Tancredo. It is great. I am so happy to hear it."[31]

CHAPTER 13

THE WORLD
JUST CHANGED

With glasses, neatly parted hair, and a chiseled chin, Eric Cantor embodied the nerdy good looks of Superman's alter ego, Clark Kent. Cantor grew up in a politically connected Republican family in Richmond, Virginia. His father was the Virginia treasurer for Ronald Reagan's 1980 presidential campaign. While studying at George Washington University, Cantor served as an intern for Republican Tom Bliley's campaign for the House of Representatives in 1981, settling into the role of driver. Bliley won and served in the seat until retiring in 2001, when Cantor replaced him. After college, Cantor got a law degree from William & Mary and a master's from Columbia in real estate development, and then worked for his father's real estate company. In 1992, at age twenty-nine, he won a seat in the Virginia House of Delegates, where he remained until running for Bliley's seat in the House in 2000. All of his campaigns between 2000 and 2012 were formalities, with no candidate coming within 17 percent of him. The most notable was his 2002 race in which he faced off against Ben "Cooter" Jones, the actor who played Cooter the mechanic on the *Dukes of Hazzard* TV show in the 1980s. Cantor won 69 to 30 percent. He made his way up the leadership ladder in the Republican caucus in the House of Representatives, becoming the second in command, the House minority whip, in 2009. When the Tea Party movement swept Republicans into the majority in the House in the 2010 midterm election, John Boehner became the Speaker of the House and Cantor the House majority leader. As majority leader, Eric Cantor represented the traditional center-right, pro-business wing of the Republican Party. However, even as he ascended to the pinnacle of power, his position was tenuous. The base of the Republican Party had shifted under his feet as the Tea Party and conservative talk radio moved further and further to the right. Within a few years, Cantor's moderate position on comprehensive immigration reform would become a liability to an extent that he could never have imagined.

ANTI-IMMIGRANT HATE GROUPS

Although John Tanton's network of anti-immigrant groups was increasingly influential in Washington, DC, Tanton himself was being ushered off the stage and tucked back into his quiet rural life in Petoskey. While the media and the Republican Party saw an organic, grassroots movement against immigration, the Southern Poverty Law Center and other immigrants' rights groups saw the Tanton Network as a concerted effort to sanitize white supremacy. John Tanton's extreme views first gained notice in 1988 when the *Arizona Republic* published his private memos about a "Latin onslaught" threatening white American culture. At the time, Tanton's group U.S. English had organized English-only ballot measures in Florida, Colorado, and Arizona for the November 1988 election.[1]

In October 1988, Perry Baker, the leader of the opposition to the English-only law in Arizona, received a copy of a memo John Tanton wrote in 1986.[2] Baker held onto it for a few weeks so that he could time the release just before the election, a quintessential October surprise. The leaked memo included the prompts for a discussion at Tanton's 1986 witan salon. The memo warned of a "Latin onslaught" that could overwhelm the white majority of the country, bringing new cultural practices including higher birth rates and more Catholicism. The discussion noted "the greater reproductive powers" of Latinos and colorfully warned, "Those with their pants up are going to get caught by those with their pants down!" The memo also asks how whites in the United States will react to these changes. Will they accept their replacement by minority groups or fight back? He wrote, "As whites see their power and control over their lives declining, will they simply go quietly into the night? Or will there be an explosion?"[3]

The reaction was swift in 1988. Tanton was widely condemned in the media, and a series of supporters left the U.S. English board, including the U.S. English director, Linda Chavez, a prominent Republican who was an official in the Reagan administration. Walter Cronkite and Saul Bellow led the exodus from the board of directors. Within days, Tanton wrote a memo to the remaining board that concluded, "If you find me guilty as charged, please accept my resignation."[4] They did.

In addition to attempting to counter the allegations, Tanton spent the month after his 1988 exposure taking the temperature of his funders. Jay Harris, whose initial gift was crucial to getting FAIR off the ground, cut ties with Tanton and FAIR. Tanton wrote back thanking him for his initial support but also suggesting an alternative: "Incidentally, if you ever wish to make any completely anonymous contributions . . ." he began. He let Harris know that he had set up a new group under the U.S. Inc. umbrella called U.S. Donor Direct Depository, which functioned to hide the source of donations to his groups.[5] Warren Buffett also cut ties with FAIR, but not as quickly as some others. In 1989, a few months after the exposure, Buffett made a new donation to FAIR but left the board later.[6]

The 1988 incident began the slow process of each of Tanton's groups beginning to distance themselves from him. Roger Conner, the first executive director of FAIR, decided to resign. Conner told the *New York Times* in 2011 that it was difficult. Tanton's charisma was "so profound that the people around him disregarded things that we should have called him on."[7] Patrick Burns, FAIR deputy director, told the *Detroit News* in 2017, "It's sad. It's like a dead cat in a well. It poisons a lot of good water. Tanton has been that cat for 30 years."[8]

By the early 2000s, Heidi Beirich of the SPLC reviewed Tanton's correspondence housed at the Bentley Historical Library at the University of Michigan. What Beirich found confirmed that Tanton was regularly in touch with white supremacists and largely shared their views even while he acknowledged the need to soften them for public consumption. Tanton corresponded with Sam G. Dickson, a lawyer for the Georgia Ku Klux Klan.[9] Tanton's group Californians for Population Stabilization received money from the Pioneer Fund.[10] Tanton frequently recommended the work of the alt-right favorite and anti-Semitic author Kevin MacDonald. Tanton corresponded with Roger Pearson, the British eugenics advocate who received Pioneer Fund support for his white supremacist journals *Mankind Quarterly* and the *Journal of Social, Political, and Economic Studies*. Tanton sent money to subscribe to Pearson's journals and also shared his own writings with Pearson.[11] Tanton arranged for Cordelia Scaife May to fund a research assistant and promotion for Peter Brimelow's *Alien Nation*, the first line of which is "There is a sense in which current immigration policy is Adolf Hitler's posthumous revenge on America."[12] Brimelow went on to found VDARE, the white supremacist website.

Tanton was particularly impressed with Brimelow and asked him to be his spokesperson three different times, essentially offering to bankroll him and his white supremacist views.[13] Tanton wrote to Brimelow in 1997 that one of his biggest concerns was that "all of Western Civilization is running at sub-replacement fertility, and will, within a generation or two disappear from the history books."[14] Tanton shared a similar fear about the great replacement with Cordelia Scaife May on October 6, 1997. She wrote to Tanton that she was worried about declining birth rates in Western countries. He agreed and wrote to her, "The idea behind the population movement was not those of us who thought population was a problem would adopt permanent sub-replacement fertility, and eventually disappear from the scene." Tanton did not want whites with low birth rates to be replaced by immigrants, "handing our territory over to the more fertile, and thereby lose the battle."[15] In a 1993 letter to Garrett Hardin, Tanton's longtime friend and the author of "The Tragedy of the Commons," Tanton wrote, "I've come to the point of view that for Euro-American society and culture to persist requires a European-American majority, and a clear one at that."[16]

The Southern Poverty Law Center released a series of reports that outlined Tanton's white supremacist connections, activities, and writing. Since 1990, the SPLC has published an annual list of hate groups across the United States, which includes well-known organizations like the Ku Klux Klan and the Aryan Brotherhood, but also over a thousand other smaller groups. The SPLC defines a hate group as "an organization that—based on its official statements or principles, the statements of its leaders, or its activities—has beliefs or practices that attack or malign an entire class of people, typically for their immutable characteristics."[17] The SPLC designated FAIR a hate group in 2007 and the Center for Immigration Studies in 2017.[18] Other Tanton-related groups that have received the hate group designation are Californians for Population Stabilization, the Social Contract Press, and ProEnglish. American Border Patrol and the Remembrance Project, which both received funding from Colcom and U.S. Inc., are also designated hate groups. Numbers USA is the only significant group from the Tanton Network that is not officially designated a hate group by the SPLC.

While Tanton remained defiant and opted to strike back at the SPLC by questioning their motives and writing long rebuttals to their claims on his personal website, the Tanton Network distanced themselves from him. CIS claimed that Tanton has not been involved in the think tank since he founded it in 1985. They wrote that Tanton "played no part in its organization and was scrupulous in allowing the early core of researchers and writers to take charge of the design. I don't believe he has ever been in the CIS offices, over all these years."[19] Numbers USA, which was a subsidiary of U.S. Inc., was spun off as a separate entity after the 2002 SPLC report on Tanton's white supremacist ties. Numbers USA claims it had no contacts with John Tanton since then. Tanton remained on the board of directors of FAIR until 2011, when his name was quietly dropped from the organization's masthead after a *New York Times* report delved into his extremist history.[20] FAIR claimed the timing was coincidental and he left due to ill health.[21] Tanton's health deteriorated as he struggled with Parkinson's disease from 2003 until he died in 2019.[22]

By the time that the Tanton Network cut ties with their founder, they already had all the tools in place to operate on their own. Tanton established enough different groups to ensure that they all appeared to be autonomous, and he secured permanent funding for them all through Scaife May's Colcom Foundation, which in 2021 has an endowment of over $420 million. Tanton had installed his close associate and biographer John Rohe at Colcom to ensure that Scaife May's and his anti-immigrant vision was enacted without interference. By 2012, Colcom funding for the Tanton Network was over $11 million and has remained above that level every year since.[23] From 2005 until 2018, Colcom gave a total of $176 million to the major groups in the Tanton Network (table 4).

TABLE 4: *Colcom Foundation donations to Tanton Network groups from 2005 to 2018*

TANTON NETWORK GROUP	AMOUNT ($)
Numbers USA	58,411,336
Federation for American Immigration Reform (FAIR)	57,338,236
U.S. Inc.	18,894,700
Center for Immigration Studies (CIS)	17,745,000
Immigration Reform Law Institute (IRLI)	12,335,000
Californians for Population Stabilization (CPS)	8,050,2200
Progressives for Immigration Reform (PFIR)	3,269,000
Total	176,043,492

SANCTUARY CITIES AND SHOW ME YOUR PAPERS LAWS

During the Obama presidency (2009–17), the Tanton Network relished their role of opposition as they rode the wave of the Tea Party movement, which shared the same base of support even if its aims were not always totally aligned. The Tanton Network staked out small victories where they could while strengthening their position with the Republican Party in Congress. They lobbied against sanctuary city designations and wrote draft bills for state legislatures that wanted to crack down on immigrants in their jurisdictions. Much of this effort was led by Kris Kobach.

Kobach, a telegenic Kansas native, has impeccable credentials with a BA from Harvard, a doctorate from Oxford, and a law degree from Yale. He was a professor at the University of Missouri–Kansas City law school, and from 2001 to 2003 he served as an advisor to US Attorney General John Ashcroft on immigration. While in the Justice Department, Kobach crafted the National Security Entry-Exit Registration System (NSEERS). NSEERS required people arriving in the United States from several Muslim-majority countries to undergo extra screening and submit to additional surveillance during their stay. The program was ended by the Obama administration in 2011 after producing zero terrorism convictions despite scrutinizing 83,000 people.[24] Kobach became the chair of the Kansas Republican Party in 2007 and served as the Kansas secretary of state from 2011 to 2019. As secretary of state, he supported a voter ID law in Kansas that he described as essential to prevent voter fraud but which critics derided as a way to suppress minority votes.

Even as he held these other positions, Kobach also worked as the lead counsel for the Tanton Network, primarily through the Immigration Reform Law Institute. IRLI and Kobach served as the organized legal wing of the Tanton Network, where they refined legal and legislative arguments against immigration. Historically, immigration enforcement has been the domain of the federal government, not local or state police. This separation of authority was established in the Passenger Cases in 1849 and confirmed in the Chy Lung decision in 1875. Kobach held the unorthodox belief that just because states could not make immigration laws did not mean they could not help the federal government enforce them. Kobach and IRLI worked closely with Lou Barletta, the mayor of Hazelton, Pennsylvania, who passed an ordinance that revoked the business licenses of companies that were found to employ undocumented immigrants. As the Hazelton case was litigated, and eventually lost by Kobach and IRLI, Barletta became a star in the anti-immigrant movement and rode his right-wing radio fame to a seat in the House of Representatives. Barletta went on to serve on the board of directors of FAIR.

Kobach also shaped several state laws cracking down on immigration by creating state statutes that mirrored federal ones. Kobach has said that he was not a mastermind but rather only provided the legal insight to support what local lawmakers wanted to do: "I did not generate the motivation to pass the law. . . . I am merely the attorney who comes in, refines, and drafts their statutes."[25] The most prominent example was SB 1070 in Arizona, which made it a misdemeanor if a legal immigrant was not carrying their required certificate of alien registration. After it was signed into law in April 2010, it was widely criticized for encouraging police to use racial profiling to inquire about individuals' immigration status during routine traffic stops or other interactions. The US Department of Justice filed a civil rights lawsuit challenging the law, which was heard before the US Supreme Court in 2012. The court struck down several of the provisions but allowed the local police to check the immigration status of people during stops.[26]

Barack Obama's second term saw another effort at comprehensive immigration reform. After Mitt Romney lost the presidential election in 2012, the consensus at the Republican National Committee was that a declining share of minority voters, particularly Latinos, had dearly cost the party. Just as George W. Bush had favored using comprehensive immigration reform as a way to repair the relationship with Latino voters in 2007, Eric Cantor and Republican leaders again tried to work with Democrats and Barack Obama to pass the legislation in 2013–14. However, by that point, the Tanton Network was well organized and ready to fight. In Congress, much of the opposition to the new round of comprehensive immigration reform flowed out of the Senate offices of Jeff Sessions, who gave eloquent speeches and cranked out policy papers replete with detailed statistics from studies done by CIS.[27] Sessions was a true believer, but behind the scenes it turned out there was an even stronger force operating in his office.

At first, it seemed like Sessions and the Tanton Network were outmaneuvered. The Senate passed the Comprehensive Immigration Reform measure 68–32 with fourteen Republican votes in June 2013. However, it languished in the Republican-led House of Representatives, where John Boehner and Eric Cantor delayed bringing it up for a vote. Even as Cantor and the rest of the leadership supported it, the rank and file did not. The Tea Party accounted for one-fourth of Republican members in the 2013–14 House of Representatives, many of whom had grown politically active by listening to the type of talk radio hosts who attend FAIR's Hold Their Feet to the Fire events. They refused to support the reform that the talk radio hosts were denouncing daily as "amnesty."

THE HOUSE MAJORITY LEADER

In the 2014 Republican primary for Eric Cantor's seat in Virginia's Seventh Congressional District, Cantor's opponent was Dave Brat, a little-known professor at Randolph Macon College in Ashland, Virginia. As with Cantor's previous opponents, Brat did not appear to stand a chance against the powerful House majority leader. Brat lacked charisma and had never held public office. The Cantor campaign's initial polling showed Cantor with a 34-point edge, and they outspent Brat forty to one. The Cantor campaign spent the same amount at steakhouses alone as the total budget of the Brat campaign.[28]

Given the financial limitations, Brat ran a single-issue campaign focused on immigration, arguing in every public appearance that a vote for

Eric Cantor was a vote for open borders.[29] Brat's singular focus on immigration drew support from several right-wing radio personalities, including Laura Ingraham and Anne Coulter. Brat also got campaign assistance from Senator Jeff Sessions, who loaned him a young aide named Stephen Miller. The strategy was to make the Republican primary a litmus test on immigration based on the knowledge that the most dedicated and partisan people vote in primaries. In the general election, moderate Republicans might not care at all about the immigration issue but would still fall in line and vote for their party's candidate anyway. Eric Cantor was not a left-wing, pro-immigrant politician, but he did support a limited path to citizenship for immigrants in the Comprehensive Immigration Reform bill. Apparently, that was enough.

On Election Day, Brat won comfortably, 55 to 44 percent, in a result that sent shockwaves through the political establishment. It was the first time in US history that a House majority leader lost their seat in a primary, and the news media spent weeks dissecting exactly what had happened. The twenty-eight-year-old Stephen Miller told the *New York Times* succinctly, "The world just changed."[30]

CHAPTER 14

IT'S TIME TO MAKE IMMIGRATION
POLICY GREAT AGAIN

On May 29, 2015, two weeks before Donald Trump descended the escalator at Trump Tower to announce his candidacy for the presidency of the United States, Stephen Miller gave the keynote speech at an award ceremony at the National Press Club in Washington, DC, for the Center for Immigration Studies, the research center John Tanton founded in 1985 that was designated a hate group by the Southern Poverty Law Center in 2017. As the event began, Miller sat on the stage and fidgeted with a can of diet cola, starting to take several sips before remembering it was empty. Mark Krikorian, the CIS director, beamed as he introduced Miller, saying he is "the communications director for Senator Jeff Sessions and is part of the team that has really—obviously led by the Senator—made the immigration issue something that is discussed in a much more sophisticated and complete way than it has been up to now."[1] With slightly askew thinning gray hair and glasses, Krikorian spoke with the confidence of someone accustomed to standing at a microphone. He had been the director of CIS since 1995 and used his rumpled, professorial appearance to gain access to the popular media, including frequent interviews on National Public Radio. Krikorian joked that Miller could talk about whatever he wants, but he hoped it was going to be about immigration. Miller, still only twenty-nine years old, was happy to oblige. He stepped up to the podium in a camel-colored suit and blue tie, his prematurely balding dark hair and sideburns trimmed short. He began his speech awkwardly, cocking his head to the side several times in a nervous tic. Miller softened the crowd with a joke targeted to his anti-immigration audience: "I'd like to thank everyone here today, and especially those at the Center for Immigration Studies, for everything they do to illuminate a debate that far too often operates, like illegal immigrants, in the shadows." A smile crept across his face as the audience laughed.

Stephen Miller was born on August 23, 1985, to a wealthy Jewish family in Santa Monica, California. He began to question his liberal upbringing after reading longtime National Rifle Association leader Wayne LaPierre's 1994 book *Guns, Crime, and Freedom*. The book lays out a defense of the Second Amendment's right to bear arms, but it goes further to critique a wide range of progressive policies that LaPierre argues result in "carnage on our streets," a phrase that was echoed by Donald Trump's inaugural address, written by Miller, which lamented "American carnage."[2] Miller's high school antics in Santa Monica suggest he has always relished the villain role, finding satisfaction in triggering liberals by saying outrageous things. He would tell Latino students in the hallway to stop speaking Spanish. He ran for the job of announcing daily news over the intercom system on a platform that students should not have to pick up their own trash because the school paid custodians to do that job.[3]

Miller came of age in the aftermath of the terrorist attacks on September 11, 2001—he was sixteen at the time—and he began to espouse extreme anti-immigrant and anti-terrorism views. He honed his smug speaking style on *The Larry Elder Show*, a local conservative talk radio show in LA. After several precocious appearances, Miller received a standing invitation from Elder to come on the show whenever he wanted; Miller appeared a total of sixty-nine times. The radio hits introduced Miller to conservative activists across LA. Years later, Steve Bannon and Andrew Breitbart would both realize they had listened to Miller on the show when he was in high school.[4] The listener that had the biggest impact on his life was David Horowitz. Horowitz is a formerly left-wing scholar who became disillusioned with academia and made a career out of criticizing universities for supposedly silencing conservative voices. His foundation, the David Horowitz Freedom Center, was largely funded by Richard Scaife, Cordelia Scaife May's brother. After September 11, Horowitz became a leading anti-Islamic voice in the United States, and his foundation is designated a hate group by the Southern Poverty Law Center. Horowitz heard Miller on *The Larry Elder Show* and got in touch.

Miller became Horowitz's acolyte and invited Horowitz to speak at Santa Monica High School. The school canceled the first appearance, which Miller decried on the radio as another instance of silencing conservative voices. The school relented and Horowitz spoke.

When Miller graduated from high school in 2003, his yearbook quote from Teddy Roosevelt harkened back to the early 1900s nativist criticism of hyphenated Americans during the first push for immigration restrictions. It read, "There can be no fifty-fifty Americanism in this country. There is room here for only 100 percent Americanism, only for those who are Americans and nothing else."[5]

Miller enrolled at Duke University, where he found a small community of students who shared his views. Miller became friends with Richard Spencer, the white nationalist leader who coined the term alt-right and who helped organize the Unite the Right rally in Charlottesville, Virginia, in August 2017. Spencer was a PhD student at Duke at the time, and Miller and Spencer were both members of the Duke Conservative Union. The two worked together to invite Peter Brimelow, the regular correspondent of John Tanton's and the founder of the white supremacist website VDARE, to campus for a debate.[6] VDARE is an SPLC-designated hate group. Richard Spencer told a reporter in 2016, "It's funny no one's picked up on the Stephen Miller connection. I knew him very well when I was at Duke. But I am kind of glad no one's talked about this because I don't want to harm Trump."[7] Richard Spencer's foundation, the National Policy Institute, is also an SPLC-designated hate group. Miller was the president of the Duke chapter of David Horowitz's Students for Academic Freedom, and he brought Horowitz to speak on campus. Miller gave the speech introducing him.[8] In 2005, Miller wrote an article for Horowitz's *Front Page* magazine about the problems of multiculturalism at Santa Monica High School, which was reprinted on Jared Taylor's white supremacist website American Renaissance, probably without Miller's knowledge.[9] Miller wrote a column for the Duke campus newspaper titled "Miller Time" that was known for provocative content designed to outrage his fellow liberal students. In 2006, he gained national attention for his outspoken support for three white players on the Duke lacrosse team who were accused, falsely it turned out, of rape by a stripper. Miller parlayed his contrarian position into interviews on cable news, including Bill O'Reilly's show on Fox News.[10]

Miller graduated from Duke in 2007 without clear plans. He had intended to go to law school, but he missed his LSAT exam while planning a 9/11 memorial on the five-year anniversary in 2006. In the summer of 2007, he went to Israel on a birthright trip, a propaganda strategy of the Israeli government that provides free trips to American Jews to shape their perspective on the country. Afterward, Miller traveled in Europe but did not have further plans. Eventually, Horowitz helped him land a job in the office of Michelle Bachmann, the Republican representative and Tea Party favorite from Minnesota.

In Congress, Miller gained a reputation for his strong anti-immigrant views and his tendency to write long, virulent emails to other congressional staffers and journalists, a practice that would get him into trouble later on. In 2009, Miller became disillusioned with Bachmann, and Horowitz introduced him to Arizona representative John Shadegg. A few months into his job with Shadegg, Horowitz heard that Jeff Sessions was looking for a new press secretary and recommended Miller for the job. With Sessions, Stephen Miller found a boss with whom he was in total agreement. Miller produced policy documents to support Sessions's anti-immigrant views, often drawn directly from reports produced by the Tanton Network, particularly CIS. Although Miller was still unknown to most Americans, he was becoming a star in the anti-immigrant community. After the defeat of comprehensive immigration reform in 2013 and Dave Brat's surprise primary victory over House majority leader Eric Cantor in 2014, Miller had developed close, friendly ties with the Tanton Network, leading to the invitation to be the keynote speaker at the CIS event in May 2015.

At the beginning of his speech at the CIS award ceremony, Miller took the time to recognize the CIS staff members in the audience, who all appeared to be close friends of his. He said, "There is no one in America who knows more about immigration enforcement than Jessica Vaughan." Vaughan is the director of policy at CIS and has worked there since 1992, often writing reports linking immigrants with crime and gang activity. Miller continued, "And, of course, Marguerite, who broadcasts all this information to the whole world." Marguerite Telford is the longtime communication director for CIS. He grinned when he got to Steve Camarota, the director of research at CIS. Camarota holds a PhD from the University of Virginia and has written hundreds of pieces on the negative aspects of immigration, mostly self-published on the CIS website. One of Camarota's few articles published in a non-CIS venue is in the *Journal of Social, Political, and Economic Studies*, an outlet for eugenics and white supremacist thought that was founded by Roger Pearson with money from the Pioneer Fund.[11] To Miller, Camarota is someone "who knows more about immigration numbers, history, demography, the economy than anyone I have ever worked with." Miller continued, "One of the great pleasures of my professional life is just being able to get on the phone with Steve and just talk, just have a conversation and just explore what's in his thoughts, what he's studying, what he's researching."

After Miller finished his speech, he turned the podium back over to CIS director Mark Krikorian, who announced that the winner of the Eugene Katz Award for Excellence in the Coverage of Immigration was the journalist Neil Munro. Munro was probably best known at that point as the journalist who in 2012 interrupted President Barack Obama in the middle of a speech in the White House Rose Garden by shouting the question, "Why do you favor foreigners over Americans?"[12] At the time of the CIS award ceremony, Munro had just left the *Daily Caller*, Tucker Carlson's right-wing news outlet, and was working at Laura Ingraham's *Lifezette*. He joined Breitbart News that fall, where he teamed up with Steve Bannon, the executive chair of the online news outlet.

THE PLATFORM FOR THE ALT-RIGHT

Stephen Miller was already friends with Steve Bannon and many other writers at Breitbart, the *Daily Caller*, and *Lifezette*. Bannon was a founding investor in Andrew Breitbart's news aggregator website in 2007, then Bannon took over the editorial side after Breitbart's unexpected death in 2011. Bannon set out to make Breitbart a voice for his nationalist vision for America. He transformed the website into a platform for the alt-right, the rebranded name for white supremacy coined by Stephen Miller's friend Richard Spencer. In the process, Bannon increased the readership from 12 million page views per month in 2012 to 192 million in 2016.[13]

As part of his communications job for Jeff Sessions, Miller would send daily emails to sympathetic journalists suggesting stories and recommending research, often from CIS, that they should cover. In 2019, Katie McHugh, a former Breitbart writer, leaked over nine hundred emails

Miller sent her from March 2015, two months before his CIS keynote, through June 2016. Steve Bannon had put McHugh in touch with Miller so that Miller could help her frame stories about immigration. Sometimes McHugh would contact Miller asking for feedback or reaction to a particular event. More frequently, Miller emailed her to suggest a particular story or to recommend an article. McHugh explained, "What Stephen Miller sent me in those emails has become policy at the Trump administration."[14]

Stephen Miller's email correspondence looks very similar to John Tanton's letters that are archived at the University of Michigan. They demonstrate that Miller was reading white supremacist news sources and recommending the articles to McHugh, as well as Neil Munro, the author Miller shared the stage with at the CIS event in April 2015. Steve Bannon was cc'd on many of the communications and replied "Wow!!!" to a message of Miller's that demonized Islam. In the emails, Miller recommended over seventy reports from the Tanton Network, which works out to once per week over the sixteen-month period. Miller also recommended articles on the SPLC-designated hate group websites VDARE and American Renaissance run by Peter Brimelow and Jared Taylor. Miller forwarded stories that proposed ending Muslim immigration to the United States and spoke highly of Calvin Coolidge, an icon for white nationalists, the president who coined the phrase "Keep America American" and signed the 1924 Immigration Act. On August 4, 2015, Miller wrote approvingly of a plan to stop all immigration to America, "like Coolidge did. [A] Kellyanne Conway poll says that is exactly what most Americans want after 40 years of non-stop record arrivals."[15]

Miller also brought up *The Camp of the Saints*, the book about refugees invading Europe that was published by John Tanton's Social Contract Press.[16] The email went to McHugh and another Breitbart journalist, Julia Hahn, who became a friend of Miller's. Hahn, like McHugh and Miller, was a young, upwardly mobile author deeply connected to the far right. Before Breitbart, she worked as a producer for Laura Ingraham's radio show and as a spokesperson for Dave Brat, the long-shot candidate who defeated then House majority leader Eric Cantor. In the following year, Hahn would follow Steve Bannon into the White House, where she served as a special assistant to the president during his full term, even after Steve Bannon left in 2017.[17] Less than three weeks after Stephen Miller recommended *The Camp of the Saints* to Hahn and McHugh in an email,

Hahn published an article about the book on Breitbart. AmRen, as American Renaissance is known to its readers, promptly republished Hahn's article on its website.[18] Steve Bannon has called *The Camp of the Saints* one of his favorite books.

THE CANDIDATE

In January 2013, Steve Bannon, Jeff Sessions, and Stephen Miller had dinner at Bannon's Washington, DC, apartment that also served as the Breitbart headquarters. They called it the Breitbart Embassy. The purpose was a postmortem on Mitt Romney's 2012 election loss and a strategy session for Barack Obama's second term. The mainstream Republican consensus was that Latinos and other minority groups in the United States voted heavily for the Democrats. If Republicans ever wanted to compete in a national election again, they needed to change their messaging and reach out to these groups. The men at the table did not buy into that theory at all. They agreed that minority groups were largely going to vote Democratic, so they were mystified as to why other Republicans wanted to give amnesty to millions more potential Democratic voters. As they sipped bourbon late into the night, they discussed an alternative theory of why Republicans lost that had been articulated by commentator Sean Trende on the RealClear-Politics website only days after the election.[19] Trende argued that despite the popular narrative that surging minority votes turned the election for Obama, the data did not support it.[20] Instead, he demonstrated that in reality 7 million white voters had sat the election out. Bannon, Sessions, and Miller reasoned that they were never going to win the minority votes, so the best bet was to fire up those missing white voters. The solution was to turn out a new constituency for the Republican Party: working-class whites, who historically voted for the pro–labor union Democrats but were culturally conservative. By demonizing immigrants, Bannon, Sessions, and Miller were convinced they could appeal to working-class whites who were losing their jobs due to globalization and who could be persuaded that they were losing their country and their culture to immigrants. If they succeeded, it was a double win for Republicans. By reducing immigration, it would reduce the number of future Democrats, and by appealing to working-class whites, they would flip the Democratic stronghold of the Great Lakes and Upper Midwest to the Republican side.

As they talked about their shared views on immigration, Bannon got to the point of the dinner date. He thought Jeff Sessions should run for president in 2016. Although he probably would not win, Bannon thought it was crucial that the immigration message of the alt-right had a voice in the debates. Sessions remained an extreme voice in the Senate and was unknown to most Americans, but his vocal opposition to immigration made him a hero on the far right. Sessions was the keynote speaker in 2007 at FAIR's annual conference, the same year FAIR was designated a hate group by the SPLC, and he became a fixture at CIS events in Washington. Sessions also developed connections to David Horowitz, the man who introduced Sessions and Miller to each other. The David Horowitz Freedom Center is labeled a hate group by the SPLC, but Jeff Sessions received their Annie Taylor Award for courage in 2014. Annie Taylor is the first person with the courage—or insanity, depending on your perspective—to take the plunge over Niagara Falls in a barrel.

Sessions ultimately decided not to take the plunge into the presidential race, not wanting to dredge back up the accusations of racism he faced during his failed judicial nomination back in 1986. Sessions and Bannon maintained their alliance, and Sessions appeared eighteen times on Breitbart radio shows between 2013 and 2016. A few months after their dinner at Bannon's apartment, they all heard Donald Trump speak at the Conservative Political Action Conference in Washington, DC. At the time, Trump was still best known as the host of the TV show *The Apprentice* and came onto the stage to its theme song, "For the Love of Money" by the O'Jays. Trump focused his speech on the economic troubles in the country and the way that trade with China was hurting working-class Americans. Then he turned to immigration. He bemoaned the 11 million "illegals" in the country, who he was sure would only vote for Democrats if they were given amnesty. Trump then asked, "Why aren't we letting people in from Europe?" He said, "No one wants to talk about this, to say it."[21] He ended the speech in 2013 with the phrase "Make America Great Again." Bannon, Sessions, and Miller were impressed that Trump made all of the arguments they had discussed at their dinner in January. However, he was flawed and had no political experience.

Even after Trump announced his campaign in June 2015, the three men were still unsure if Trump could be their entry point into mainstream presidential politics, but they monitored his campaign carefully. Despite rising to the top of many Republican primary polls in the summer of 2015, most commentators treated Trump as a reality star in the race for the publicity, not a serious candidate for president. Pundits and columnists assured uneasy elites that there was no way that Trump would actually be the Republican nominee. The conventional wisdom was that his candidacy was a marketing ploy to get free publicity and that he would drop out of the race before the first votes were counted in early 2016 in order to avoid the inevitable embarrassment of a loss.

Donald Trump brought up the idea of running for president for decades, often prefacing it with the notion that many, always unspecified, people were urging him to do it, but beyond being famous there was little to suggest he would be a successful candidate. In the 1990s, Donald Trump performed the role of ultrawealthy New York real estate mogul on TV and in films even as his actual real estate investments went bankrupt. He appeared briefly in the blockbuster *Home Alone 2*, but also in several soft-core pornographic films.[22] His big break happened as reality television took off in the 2000s. In 2004, Donald Trump was cast as the boss on the business-themed reality show *The Apprentice*, which became a hit. The show gave Trump the chance to continue to play the role of billionaire real estate mogul on TV, as he had been doing for decades. *The Apprentice* proved to be popular, and the production values of the show perfected Trump's image as a strong and wealthy executive, even as his actual businesses such as Trump University, Trump Vodka, and Trump Steaks continued to fail.

As *The Apprentice* turned Donald Trump into a national celebrity, he waded into presidential politics, but he seemingly shot himself in the foot at the start by coming off as a racist conspiracy theorist. In March and April 2011, as the Republican presidential field was taking shape, Donald Trump spent six weeks as a birther.[23] The birther conspiracy theory claimed that President Barack Obama was not actually born in the territorial United States and was therefore not eligible to be the president under the "natural born citizen" requirement. Obama's mother, Ann Dunham, was an American citizen, so no matter where Barack Obama was born, he would have been a US citizen. The birther theory claims that the eighteen-year-old Dunham and Obama's twenty-five-year-old father, a Kenyan graduate student at the University of Hawai'i, somehow foresaw that their mixed-race son was destined to grow up to be the president of the United States. According to the theory, Obama was born in Kenya but his parents secretly brought him to Hawai'i and recorded his birth there so he would meet the natural-born citizen requirement for the presidency.

As Obama was first running for president in 2008, the issue of his birthplace came up. The campaign answered it by releasing a short-form copy of his certificate of live birth at Kapiolani Hospital in Honolulu. Donald Trump revived the issue in the spring of 2011 as he did a string of television interviews casting doubts about Obama's birthplace, almost all on morning shows that focus more on entertainment rather than hard news.[24] On March 23, 2011, on *The View*, Trump said, "Why doesn't he show his birth certificate? There's something on that birth certificate that he doesn't like." On March 28, on *Fox and Friends*, he said, "All of the sudden a lot of facts are emerging, and I'm starting to wonder myself whether or not he was born in this country." He went on Laura Ingraham's radio show on March 30 and went further, suggesting, "Now, somebody told me—and I have no idea if this is bad for him or not, but perhaps it would be—that where it says 'religion,' it might have 'Muslim.' And if you're a Muslim, you don't change your religion, by the way." He went on both the *Today Show* and *Morning Joe* on April 7, suggesting more evidence would be released shortly.

Fed up with the distraction, President Obama released his long-form birth certificate on April 27, 2011, seemingly putting the matter to rest. Trump was triumphant and took credit for finally forcing Obama to produce the birth certificate after years of questions about it. Obama exacted his revenge a few days later at the Annual White House Correspondent's Dinner in Washington, DC, on April 30. The dinner is a lighthearted affair that includes a comedian who typically pokes fun at the president and then the president also gives a speech with jokes. Obama used the opportunity to skewer Trump, who sat uncomfortably at his table as the audience laughed at him. Obama first said he was glad to help Trump settle the birther issue, so Trump could focus on more pressing matters like whether the moon landing was faked. Trump grew increasingly uncomfortable as the jokes kept coming. Obama laughed at the insignificance of Trump's work, pointing to the ridiculous firing decision between washed-up celebrities on the latest season of *Celebrity Apprentice*. Obama went so far as to mock Trump's presidential ambitions by showing an image of the White House if Trump were to win, which was gilded like Trump's ostentatious casinos and buildings. Trump seethed.

BUILD THE WALL

The early months of the Trump campaign in 2015 were described as chaotic and disorganized. However, there was much more careful planning than many people appreciate, and it began years in advance. His 2013 CPAC speech already included his nativist campaign themes and the phrase "Make America Great Again." As John Tanton saw in the early 1980s when he suggested to his colleagues at FAIR that they should focus more on cultural and identity issues, Trump used the birther conspiracy theory to confirm that there were many Americans who shared his politically incorrect views about race and immigration. A poll in 2011 found that half of Republicans believed Obama was not born in the United States.[25] Trump recognized that these people were the base of the Republican Party and made a drastic change in his political giving.[26] Historically, he gave to politicians in his home state of New York without regard to their political party. From 2006 to 2010, Trump gave $283,250 to Democrats and $218,250 to Republicans. In 2011, this shifted almost completely to Republicans, and he donated to obscure races across the United States. From 2011 to 2016, Trump gave $630,150 to Republicans and only $8,500 to Democrats. In 2014, Trump donated the maximum allowable amount to the reelection campaign of Jeff Sessions, even though Sessions was the only senator in the country running unopposed in both the primary and general election.[27] Sessions returned the favor by appearing at a Trump rally in Alabama in August 2015. Sessions did not officially endorse Trump, but he donned a white "Make America Great Again" hat at the event.

As Donald Trump elbowed his way through the Republican primary in the fall of 2015, he continued to demonize immigrants in his campaign events. His campaign slogan, in addition to "Make America Great Again," which echoes Calvin Coolidge's "Keep America American" of the 1920s, became "Build the wall." The phrase was the idea of Sam Nunberg, an early advisor who wanted a device to keep Trump on the topic of immigration in his speeches. The genius of Trump's campaign was that he managed to take a whole series of simmering economic and social grievances of poor whites, including the outsourcing of jobs abroad and the growth of immigrant workers in the United States, and boil them down to a simple political slogan. The wall was an inspired choice because it became a concrete object, literally, that would materialize all of the abstract grievances of his base. It not only validated their feelings toward immigrants but also provided a simple, one-stop solution. Build the wall. Stop immigration. Make America great again.

Trump's followers relished his willingness to say the things that they were thinking but that were too politically incorrect to say. By voicing those beliefs, he validated them and gave his followers permission to say them too. Trump knew from his decades of practice wooing the media that he had to say inflammatory things to get their coverage, so he obliged with a new outrage to drive each news cycle. The Democrats also obliged by making what they thought were critical ads highlighting his extremist message, but for many of his supporters that further endeared him to them, akin to the boost that Jeff Sessions got after the elitist senators rejected him for a judgeship in 1986.

In December 2015, Trump upped the ante further on his anti-immigrant language. After a mass shooting in San Bernardino, California, killed fourteen people and injured twenty-four, Trump proposed a complete ban on Muslims entering the United States. Earlier in the fall, he had already suggested surveillance of mosques and a national database to track Muslims in the country. His campaign press release said, "Donald J. Trump is calling for a total and complete shutdown of Muslims entering the United States until our country's representatives can figure out what is going on."[28] By that point, Trump was the front-runner in the Republican campaign, and the hope that he would fade before the spring primaries seemed naive. His fellow candidates condemned the statement. South Carolina senator Lindsey Graham tweeted, "Every candidate for president needs to do the right thing & condemn @realdonaldtrump's statement." Former Florida governor Jeb Bush tweeted, "Donald Trump is unhinged. His 'policy' proposals are not serious."

While mainstream politicians and the media continued to condemn Donald Trump's racial language and to express bafflement at his success, the Tanton Network took notice. They had concerns about the explicit racial language, which they had spent years hiding and denying, and they did not think a border wall was a priority. Numbers USA initially gave Trump a "C" on their immigration scorecard in the summer of 2015.[29] However, as they realized that Donald Trump had a real chance of winning the Republican Party's presidential nomination, they saw a once-in-a-lifetime opportunity for their extreme views to become the official policies of the United States.

John Rohe, the vice president for philanthropy at Colcom, flooded the Tanton Network with funds.[30] In the fiscal year that ended June 2015, just as Donald Trump announced his candidacy, Colcom gave a total of $23,306,891. Of that, a little more than half, $12,842,000, went to anti-immigration groups, and all but $390,000 of that went to the Tanton Network. The largest four recipients were Numbers USA with $3.89 million, FAIR $3.59 million, CIS $1.742 million, and U.S. Inc. $1.1 million. In the fiscal year that ended in June 2016, Colcom's anti-immigrant funding almost doubled to $21 million. FAIR received $7.48 million and Numbers USA $6.78 million. As the election kicked into high gear in the fall, Colcom gave another $20 million to the Tanton Network in the 2016–17 fiscal year. Over the 2015–18 period, donations from Colcom accounted for 81 percent of Numbers USA fundraising, 56 percent for FAIR, 61 percent for CIS, and 76 percent for the Immigration Reform Law Institute. In the 2016 election year alone, the Tanton Network spent over $45 million to publish reports, furnish experts for the media, and conduct grassroots organizing for the need for more immigration restrictions.

By early 2016, it was clear that Trump was a serious contender for the Republican nomination, and anti-immigrant politicians and analysts who were initially wary began to join his campaign. On February 28, 2016, Jeff Sessions became the first senator to endorse Donald Trump for president of the United States, two days before eleven states held their primaries on Super Tuesday, including Sessions's home state of Alabama.[31] Sessions again donned a MAGA hat at a rally, this time opting for the traditional red. Even with Sessions's reputation as a fringe figure, the media treated it as a significant event because up until then the establishment of the Republican Party had maintained its distance from Trump, hoping, in vain it would turn out, that one of the more mainstream candidates still in the race would turn back the Trump surge.

In reality, Sessions's official endorsement was a lagging indicator and was timed to have the most impact on the Alabama primary on Super Tuesday. The most significant signal that Sessions and the Tanton Network had embraced Trump happened in January 2016 when Stephen Miller left Sessions's Senate staff to join Donald Trump's campaign as a senior advisor. Stephen Miller has a gift at ingratiating himself with his bosses, and after joining the Trump campaign, he quickly settled into a prominent role for Donald Trump. Miller wrote Trump's speeches and appeared twenty-one times on Breitbart radio shows between February and May 2016 alone.[32] As Trump's campaign rallies became raucous events, Miller was installed as Trump's warm-up act, the last speaker before Trump appeared. In each speech, Miller would go through the laundry list of campaign slogans and anti-immigrant talking points to prime the audience for the appearance of Donald Trump himself. While he had been an awkward speaker at the CIS event the previous year, he honed his speaking style and relished the cheers for his hard-line immigration positions. At event after event, the crowd would start to chant "Build that wall, build that wall" as Miller built to a crescendo in his speech about how under Donald J. Trump that "wall is gonna get built" and open borders will be gone forever. Miller would nod his head as the crowd's roar washed over him.

THE TANTON NETWORK TAKEOVER

After finally prevailing in the Republican primaries, over the summer of 2016, Trump's campaign seemed to be pulled in two directions. The pro-Russia wing, led by then campaign manager Paul Manafort, was focused on foreign policy issues around NATO, the UN, and European politics. The anti-immigrant wing, led by Stephen Miller and Jeff Sessions, was focused singularly on immigration and the need to build the wall. In August 2016, Manafort's past corrupt dealings with Ukrainian oligarchs were exposed and he was removed as Trump's campaign chair. As Trump decided whom to hire, he met with Steve Bannon of Breitbart News, who told Trump his campaign was in disarray and needed to return to its foundation of anti-immigrant and anti-China rhetoric.[33] Trump was impressed and hired Steve Bannon to be the CEO of the campaign. Kellyanne Conway, who had long been the pollster for the Tanton Network, was named Trump's third campaign manager.[34] The anti-immigrant wing had won, and the strategy throughout the fall was to demonize immigrants in order to swing poor white voters over to Trump's campaign.

On Monday, August 22, 2016, less than two weeks into their new roles with the campaign, Bannon and Conway convened a meeting at Trump Tower to develop Trump's immigration positions in advance of a major policy speech.[35] Every single person in the room had a connection to John Tanton, except for Donald Trump himself. In addition to the candidate, the others present from the campaign were Bannon, Conway, Jeff Sessions, and Stephen Miller. They also invited three outside experts to consult on their immigration policy: Roy Beck, the president of Numbers USA; Steve Camarota, the CIS analyst with whom Miller had expressed his deep friendship at the CIS event the previous summer; and George Borjas, a conservative Harvard economist who had written reports for CIS since as early as 2002 and who had been interviewed several times at CIS venues, often by Camarota. The takeover of the campaign by the Tanton Network was complete.

In a sense, Trump's campaign for the presidency mirrored Dave Brat's surprise defeat of Senate majority leader Eric Cantor in 2014. In both cases, polished, mainstream politicians like Cantor and Jeb Bush turned out to be no match for a neophyte candidate who made immigration the singular issue in the Republican primary. Neither Brat nor Trump were ideal candidates. While Brat lacked charisma and had zero name recognition, Trump brought along a ton of baggage including a slew of accusations of sexual assault, which culminated with the release of a recording of him from the TV show *Access Hollywood* in which he bragged about grabbing women by the pussy. However, by that point he was the Republican candidate. While many moderate Republicans may not have shared Brat's and Trump's racial depictions of the threat of immigration and would have preferred many of the other more mainstream candidates, they would still fall in line and vote for the Republican candidate over any Democrat, particularly a Democrat as villainized on the right as Hillary Clinton.

Polls leading up to the 2016 election suggested it would be close but uniformly predicted a Clinton victory. On Election Day, news reports showed women visiting the grave of Susan B. Anthony, the women's suffrage activist, as a pilgrimage to celebrate the anticipated election of the first female president. The Clinton election-night rally was held in the all-glass Jacob K. Javits Convention Center in Manhattan to symbolize the glass ceiling in American politics she was about to break. Even in the early hours of the results, the exit polls suggested Clinton had won. As the night wore on, Trump racked up a series of razor-thin victories in key states, starting with Florida and followed by Wisconsin, Michigan, and Pennsylvania. Although Clinton won the popular vote by more than 3 million, Trump won in the Electoral College and became the forty-fifth president of the United States.

At the beginning of the 2016 election cycle, FAIR and CIS released a series of policy proposals in order to shape the debate about immigration in the coming administration. CIS released its list in April 2016, even before Trump won the Republican nomination and when Hillary Clinton was heavily favored to be the next president. The CIS list included seventy-nine points and was titled "A Pen and a Phone," a reference to what Barack Obama said was all he needed to implement his agenda through executive orders without congressional approval. The list runs the gamut of longtime Tanton Network goals including ending family reunification visas, which they call chain migration, reducing the refugee quota, and allowing US Immigration and Customs Enforcement (ICE) more latitude to round up undocumented immigrants in the United States. CIS executive director Mark Krikorian explained at the time to the *Daily Beast*, "We're a think tank. Our job is to put stuff out there. Our job is to put a message in a bottle and hope somebody finds it."[36] Krikorian and Dan Stein, the FAIR president, could never have imaged that their own employees would be the ones to find the bottle.

Two of the four authors of the FAIR document, Robert Law and Sarah Rehberg, joined the administration itself and were able to implement their own suggestions. A third author, Matt O'Brien, was appointed as an immigration judge. Julie Kirchner, the FAIR executive director at the time the wish list was written, also joined the administration, along with over a dozen other Tanton Network officials. Jon Feere, who had been a legal policy analyst with CIS since 2002, took a leave of absence to join the Trump campaign in the fall of 2016. After the election, Feere was one of the Trump administration's first hires as a senior advisor at ICE. On Inauguration Day, January 20, 2017, Feere posted a final farewell message on his Twitter account: "It's time to make immigration policy great again." The Tanton Network, which for decades had been on the fringes of American politics, suddenly found themselves at the levers of power in the United States, and they did not waste any time.

CHAPTER 15

THE INVISIBLE WALL

Hassan Ahmad could not believe what he was reading. He knew that Donald Trump had campaigned on an anti-immigrant platform, but he did not expect that Trump would institute a Muslim ban in his first week in the White House. Ahmad rubbed his forehead as he read the details. The executive order paused refugee resettlement for 120 days, reduced the refugee quota from 110,000 to 50,000, permanently banned refugees from Syria, and banned foreign nationals from Iraq, Iran, Libya, Somalia, Sudan, Syria, and Yemen from entering the United States for ninety days. It also went into effect immediately, meaning that people from these countries could have boarded a plane with a valid visa and then landed in the United States without one. Ahmad, a native North Carolinian who studied law at Tulane, had practiced immigration law for fifteen years. The idea of banning immigrants riled him up. However, as a Muslim himself, the targeting of Muslims felt personal. He lived less than ten minutes from Dulles International Airport in northern Virginia, so he grabbed his cell phone and headed to the airport to see what he could do. His years as an immigration attorney had already taught him that US Customs and Border Protection officials could be difficult to work with, but he was not prepared for what he found at the airport.

Even the Trump transition team officials who had written the draft of the executive order were caught off guard by the rapid implementation.[1] During the transition, Senator Jeff Sessions's thirty-three-year-old legal advisor Gene Hamilton was tapped to lead a group of staffers who wrote a series of draft executive orders on immigration that could be considered early in the Trump administration. Hamilton worked with Stephen Miller in Sessions's office, and they had developed a list of other congressional staffers and government officials that shared their views on immigration. Hamilton secretly invited them to join the group.[2] These included Andrea Loving, George Fishman, Dimple Shah, and Art Arthur from the staff of Virginia Republican representative Bob Goodlatte. Goodlatte was the chair of the House Judiciary Committee and had previously appeared at Center for Immigration Studies events.[3] Shah went on to positions in the Trump administration as deputy general counsel in the Office of the General Counsel at the Department of Justice and the assistant secretary for international affairs in the Office of Strategy, Policy, and Plans at the Department of Homeland Security. Arthur later left Goodlatte's staff and became a resident fellow in law and policy at CIS. In 2019, he was then called to testify as an expert witness in front of the House Immigration Subcommittee. Hamilton also brought in Kathy Nuebel Kovarik from Iowa senator Chuck Grassley's staff, whom Hamilton had worked with on the Senate Judiciary Committee. Lee Francis Cissna and Tracy Short, who were already in government positions, joined the team. They all shared a bond developed from years as outcasts on the fringes of the immigration debate who, like Jeff Sessions, Steve Bannon, and Stephen Miller, finally saw the opportunity to make changes in an area they felt passionately about. The Hamilton group set about writing drafts of a range of different executive orders that President Trump could sign in order for him to begin to fulfill his campaign promises without having to wait on the slower legislative process. The draft executive orders included ways to build his border wall, end DACA, end temporary protected status for a range of immigrant classes, and institute a ban on refugees and immigrants who could potentially be terrorists. The Hamilton group was surprised when what they thought were first drafts that would be revised and thoroughly vetted by lawyers and career officials were instead implemented virtually unchanged in the first weeks of the Trump administration.

After the short drive from his house, Hassan Ahmad stepped into chaos at the arrival hall of Dulles Airport on Saturday, January 28, 2017. As word of the immediate ban on arrivals from the seven Muslim-majority countries spread over social media, crowds of protesters streamed into the terminal. Only a week earlier, millions of Americans had been in the streets as part of the Women's March, and many were energized to continue to protest against Donald Trump. Dulles Airport police officers, who were accustomed to watching exhausted travelers quietly gather their luggage after long-haul flights from around the world, eyed the growing crowd of protesters and lawyers warily. The protesters waved signs and chanted, "Let them in." Each time someone walked out of the international arrival doors, the crowd would cheer. The arriving passengers were jet-lagged and confused, many unaware that a Muslim ban had been put in place. Ahmad and the lawyers tried to gather information from the bewildered travelers about whether any of their fellow passengers had been detained. Ahmad heard about a family of four from Iraq with green cards, whose father had been a translator for the US Army, who were detained but eventually allowed through. Ahmad got another call from a wheelchair-bound seventy-one-year-old Iranian man with a heart condition who seemed like he might be turned back. The airport worker pushing his wheelchair had kindly allowed the man to borrow his cell phone. Ahmad went to Facebook to get in touch with the offices of US senators who could help. As word got out, elected officials began to arrive at the airport, including Virginia's governor Terry McAuliffe and Attorney General Mark Herring as well as New Jersey senator Cory Booker.

That evening, federal judge Leonie Brinkema issued a temporary restraining order saying that people detained under the new executive order at Dulles had to be given access to their lawyers. As the evening wore on, CBP officials continued to refuse to allow Ahmad and the other lawyers to meet with the fifty to sixty people being detained at the airport. The raucous protesters chanted, "Let them see their lawyers, let them see their lawyers" and "Due process now." The low ceilings and tile floors of the baggage claim area magnified and jumbled the chants, adding to the sense of confusion. Ahmad was struck by how quickly things had changed. Only the week before he had easily been able to access the area where detainees were held to visit clients, but now it was guarded by two heavily armed agents. It was something Ahmad never expected to see in the United States: "It reminded me of some of my asylum cases, where my clients would tell me stories about checkpoints, registration, being targeted, being told different things by different officials, about the law simply not working. Except this was Virginia, minutes from my home."[4] The same scenes played out across the country as families were separated, Muslims felt targeted, and the reality of the Trump administration began to sink in.

"THE WALL IS A WALL"

The chaotic rollout of the Muslim ban signaled the new approach of the Trump administration. For Jeff Sessions, Steve Bannon, and Stephen Miller the operative word was speed. The administration was disdainful of the institutional knowledge of career officials and rarely consulted them before unveiling a new policy. Rather than careful consideration, the focus was on strict interpretations of laws and rapid implementations. The Muslim ban was revised twice and litigated in the courts but upheld by the Supreme Court in *Trump v. Hawaii* on June 26, 2018. The 5–4 ruling delivered by Chief Justice John Roberts concluded, "Under these circumstances, the Government has set forth sufficient national security justification to survive rational basis review."[5] Many of the Trump administration's immigration crackdowns would follow a similar process of litigation and revisions, with some passing muster while others, such as the attempt to end the DACA program, were thwarted by the US Supreme Court.

Sessions, Bannon, and Miller had each taken up key positions in the new administration that would allow them to carry out their anti-immigrant vision. Jeff Sessions was Donald Trump's first cabinet nominee and was confirmed as the attorney general of the United States on February 9, 2017. The Tanton Network was thrilled that their strongest ally in the Senate was now directing the entire Department of Justice, which included the ability to decide how strictly to enforce immigration laws. The FAIR newsletter explained,

> In the Senate, Sessions spearheaded successful efforts to derail massive amnesty legislation under both Presidents George W. Bush and Barack Obama. In 2006, 2007 and again in 2013, Sessions argued passionately against legislation that promoted the interests of illegal aliens and cheap labor employers over those of the American people. FAIR worked closely with Sessions and his staff during these legislative battles and we look forward to working with him, as attorney general, to ensure that immigration laws that were enacted to protect the interests and security of the American people are carried out.[6]

It must have also been a head-spinning turn of events for Sessions, who became the top law enforcement official in the country after having been rejected for a judgeship by the Senate in the 1980s.

Miller and Bannon took positions in the White House that did not require Senate confirmation. Stephen Miller was named senior advisor to the president and the White House director of speechwriting. Steve Bannon became the White House chief strategist and a senior counselor to the president. Sessions, Bannon, and Miller recognized that their time was limited both by the fact that they may never find themselves in power again and because new presidents have a relatively small window early in their terms to implement significant changes to policy.[7] By the second year, the US congressional midterm elections are in full swing, so early in the first year is the time to get things done. Bannon did not last even that long and was ousted from the White House after only eight months in August 2017. Sessions incurred the wrath of Donald Trump after he recused himself from the Russia investigation and eventually resigned as attorney general the day after the midterm elections on November 7, 2018. Nevertheless, Sessions was able to implement significant policy changes during his term including the no-tolerance policy that resulted in family separations at the border.[8] Miller was a survivor and even overcame the release of his controversial emails in late 2019 that detailed his connections to white nationalists and SPLC-designated hate groups such as American Renaissance, VDARE, FAIR, and CIS.[9]

In the first years of his presidency, Donald Trump, his supporters, and the media fixated on his pledge to build a border wall. Trump authorized the construction of six border wall prototypes near San Diego, at a cost of $20 million, to demonstrate action on the border wall issue and to illustrate the different types of walls that were possible. All were thirty feet tall and imposing, but not exactly the beautiful wall Trump had promised. They were mostly made of concrete, but a few had blue and red metal sections. One had spikes on the top. The prototypes were taken down in 2019 with none having been built on the border itself. In January 2018, Trump's chief of staff, John Kelly, told lawmakers privately and then stated publicly on Fox News that Trump's campaign pledges on the wall were not "fully informed" and his thinking had "evolved." Kelly said, "Campaign to governing are two different things."[10] Trump was furious and tweeted in response to Kelly's public statements, "The Wall is the Wall."[11]

Many Americans assume the presidency is extremely powerful, but the US Congress has control over taxation and appropriations, which means they decide what is funded. During his first two years in office, Trump found that even with Republican control of Congress he could not get funding for his border wall project. Increasingly frustrated, and goaded by right-wing voices in the media, Trump insisted on border wall funding in a budget bill in December 2018, which forced a government shutdown over the holiday season. The government remained closed for thirty-five days but Trump eventually relented even though additional funding for his border wall was not authorized. On February 15, 2019, Trump used one of the powers of the presidency to declare a state of emergency in order to redirect funds toward border wall construction. The emergency proclamation allowed the US Department of Defense to divert congressionally approved military funds to border wall construction. The decision was immediately contested in the courts, but in July 2019, the US Supreme Court ruled in a short 5–4 opinion that the emergency was legal. The Trump administration built approximately four hundred miles of border wall, often replacing smaller vehicle barriers with thirty-foot-high walls.[12]

THE FRIDAY GROUP

While Trump and his supporters were drawn to the idea of building a border wall, Stephen Miller and the Tanton Network were more interested in establishing an invisible wall behind the scenes through changes to immigration policy and enforcement that would have a much more significant impact. At first, Miller clashed with other officials like National Security Advisor H. R. McMaster and Chief Economic Advisor Gary Cohn, but he later agreed that he would not get into their areas of national security and economics if they left immigration to him.[13] As he settled into his role as a senior advisor to the president and the head of the Domestic Policy Council, Stephen Miller organized a regular Friday meeting with other immigration officials in the Roosevelt Room, which is directly adjacent to the Oval Office in the West Wing of the White House.

Miller and his Friday group set to work to change immigration policy from the inside. Many of the regular attendees were drawn from Gene Hamilton's immigration transition team, who had now taken up positions across the White House, the Department of Justice, and the Department of Homeland Security.[14] These included Hamilton, Lee Francis Cissna, Dimple Shah, Tracy Short, and Kathy Nuebel Kovarik. New members were Julia Hahn, the Breitbart writer who wrote the feature on *The Camp of the*

Saints and served as Bannon's eyes and ears in the White House; Jon Feere, the longtime CIS staffer who worked on the Trump campaign and was now a senior advisor at ICE; and Andrew Veprek, a foreign service officer who would become Stephen Miller's close associate and be promoted to deputy assistant secretary in the Bureau of Population, Refugees and Migration in 2018 and then appointed to the National Security Council in 2020.[15]

Beyond the members of the Friday working group, there were over two dozen other officials with ties to the Tanton Network who were hired into positions in the campaign, the transition, and across the administration. Seventeen were employees of Tanton Network groups, marking the first time ever that known members of an SPLC-designated hate group were hired for a government position (table 5). In previous administrations, both Republican and Democratic, working for a hate group would have resulted in an immediate disqualification. These Tanton-connected officials had positions in a range of agencies, but most were clustered in a few critical offices that handle immigration policy and enforcement in the White House, the Department of Justice, and the Department of Homeland Security. This included many mid-level staffers from FAIR and CIS as well as senior Tanton Network figures such as Julie Kirchner. Kirchner was the executive director of FAIR for over a decade before joining the Trump administration. At least eleven more Trump campaign, transition, or administration officials wrote articles for or spoke at an event organized by a Tanton Network group (table 6). Dan Stein, the president of FAIR, explained to CBS News, "It certainly is delightful to see folks that we've worked with in the past advance and contribute to the various efforts of the administration, most of which we support."[16]

TABLE 5: *Trump administration officials who worked for a Tanton Network group*

NAME	TRUMP ADMINISTRATION ROLE	TANTON NETWORK ROLE
Arthur, Art	Transition immigration group	CIS fellow (after Trump administration role)
Barletta, Lou	Transition team	FAIR board member
Beck, Roy	Campaign advisor	Numbers USA president
Camarota, Steve	Campaign advisor	CIS, director of research

(continues)

TABLE 5: *Trump administration officials who worked for a Tanton Network group* (continued)

NAME	TRUMP ADMINISTRATION ROLE	TANTON NETWORK ROLE
Conway, Kellyanne	Campaign manager, senior advisor to the president	Pollster for CIS, FAIR, Numbers USA
Feere, Jon	Legal advisor, ICE	CIS staffer for over fifteen years
Homan, Thomas	Acting director of ICE	Spoke at CIS event while in office, now fellow with IRLI (after Trump administration role)
Kirchner, Julie	USCIS ombudsman, DHS Office of Civil Rights Violations	FAIR executive director for over a decade
Kobach, Kris	Transition team, Voter Fraud Commission	Legal counsel for FAIR, IRLI
Jacobs, Elizabeth	Senior advisor to the chief counsel, USCIS	FAIR lobbyist
Law, Robert	Chief of the Office of Policy and Strategy, USCIS	FAIR lobbying director
Morgan, Mark	Chief of the Border Patrol, acting director of ICE, acting director of CBP	FAIR senior fellow (after Trump administration role)
Noronha, Maya	Special advisor, Department of Health and Human Services	FAIR lobbyist
O'Brien, Matthew	Immigration judge	FAIR director of research
Overcash, Colton	Senior advisor for strategy and policy, director of strategic engagement and communications, DHS	FAIR legislative advisor
Rehberg, Sarah	Assistant secretary for border security and immigration, DHS	FAIR director of state and local relations
Smith, Ian	Policy analyst, DHS	IRLI investigative associate
Zadrozny, John	Acting chief of staff, USCIS	FAIR legislative counsel

TABLE 6: *Trump administration officials who wrote for or spoke at a Tanton Network group*

NAME	TRUMP ADMINISTRATION ROLE	TANTON NETWORK ROLE
Borjas, George	Campaign advisor	CIS contributor
Cissna, Lee Francis	Director, USCIS	Spoke at a CIS event while in office
Cuccinelli, Ken	Interim director, USCIS, interim deputy director, DHS	Spoke at a CIS event while in office
Miller, Stephen	Senior advisor to the president	Keynote speaker at CIS event
McHenry, James	Executive office of immigration review director (DoJ)	Spoke at CIS event
Morgan, Mark	Acting commissioner of customs and border protection	Conducted an interview with CIS for their newsletter
Mortensen, Ronald	Nominated but not confirmed assistant secretary of state for bureau of population, refugees, and migration	Frequent CIS newsletter contributor
Richwine, Jason	Deputy undersecretary of commerce for standards and technology	Weekly CIS newsletter contributor
Sekulow, Jay	Trump's personal lawyer, impeachment lawyer	Co-wrote an amicus brief with IRLI for SB 1070
Sessions, Jeff	Attorney general	FAIR award recipient, regular attendee at CIS events
Vitiello, Ronald	Acting director, ICE	Attended FAIR event while in office

Outside the administration, the Colcom Foundation further expanded their funding for the Tanton Network to $34.4 million in 2018, which accounted for 82 percent of the funds Colcom distributed that year. That was up from only $7.7 million to the Tanton Network eight years earlier in 2010.[17] The biggest recipients were FAIR and Numbers USA, which received $13 million and $12.45 million, respectively. In addition to sending experts to testify before Congress, the Tanton Network used the funds to expand their reach into mainstream media outlets. CIS director Mark

Krikorian is regularly interviewed on National Public Radio despite the fact that he leads an SPLC-designated hate group. At the 2019 Conservative Political Action Conference, Trump cited a FAIR report that said "illegal aliens are incarcerated at three times the rate of legal residents," which is false.[18] Though CIS was an SPLC-designated hate group, the *New York Times* published an op-ed by CIS employee Jerry Kammer in January 2020.[19]

Beyond placing many key figures in the administration and expanding its media outreach, the Tanton Network found that it had direct access to the administration itself. Dan Stein, the president of FAIR, said, "As you might imagine, the communication is much better now, and people are asking us to attend all kinds of different meetings." Roy Beck of Numbers USA explained, "What they're trying to do meshes with what our organization has always tried to do."[20]

The closed circle of immigration decision-making becomes clear with legislation like the RAISE Act proposed by Arkansas Republican senator Tom Cotton and written in part by Julie Kirchner, the former executive director of FAIR.[21] The bill did not pass, but it would have dramatically reduced immigration to the United States and shifted it away from family reunification toward skill-based workers. In announcing the White House's support for the bill, Stephen Miller cited the research of CIS contributor and Harvard professor George Borjas and Steve Camarota of CIS, both of whom had been at the August 2016 Trump campaign immigration policy meeting. The White House created a webpage with praise for the RAISE Act, which included a statement of support from government officials including Attorney General Jeff Sessions. The website includes only two statements from nongovernment officials: Numbers USA president Roy Beck and FAIR president Dan Stein, who says, "These changes will truly make immigration great again."[22]

THE ANTI-IMMIGRANT PRESIDENCY

The policies of the Trump administration often seemed scattershot, as if they were lacking an overarching purpose. After Trump's term ended, many analysts suggested that he was largely an ineffective president, stymied by the constant drumbeat of scandals including Russian election meddling, the Robert Mueller probe, his dealings with Ukraine that led to his first impeachment, the incompetent handling of the coronavirus pandemic, the incitement of the attack on the Capitol Building, and his second impeachment. However, when viewed through the lens of the great replacement, the immigration-related changes come into focus. By the end of the fourth year, Stephen Miller and the Friday group had implemented most of the proposed immigration policies from the wish lists FAIR and CIS wrote in 2016, along with many additional changes.

The nonpartisan Migration Policy Institute released a report at the end of Trump's term that identified over four hundred new immigration restrictions.[23] An analysis by Stanford University professor Lucas Guttentag documented over one thousand total changes to immigration policies.[24] In addition to the widely reported policies such as the Muslim ban, the border wall, and the no-tolerance policy that led to family separations at the border, there were hundreds of other less visible restrictions that affected all types of immigration to the United States. These smaller changes ran the gamut from arcane visa rules to expanded enforcement capabilities for the Border Patrol and ICE.

A few examples will suffice. The refugee quota was reduced from 110,000 in President Obama's final year to 15,000 in fiscal year 2021. US asylum policy was completely revamped, including metering the number of requests at ports of entry and restrictions on what counts as a credible fear. The administration also put in place the euphemistically named Migrant Protection Protocols that required asylum applicants to remain in Mexico while their applications were considered, often living in squalid camps. Many people lost their only chance at protection when they were deported or had their asylum applications denied by extremely strict immigration judges appointed by the Trump administration. In FY 2020, 71.6 percent of asylum claims were denied, the highest rate ever. In 2016, it was 54.6 percent.[25] The administration scrutinized all classes of visa applications more closely, resulting in higher rejection rates. In 2015, under the Obama administration, 94 percent of H1B visas for skilled workers were approved. In 2019, it was down to 68 percent. In 2020, US Citizenship and Immigration Services (USCIS) closed all of their offices overseas at the same time that they began to require in-person interviews for green card applications. As the coronavirus pandemic spread globally, the administration used it to further crack down on immigration. All asylum processing at the border was ended, many immigrant work visas like H1B were paused, and even student visas for universities were threatened if the university opted for all online instruction.

The devil is often in the details, and seemingly inconsequential changes illustrate the extent of the effort to reduce immigration to the United States. In 2019, USCIS instituted a new policy that automatically rejected documents if any fields were left blank.[26] This might seem reasonable to an extent, but it was not. For example, the forms had lines for things like apartment numbers, middle names, and the ages and current residences of four siblings. If someone lived in a house or did not have an apartment number, did not have a middle name, or had fewer than four siblings, they might reasonably skip over these spaces. If they did, their application was ruled incomplete and rejected on the premise that the applicant needed to write N/A in every blank that did not apply to them. Even if they wrote NA instead of N/A, it was rejected. The no-blanks policy led to the rejection of 50 percent of applications after it was implemented.[27]

USCIS also began to regularly update forms, often making very small changes. If an applicant used an old form, even if the new form came out after they mailed their documents, their application was rejected. In the summer of 2020, USCIS ended its contract with one of two printing companies that produce documents like green cards.[28] The result was months of delays in which immigrants did not receive the documents they needed. This meant they could not apply for work, but it also opened them up to deportation. Immigrants are required to carry these documents at all times, and failure to do so can result in removal from the United States. Consequently, by canceling the contract and not finding additional capacity, USCIS exposed people legally in the country to the possibility of deportation through no fault of their own.

The enduring legacy of the Trump administration will be a sharp reduction in immigration to the United States. Donald Trump was voted out of office after one term, but the impact of the changes his administration implemented will linger even as the policies themselves are reversed. By the summer of 2020, legal immigration to the United States had declined by 49 percent compared to levels at the end of the Obama administration.[29] Steve Camarota of CIS calculated that from 2010 to 2017, immigration increased the population of the United States by 650,000 people per year. In the first two years of the Trump administration, it only increased by 200,000 per year.[30] The Migration Policy Institute found that beyond the sharp reduction in refugee admissions and the use of the pandemic as an excuse to shut down normal visa processing in 2020, it was likely to take many years to fully account for the impact of all of the small but significant changes to immigration policies.[31]

In the end, the Trump administration represented the culmination of the Tanton Network's decades-long effort to move extreme anti-immigrant policies back into the mainstream of American politics. What began in the 1970s as the quixotic mission by a small-town ophthalmologist in upstate Michigan to get environmentalists to pay more attention to immigration grew into a national movement. Along the way, a ragtag group of allies in the conservation and white supremacist movements, but with funding from some of the wealthiest people in the world, managed to co-opt one of the two major political parties in the country and carry their desire to protect "a European-American majority" all the way to the White House. What had been fringe white supremacist ideas about the danger of immigration once again became the official policy of the United States of America.

THE GREAT REPLACEMENT

J im Acosta, CNN's chief White House correspondent, was the last person Stephen Miller called on in his appearance in the White House briefing room on August 2, 2017.[1] Miller, wearing a dark gray suit and a blue, black, and white striped tie, was there to tout the RAISE Act, which did not pass but would have severely curtailed legal immigration to the United States by restricting family reunification visas and adding a new points-based system for green cards that favored skilled workers who spoke English. Miller had already parried questions from Fox News and the *New York Times* about whether the proposal was politically feasible or should even be a priority given other pressing issues in the country. Acosta, whose father was a Cuban immigrant, had a more pointed question. He asked, "What you're proposing, or what the president's proposing, here, does not sound like it's in keeping with American tradition when it comes to immigration. The Statue of Liberty says: 'Give me your tired, your poor, your huddled masses yearning to breathe free.' . . . Aren't you trying to change what it means to be an immigrant coming into this country, if you are telling them they have to speak English?"

Miller, who had relished debates with offended liberals since his high school days, pounced. Miller countered that Acosta was not just wrong about history but was also showing his liberal cosmopolitan bias. He reminded Acosta that speaking English was already a requirement to be naturalized as a US citizen. Then Miller turned to the Statue of Liberty, which had long been a bone of contention for white nationalist and anti-immigrant groups.[2] Miller said, "I don't want to get off into a whole thing about history here, but the Statue of Liberty is a symbol of liberty enlightening the world. It's a symbol of American liberty enlightening the world. The poem that you're referring to was added later. It's not actually part of the original Statue of Liberty."

The Statue of Liberty was a gift from France that was meant to commemorate the end of slavery and the United States' centennial in 1876. The idea for the monument originated from a conversation between slavery abolitionist Édouard René de Laboulaye and the sculptor Frédéric Auguste Bartholdi in 1865. Bartholdi designed the copper statue and titled it *Liberty Enlightening the World*, as Miller correctly pointed out. The metal frame was made by Gustave Eiffel, whose tower at the 1889 Universal Exposition in Paris would cement his name into the identity of the city. *Liberty Enlightening the World* depicts the Roman goddess of liberty, *Libertas*, who holds a tablet with July 4, 1776, written in Roman numerals. At her feet lay a broken shackle and chains to symbolize the end of slavery. Delays in fabrication meant that only the torch was ready for display during the US centennial celebrations in 1876. The statue was finally installed in 1886 on Bedloe's Island, an abandoned army base off the coast of New Jersey. President Grover Cleveland presided over the dedication ceremony on October 28, 1886, saying that a "stream of light shall pierce the darkness of ignorance and man's oppression until Liberty enlightens the world."[3] There was no mention of immigration.

Despite standing 305 feet (93 meters) tall and having its own power plant to provide electricity to light up the torch at night, the Statue of Liberty was almost two miles south of Battery Park on the southern tip of Manhattan and turned out to be not that visible from New York City. However, it is much more visible to boats approaching New York by sea. Bedloe's Island was adjacent to another disused military outpost on Ellis Island, which was repurposed in 1892 as the primary arrival point for the millions of immigrants coming to the United States from Europe. For these immigrants, the Statue of Liberty became the symbol of welcome to the new country, holding up a torch to safely guide them to their final destination.

The famous lines from Emma Lazarus's poem "The New Colossus" that Jim Acosta quoted at the briefing were added to the Statue of Liberty in 1903.[4] Lazarus, an advocate for Jewish refugees from pogroms in Europe and Russia, had written the poem in 1883 as part of the fundraising drive to complete the base of the statue, but it had largely been forgotten. The poem reads in part,

> . . . *"Give me your tired, your poor*
> *Your huddled masses yearning to breathe free,*
> *The wretched refuse of your teeming shore.*
> *Send these, the homeless, tempest-tost to me,*
> *I lift my lamp beside the golden door!"*

Lazarus died of cancer in 1887, at only thirty-eight, and her obituaries did not mention what would become her most famous poem. In the early 1900s, Lazarus's friend Georgina Schuyler noted that even though the original purpose of the statue was to symbolize freedom, its proximity to Ellis Island had transformed it into a symbol of welcome to the immigrants arriving there, just as Lazarus had originally interpreted it. In 1901, Schuyler began an effort to honor her friend by adding the poem to the monument, and in 1903, a small plaque was added inside the base with the words of Lazarus's poem, reimagining Lady Liberty as the "Mother of Exiles."

After the 1924 national origins quotas slashed immigration to the United States and then air travel replaced ships as the primary mode of transatlantic travel, arrivals at Ellis Island dwindled and the facility was closed in 1954. In 1956, Bedloe's Island was renamed Liberty Island. On May 11, 1965, Lyndon Johnson signed a proclamation making Ellis Island part of the Statue of Liberty National Monument. The proclamation read,

> The Statue of Liberty is a symbol to the world of the dreams and aspirations which have drawn so many millions of immigrants to America. . . .
> To all Americans the Statue of Liberty stands eternal as the symbol of the freedom which has been made a living reality in the United States for men of all races, creeds, and national origins who have united in allegiance to the Constitution of the United States and to the imperishable ideals of our free society.[5]

When Johnson signed the Hart-Celler Immigration Act later that year on October 3, 1965, he chose to do so on Liberty Island at the base of the

Statue of Liberty. An immigration museum was installed inside the Statue of Liberty in 1972 and remained in operation until 1991, when it was replaced by the larger immigration museum on Ellis Island. Even though it was not how it was originally conceived, the Statue of Liberty has become the preeminent symbol of the immigrant origins of the United States.

In the White House Briefing Room in 2017, things got tense as Acosta and Miller bantered back and forth, speaking over each other while proclaiming the moral high ground. Miller ended up a little flustered and exasperated: "Jim, Jim. Your statement is shockingly ahistorical in another respect too." Acosta, his voice dripping with righteous indignation, asked if the English requirement meant that the United States was only going to allow immigrants from Great Britain and Australia. Miller was incredulous.

> Jim, it's actually—I have to honestly say I am shocked at your statement that you think that only people from Great Britain and Australia would know English. It's actually—it reveals your cosmopolitan bias to a shocking degree that in your mind—No, this is an amazing moment. This is an amazing moment. That you think only people from Great Britain or Australia would speak English is so insulting to millions of hard-working immigrants who do speak English from all over the world. It just shows your cosmopolitan bias.

Acosta replied, "It just sounds like you're trying to engineer the racial and ethnic flow of people into this country through this policy."

The charge of racism sent Miller over the top. "Jim, that is one of the most outrageous, insulting, ignorant, and foolish things you've ever said, and for you that's still a really—the notion that you think that this is a racist bill is so wrong and so insulting. Jim, the reality is, is that the foreign-born population into our country has quadrupled since 1970. That's a fact." Miller had explained earlier in the briefing that the problem was not just that these foreign-born people had come to the country, but that they were replacing native-born Americans. In response to a question from Glenn Thrush of the *New York Times*, Miller said, "Maybe it's time we had compassion, Glenn, for American workers. President Trump has met with American workers who have been replaced by foreign workers."

As Miller regained his composure, he turned the podium back over to Press Secretary Sarah Huckabee Sanders, saying, "I apologize, Jim, if things got heated, but you did make some rough insinuations. So, thank you. Thank you. And I'll hand it over to Sarah. I think that went exactly as planned. I think that was what Sarah was hoping would happen." The reporters in the room laughed, apparently not noticing that Miller had just used the podium of the White House Briefing Room to lay out the argument against the great replacement of native-born whites by foreign-born immigrants.

THE GREAT REPLACEMENT

Immigration laws are a central, but often unrecognized, part of the white supremacist vision of the United States as a white country. The idea of restricting immigration to protect a white identity connects the immigration crackdown of the Trump administration, the eugenics and race pseudoscience of the immigration restrictions in the 1920s, and the anti-Chinese movement of the 1880s. In the great replacement version of America, new immigrants are not seen as like-minded workers drawn to the ideal of the American dream. Instead, they are an existential threat to the white character of the country. Although immigration restrictions are described as protecting American jobs, they are fundamentally about protecting white supremacy. In this framing of immigration, the arrival of every new nonwhite immigrant contributes to what has been called "the passing of the great race," "suicide of the West," "death of the West," "race suicide," and "white genocide." Protecting the white identity of the United States was why the first immigration laws were passed at the end of the nineteenth century, and every new version since has continued to serve this purpose.

There are strikingly similar themes about the great replacement in the speeches and writings of the immigration restrictionists in each era described in this book. The first commonality is the description of immigration as an invasion. The use of the word "invasion" takes what could otherwise be seen as a normal activity, migrating for work, and turns it into a military threat that, in turn, requires a militarized response. The fear of invasion is based on the claim that nonwhite groups have a numerical advantage and would overwhelm the numbers of the white population in America. In 2019, Donald Trump said of immigration, "This is an invasion. I was badly criticized for using the word invasion. It's an invasion."[6] His campaign ads reiterated the message, "We have an INVASION! So we are BUILDING THE WALL to STOP IT. Dems will sue us. But we want a SAFE COUNTRY! It's CRITICAL that we STOP THE INVASION."[7] The title of John Tanton's book, coauthored with Wayne Lutton in 1994, was *The Immigrant Invasion*. Jean Raspail's 1973 novel *The Camp of the Saints*, which was published in the United States by John Tanton and was a favorite of Stephen Miller and Steve Bannon, warned of an immigrant invasion of Europe. In 1951, President Harry Truman's Commission on Migratory Labor described seasonal Mexican labor migration as an invasion: "The magnitude of the wetback traffic has reached entirely new levels in the past 7 years. . . . In its newly achieved proportions, it is virtually an invasion."[8] In 1924, as the Senate debated placing quotas on immigration to severely limit arrivals from everywhere but Northern Europe, Senator John Shields of Tennessee explained,

> The immigrants we are receiving today are of a different character from those that came in the early history of our country, and the great numbers in which they are arriving is a cause for serious alarm and menaces the purity of the blood, the homogeneity, and the supremacy of the American people and the integrity and perpetuity of our representative form of government. . . . The people of the United States recognize in these great hordes of new immigrants a foreign invasion fraught with consequences as disastrous and humiliating as those of a military invasion.[9]

In 1882, as the Senate debated the Chinese Exclusion Act, Senator Miller of California laid out the threat: "When, in the progress of unlimited immigration, this country becomes well filled with Chinese; whose scouts and spies are now in every city and town in all the States giving information to their masters who are conducting this oriental invasion."[10]

The great replacement is often couched in the need to protect Western civilization. This idea underlies President Calvin Coolidge's campaign slogan from the 1920s to "Keep America American" and Donald Trump's pledge in 2020 to "Keep America Great." In a speech in Warsaw, Poland, in 2017, Donald Trump said,

> Today we're in the West, and we have to say there are dire threats to our security and our way of life. . . . The fundamental question of our time is whether the West has the will to survive. Do we have the confidence in our values to defend them at any cost? Do we have enough respect for our citizens to protect our borders? Do we have the desire and the courage to preserve our civilization in the face of those who would subvert and destroy it?[11]

Senator Shields made this argument in 1924: "If we permit the great American type of citizenship to be diluted, mongrelized, and destroyed, our civilization and free institutions will not survive. No mongrel race has ever achieved greatness in peace or war."[12] Likewise, Senator Miller said in 1882, "We ask of you to secure to us American Anglo-Saxon civilization without contamination or adulteration with any other."[13]

Not all immigrants are demonized in the great replacement view of America. While nonwhite immigration must be stopped at all costs, white immigrants from Europe are continuously welcomed. In 1882, Senator Miller ended his speech introducing the Chinese Exclusion Act by saying he would trade the Chinese for "any white people under the sun." In 1924, the cosponsor of the Johnson-Reed Immigration Act, Senator David Reed of Pennsylvania, celebrated that the law meant that "75 per cent of our immigration hereafter will come from Northwestern Europe."[14] In a 2015 interview with Steve Bannon on Breitbart radio, Jeff Sessions said the 1924 law "was good for America" and should be a model for future immigration restrictions.[15] In his leaked emails, Stephen Miller suggested that the United States should use Calvin Coolidge's support of the 1924 law as a model to refocus immigration on Europe, not the rest of the world.[16] In 2018, in a conversation with congressional leaders in the Oval Office, Donald Trump asked, "Why are we having all these people from shithole countries come here?" Instead, he suggested, the United States should take more people from Norway.[17]

In each era, advocates for immigration restrictions created mechanisms to remove undesirable people from the country. The Trump administration expanded the US Border Patrol and ICE to round people up near the border and in the interior of the country. Trump said in reference to potential gang members, "These aren't people, these are animals and we're taking them out of the country at a rate that's never happened before."[18] In the 1950s, roundups like Operation Wetback sent millions of Mexicans back across the border. From 1892 until 2018, the United States formally deported 8.3 million people, a figure that does not include the millions of additional people who were voluntarily removed by the Border Patrol near the border.[19] The removal logic is also present in the sustained effort in the nineteenth and twentieth centuries to return freed slaves to Africa. Even after former slaves were extended American citizenship in 1870, the American Colonization Society continued to send free African Americans to Liberia. As late as the 1940s, the Greater Liberia Act, which would have removed all African Americans from the United States, was introduced in the Senate. In 2019, Donald Trump tweeted that "'Progressive' Democratic Congresswomen," a reference to Representatives Alexandria Ocasio-Cortez of New York, Ilhan Omar of Minnesota, Rashida Tlaib of Michigan, and Ayanna Pressley of Massachusetts, should "go back and help fix the totally broken and crime infested places from which they came."[20]

ANTI-IMMIGRANT VIOLENCE

Beyond policies to limit the entry of and deport nonwhite immigrants, the great replacement ideology has also led to sustained violence against nonwhite people in the United States and at its borders. The reign of terror carried out by state militias like the Texas Rangers and the US Army to clear Native Americans and former Mexican citizens in the nineteenth century was a mechanism to eliminate nonwhite people from the newly conquered territory of the United States.[21] The ethnic cleansing of the Chinese across the western United States in the decades after the Chinese Exclusion Act was a mechanism to remove nonwhite settlers from the country.[22] The thousands of lynchings in the decades after the Civil War were a mechanism to terrify and eliminate African Americans from the country. The US Border Patrol was established two days after the national origins quotas became law in 1924 to enforce the new racial entry rules for the United States and remove those who violated them. The militarization of US borders has led to thousands of deaths as people attempting to migrate are funneled into ever more dangerous routes. Globally, tens of thousands of people have died at the borders of Europe, Australia, and the United States as their unseaworthy ships sink in the Mediterranean or they are left to die of dehydration by smugglers in the deserts of North Africa or the US Southwest.[23]

The use of violence to terrorize nonwhite immigrants has continued through the present day. In the past decade, a series of attacks have been carried out by radicalized young men in the United States and around the world under the banner of the great replacement. In August 2019, a twenty-one-year-old man killed twenty people and injured dozens more at a Walmart store in El Paso, Texas. Minutes before the attack, he posted a 2,300-word manifesto titled "The Inconvenient Truth" that was steeped in the anti-immigrant ideas of the great replacement. He wrote, "This attack is a response to the Hispanic invasion of Texas. . . . I am simply defending my country from cultural and ethnic replacement brought on by an invasion."[24] A few months earlier on April 27, 2019, in Poway, California, a nineteen-year-old man entered a synagogue where he killed one person and injured three more. Minutes before the attack, he also left a manifesto, titled "An Open Letter," that said the attack was in re- sponse to the "genocide of the European race."[25] In November 2018, a forty-six-year-old man stormed the Tree of Life Synagogue in Pittsburgh, Pennsylvania, killing eleven people and injuring six. Moments before, he posted a message explaining the attack. He said the Hebrew Immigrant Aid Society "likes to bring invaders that kill our people. I can't sit by and watch my people get slaughtered. Screw your optics, I'm going in."[26]

These attacks have not just happened in the United States but also in a number of other European and white settler countries. In July 2011, a thirty-two-year-old Norwegian man killed seventy-seven people af- ter detonating a bomb in Oslo and then stalking teenagers at summer camp organized by the Norwegian Labor Party on the island of Utøya. Before the attack, he emailed a 1,500-page manuscript titled "2083—A European Declaration of Independence" to friends and journalists. The manifesto argued that European culture was under threat from an inva- sion by Muslims. He wrote, "This irrational fear of nationalistic doctrines is preventing us from stopping our own national/cultural suicide as the Islamic colonization is increasing annually."[27] In March 2019, a twenty- eight-year-old Australian man livestreamed an attack on the Al-Noor

Mosque in Christchurch, New Zealand, as he killed fifty-one people and injured forty-nine more. He also left a seventy-four-page manifesto in which he referred to himself as an "ethno-nationalist" and "eco-fascist." To the killer, Donald Trump was "a symbol of renewed white identity and common purpose." The first lines of the manifesto could have been written by John Tanton. The killer wrote, "It's the birthrates. It's the birthrates. It's the birthrates. If there is one thing I want you to remember from these writings its [sic] that the birthrates must change. Even if we were to deport all non-Europeans from our lands tomorrow, the European people would still be spiraling into decay and eventually death. . . . We are experiencing an invasion on a level never seen before in history."28

The New Zealand manifesto was titled "The Great Replacement."

THE FIRST STEP

Throughout the presidency of Donald Trump, "This is not who we are" and "This is not what America is about" were common refrains that sought to distance the character and values of the United States from the racist words and actions of the president. For some, Donald Trump's defeat in 2020 confirmed that he was an aberration and that the United States was returning to its foundations of openness and diversity. This is naive. As this book has demonstrated, anti-immigrant nativism is a recurring feature in the history of the country, and Donald Trump was only the latest iteration in a much longer-term historical trend. His election did not initiate the use of immigration restrictions for racial purposes, and his loss did not end it. Donald Trump was voted out, but many politicians who endorsed his crackdown on immigration still won, leaving broad support in Congress and in rural areas for using immigration restrictions to enforce the white borders of the United States.

The central dispute of this book is which version of the United States will emerge in the twenty-first century. For many of the anti-immigrant figures, the United States is a white country that was founded by white men and is meant for the white progeny of those original settlers from England and Northern Europe. The threat of race suicide or white genocide requires immigration laws to prevent the great replacement of the white population by people from foreign lands. This version is symbolized by the Pioneer Fund's mission statement to support "children who are deemed to be descended predominantly from white persons who set-tled in the original thirteen states," and by the white supremacist oath of the Fourteen Words, "We must secure the existence of our people and a future for white children." As the white nationalists shouted in Charlot-tesville in 2017, "One people, one nation, end to immigration" and "You will not replace us." That is the version of America they want to make great again.

For others, the future of the United States is not in the deeds of its founders but in their words. The founding documents promise a country where all men are created equal and where there are no limits on im-migration. This version of America, rooted in equal rights, is evident in the abolitionist movement and the Underground Railroad that worked to free people from slavery. It is evident in the Emancipation Proclamation, the Civil War, and the promise of citizenship that was extended to Black Americans in 1870. It is evident in the civil rights movement in the 1950s and 1960s that upended Jim Crow laws and the system of segregation. It is evident in the uprising of 2020 against the use of the police to enforce a racial order. It is evident in a population that is 13 percent foreign-born as different ideas, foods, and ways of life come together to make a uniquely American experience. It is evident in the election of Barack Obama as the first Black president of the United States and Kamala Harris as the first Black and South Asian American vice president, whose parents were both immigrants to the country.

Almost 250 years after Thomas Jefferson wrote that "all men are cre-ated equal," the country is still trying to live up to that ideal even though Jefferson himself failed. Just as the founding documents of the United States were not true when they were written, Emma Lazarus's poem about welcoming immigrants to the United States was not true when it was added to the base of the Statue of Liberty in 1903. It is still not true today, but it could be. The first step toward that aspiration is to recognize that because immigration restrictions are a tool of white supremacy, then free movement must be the position of anyone opposed to it.

ACKNOWLEDGMENTS

M y previous book, *Violent Borders*, was published in October 2016, just a month before the election of Donald Trump as the president of the United States. That book started with the question of why there are so many migrant deaths today, and I argued that the act of drawing a border itself was inherently violent. By creating the inside/outside space of state territory, a border is a mechanism to restrict access to resources and opportunity by preventing the movement of other people. In the process, economic, cultural, and political privileges are protected for some at the expense of many others. The book concluded that while the precise configuration of violence at political borders was new, the use of movement restrictions to protect privileges was not. Earlier systems of exploitation, including slavery, serfdom, poor laws, and vagrancy laws, were all based on violently restricting the movement of some people in order to protect the privileges of an elite group.

As I watched Donald Trump build his entire 2016 presidential campaign on demonizing immigrants on racial grounds, I realized that *Violent Borders* did not adequately consider the role of race as one of the privileges that were protected by movement restrictions at borders. As I thought about this gap in my previous book and read more about the history of race in American immigration policy. I worked my way through the archives of the United States' first immigration laws, I saw the parallels between the debates then and now. It became clear that immigration laws were never benign rules about who could migrate to the country. Instead, as *White Borders* demonstrates, immigration rules were fundamentally about race from the very beginning.

Several books were essential for my research and deserve particular recognition. Mae Ngai's *Impossible Subjects: Illegal Aliens and the Making of Modern America* (2004) provided a key overview of the relationship between racism and immigration policy. My understanding of the Chinese Exclusion Act was heavily influenced by Andrew Gyory's *Closing the Gate: Race, Politics, and the Chinese Exclusion Act* (1998). The book provides an authoritative guide to the politics in the United States that led to the country's first immigration acts. Daniel Okrent's *The Guarded Gate: Bigotry, Eugenics, and the Law That Kept Two Generations of Jews, Italians, and Other European Immigrants Out of America* (2019) is an excellent study of the nativist turn that led to the 1924 Johnson-Reed Immigration Act. Another amazing find that opened up the entire world of funding for white supremacy in the middle of the twentieth century was William Tucker's *The Funding of Scientific Racism: Wickliffe Draper and the Pioneer Fund* (2002). Jean Guerrero's *Hatemonger: Donald Trump and the White Nationalist Agenda* (2020) and Julie Hirschfeld Davis and Michael Shear's *Border Wars: Inside Trump's Assault on Immigration* (2019) both came out as I was finishing the last sections of the book. Together they clarified the profound role Stephen Miller has had on the country's immigration policy. Finally, two books that helped me think about race in a historical frame were Ibram Kendi's *Stamped from the Beginning: The Definitive History of Racist Ideas in America* (2016) and Nell Irvin Painter's *The History of White People* (2010).

———

Writing a book always means relying on the work of many other people, even though a single name ends up on the cover. First and foremost, I want to thank my family for their continuing support of my research and writing. My partner, Sivylay, always gives me the time and space to write and is patient when I am traveling to visit distant archives or historical sites. Sivylay read and commented on the entire draft, catching typos and confusing phrases throughout. My children, Rasmey and Kiran, also gamely came along for many of those trips. Sometimes, like panning for gold at the site of Sutter's Mill, they actually turned out to be fun. Thanks to my parents, Celia and Wally, for their enduring support. Thanks to my brother, Brent, who read an early draft of this book and helped clarify what the argument actually was.

Corey Johnson and Md. Azmeary Ferdoush read and commented on the entire book. Anna Law, Thomas Belfield, Carly Goodman, and Hassan Ahmad read sections of the book at different stages of its development. Thanks for your time and your incisive comments. The book is better for it.

Thanks to my agent, Julia Eagleton, and both the Gernert Company and Janklow & Nesbit for supporting and promoting the book. Julia was a tireless editor of the proposal and helped make it substantially better. Thanks to Gayatri Patnaik and Beacon Press for believing in the book and bringing it into the world. Lori Rider did an excellent job with the copyedits. Thanks also to Susan Lumenello and the production team, Sanj Kharbanda and the marketing team, and Carol Chu and the design team at Beacon.

Thanks to everyone who agreed to be interviewed for the project, including Heidi Beirich, Hassan Ahmad, and Eddie Bejarano as well as others who wished to remain anonymous. The decades of work by the Southern Poverty Law Center to document the writings and actions of the anti-immigration movement in the United States were crucial to this project.

I gave presentations on this research at the School of Geography, Development, and Environment at the University of Arizona in March 2019 and at the Center for Middle East and North African Studies at the University of Michigan in September 2019, before the coronavirus pandemic limited travel. Thanks to Orhan Myadar, Stefano Bloch, and Daniel E. Martínez in Tucson and Ryan Szpiech in Ann Arbor for hosting me and facilitating my research during the visits. Thanks also to the audiences for helpful questions and discussion.

Much of the research for this book was carried out in archives. The archives of John Tanton, John Trevor Sr., and John Trevor Jr. are all held at the Bentley Historical Library at the University of Michigan. Despite the dreary material in the documents, the staff and facility are excellent. Unfortunately, only the first fourteen boxes of the John Tanton Papers are currently available for review, with the remaining ten boxes closed until 2035. Thanks to Hassan Ahmad for pursuing the legal fight to access those files now. ProPublica built an archive of tax documents for nonprofit groups in the United States. These documents are publicly available, but organizing them into a searchable database is a true public service. The final archive I used was at the Center for Sacramento History, which houses the personal and business records of V. S. and C. K. McClatchy. Sean Heyliger was helpful in organizing access to the files.

Thanks to the Social Science Research Institute at the University of Hawai'i at Manoa for a Research Support Award in 2018–19 that funded the early research for this project. I owe particular gratitude to my graduate research assistant Md. Azmeary Ferdoush who located many old congressional records, manuscripts, tax documents, and reports about the various people and organizations that feature in this book. Thanks also to Kevin Morris for research assistance on old case files in the law library. I also appreciate one of my students, Jane Taafaki, for pointing me to some early sources on immigration restrictions in the colonial period. Thanks to Brooke Binkowski for providing resources on John Tanton in the early stages of the project.

Finally, mahalo nui loa to my colleagues in the Department of Geography and Environment at the University of Hawai'i at Manoa. The wonderful group of people in the geography community make it an excellent place to live and work.

NOTES

PROLOGUE

1. All quotations come from raw video of the event, https://www.youtube.com
/watch?v=-y7nhXS_q3o, accessed November 5, 2020.

2. David Niewert, "When White Nationalists Chant Their Weird Slogans,
What Do They Mean?" Southern Poverty Law Center Hatewatch, October 10,
2017, https://www.splcenter.org/hatewatch/2017/10/10/when-white-nationalists
-chant-their-weird-slogans-what-do-they-mean.

3. Lauren Jones, "Let Freedom Ring: UVA Professor Rediscovers Sacred Story
Behind Jefferson Statue," *UVA Today*, July 2, 2014.

4. Southern Poverty Law Center, "Whose Heritage? Public Symbols of the
Confederacy," February 1, 2019, https://www.splcenter.org/20190201/whose
-heritage-public-symbols-confederacy.

5. Roger Taney, *Dred Scott v. United States*, US Supreme Court, 60 US 393 (1857).

6. Jason Kessler interview with News2Share, https://www.facebook.com
/N2Sreports/videos/jason-kessler-interview/1491896640918220, accessed November 5, 2020.

INTRODUCTION

1. Raw video of the announcement at C-SPAN, https://www.c-span.org
/video/?326473-1/donald-trump-presidential-campaign-announcement, accessed
November 5, 2020.

2. Julie Hirschfeld Davis and Michael Shear, *Border Wars: Inside Trump's Assault
on Immigration* (New York: Simon & Schuster, 2019), 27.

3. Books by Dan Denvir and Elizabeth Cohen provide an overview of this process. Elizabeth Cohen, *Illegal: How American's Lawless Immigration Regime Threatens
Us All* (New York: Basic Books, 2020); Daniel Denvir, *All-American Nativism: How
the Bipartisan War on Immigrants Explains Politics as We Know It* (New York: Verso,
2020). Just as the final edits were completed on this book, Brendan O'Connor
published a book detailing the Tanton Network and nativism. Brendan O'Connor,
Blood Red Lines: How Nativism Fuels the Right (New York: Haymarket Books, 2021).

4. Colcom 990 forms, including donations for 2015 and 2016, https://projects.
propublica.org/nonprofits, accessed February 25, 2021.

5. John Tanton letter to Garrett Hardin, December 10, 1993, John Tanton
Papers, Bentley Historical Library, University of Michigan.

6. Carly Goodman, "John Tanton Has Died. He Made America Less Open to Immigrants—and More Open to Trump," *Washington Post*, July 18, 2019.

7. Ta-Nehisi Coates, "The First White President," *Atlantic*, October 2017.

8. *Congressional Record*, February 28, 1882, 1486.

9. Larry Auster, *The Path to National Suicide: An Essay on Immigration and Multiculturalism* (Monterey, VA: American Immigration Control Foundation, 1990); Patrick Buchanan, *The Death of the West: How Dying Populations and Immigrant Invasions Imperil Our Country and Civilization* (New York: St. Martin's Griffin, 2001); Madison Grant, *The Passing of the Great Race* (New York: Charles Scribner's Sons, 1916); Renaud Camus, *Le grand remplacement* (Paris: David Reinharc, 2011).

10. In this book, the term "immigration restriction" is used to describe national rules about who can enter the United States. Some of the earlier chapters also describe state-level restrictions that are the antecedents of federal laws, but the focus is on how national immigration policy operates. The book also describes other restrictions on nonwhite populations including Jim Crow laws targeting African Americans and a series of restrictions on Chinese immigrants designed to make their lives difficult even before the national Chinese Exclusion Act was passed.

11. Nikole Hannah-Jones, "The 1619 Project," *New York Times*, August 14, 2019.

12. Adam Serwer documents the reaction in "The Fight Over the 1619 Project Is Not About the Facts," *Atlantic*, December 23, 2019.

13. Jared Taylor, "What the Founders Really Thought About Race," National Policy Institute, January 17, 2012.

14. David Reed, "America of the Melting Pot Comes to an End," *New York Times*, April 27, 1924.

15. US Senate, Subcommittee on Immigration and Naturalization of the Committee on the Judiciary, Opening statement by Sen. Edward Kennedy (Washington, DC: Government Printing Office, 1965), February 10, 1965, 1–3.

16. Camus, *Le grand remplacement*.

17. *Congressional Record*, February 28, 1882, 1548.

CHAPTER 1: GO WEST, YOUNG MAN

1. Details about the gold rush are drawn from public sources as well as Mark Eifler, *The California Gold Rush: The Stampede That Changed the World* (London: Routledge, 2016), and Philip Bekeart, *James Wilson Marshall, Discoverer of Gold* (San Francisco: Society of California Pioneers, 1924).

2. Bekeart, *James Wilson Marshall*, 14.

3. James Marshall's first-person account of finding gold is available here, http://malakoff.com/marshall.htm, accessed November 5, 2020.

4. Many of the details on James and V. S. McClatchy's lives are drawn from Steve Wiegard, *Papers of Permanence: The First 150 Years of the McClatchy Company* (Sacramento: McClatchy Company, 2007).

5. US Census data available at https://www.census.gov.

6. Some identity documents were crucial in this era, for freed slaves, for example, who had to regularly show proof of their freedom. See Kate Masur, "State Sovereignty and Migration before Reconstruction," *Journal of the Civil War Era* 9, no. 4 (2009): 588–611.

7. Michael LeMay and Elliot Barkan, *U.S. Immigration and Naturalization Laws and Issues: A Documentary History* (Santa Barbara, CA: Greenwood, 1999), 42.

8. Robert Williams, *Horace Greeley: Champion of American Freedom* (New York: New York University Press, 2006).

9. Williams, *Horace Greeley*, xvii–xviii.

10. George Tinkham, *California Men and Events: Time 1769–1890* (Stockton, CA: Record Publishing Company, 1915), 69.

11. Steven Avella, *Charles K. McClatchy and the Golden Era of American Journalism* (Columbia: University of Missouri Press, 2016), 32.

12. "Timeline of Chinese Immigration to the United States," Bancroft Library, University of California at Berkeley, https://bancroft.berkeley.edu/collections /chinese-immigration-to-the-united-states-1884-1944/timeline.html, accessed November 5, 2020.

13. "Chinese Immigration in 1852," *Annals of San Francisco*, April 1855, Found SF, http://www.foundsf.org/index.php?title=Chinese_Immigration_in_1852, accessed November 5, 2020.

14. For data on the number of Chinese workers, see Immigration Direct, "Chinese Immigration and the Transcontinental Railroad," https://www.uscitizenship .info/Chinese-immigration-and-the-Transcontinental-railroad, accessed November 5, 2020.

15. Campbell Gibson and Kay Jung, "Historical Census Statistics on Population Totals by Race, 1790–1990," Population Division, Census Bureau working paper (2002), 56, https://www.census.gov/content/dam/Census/library/working -papers/2002/demo/POP-twps0056.pdf; Philip Choy, Lorraine Dong, and Marlon Hom, *The Coming Man: 19th Century American Perceptions of the Chinese* (Seattle: University of Washington Press, 1994), 19.

16. The sequence of events is from three *New York Times* reports on the massacre in October 1871; Paul De Falla's article "Lanterns in the Sky" in *Historical Society of Southern California Quarterly* 42, no. 1 (1960): 57–88; and John Johnson Jr.'s "How Los Angeles Covered Up the Massacre of 17 Chinese," *LA Weekly*, March 10, 2011.

17. De Falla, "Lanterns in the Sky," 70–73.

18. "War of Races," *New York Times*, October 26, 1871.

19. Williams, *Horace Greeley*, 173.

20. Dred Scott v. Sandford, 60 US 393 (1857).

21. Quoted in Ibram Kendi, *Stamped from the Beginning: The Definitive History of Racist Ideas in America* (New York: Nation Books, 2016), 3.

22. Douglas Blackmon, *Slavery by Another Name: The Enslavement of Black Americans* (New York: Doubleday, 2008).

23. Thomas Jefferson, *Notes on the State of Virginia* (London: John Stockdale, 1785), 154.

24. The Library of Congress has extensive holdings about the American Colonization Society at "The African-American Mosaic: Colonization," https://www .loc.gov/exhibits/african/afam002.html, accessed November 5, 2020.

25. Andrew Gyory, *Closing the Gate: Race, Politics, and the Chinese Exclusion Act* (Chapel Hill: University of North Carolina Press, 1998), 4.

CHAPTER 2: LEWD AND DEBAUCHED
1. Fessenden Otis, *Isthmus of Panama: A History of the Panama Railroad and the Pacific Mail Steamship Company* (New York: Harper & Brothers, 1867).

2. "From Hong Kong to San Francisco," *New York Times*, February 28, 1861.

3. "Liners to America," *On the Water* exhibition, Smithsonian National Museum of American History, https://americanhistory.si.edu/onthewater/exhibition /5_2.html, accessed November 9, 2020.

4. Some details collected from the script of the play *22 Lewd Chinese Women*. See Elizabeth Yuan, "'22 Lewd Chinese Women' and Other Courtroom Dramas," *Atlantic*, September 4, 2013.

5. State of California, *Acts Amendatory of the Codes of the Twentieth Session of the Legislature, 1873–4* (Sacramento: G. H. Springer, 1874).

6. Chy Lung v. Freeman, 92 U.S. 275 (1875).

7. Ernest Eitel, *Europe in China: The History of Hong Kong from the Beginning to the Year 1882* (London: Luzac, 1895), 513.

8. John Winthrop, "A Defence of an Order of the Court," in Emerson Proper, *Colonial Immigration Laws: A Study of the Regulation of Immigration by the English Colonies in America* (PhD thesis, Columbia University, 1900).

9. Brittney Lane, "Testing the Borders," *Pepperdine Law Review* 39 (2012): 491.

10. LeMay and Barkan, *U.S. Immigration*, 2–4.

11. Anna Law, "The Historical Amnesia of Contemporary Immigration Federalism Debates," *Polity* 47 (2015): 302–19.

12. Hidetaka Hirota, *Expelling the Poor: Atlantic Seaboard States and the Nineteenth-Century Origins of American Immigration Policy* (Oxford: Oxford University Press, 2017), 9.

13. LeMay and Barkan, *U.S. Immigration*, 21–23.

14. Anna Law, "Lunatics, Idiots, Paupers, and Negro Seamen," *Studies in American Political Development* 28 (2014): 107–28.

15. Scott Stuck, "Elkison v. Deliesseline: Race and the Constitution in South Carolina, 1823," *North Carolina Central Law Journal* 2 (1984): 361–405.

16. Michael Schoeppner, *Moral Contagion: Black Atlantic Sailors, Citizenship and Diplomacy in Antebellum America* (Cambridge: Cambridge University Press, 2019).

17. New York v. Miln, 36 U.S. (ll Pet.) 102, 112 (1837), quoted in Lane, "Testing the Borders," 494.

18. People v. Hall, 4 Cal. 399 (1854).

19. People v. Downer et al., 7 Cal. 169 (1857).

20. R. Scott Baxter, "The Response of California's Chinese Populations to the Anti-Chinese Movement," *Historical Archaeology* 42, no. 3 (2008): 29–36.

21. Lin Sing v. Washburn, 20 Cal. at 536 (1862).

22. Burlingame-Seward Treaty (1868), https://www.loc.gov/law/help/us -treaties/bevans/b-cn-ust000006-0680.pdf, accessed November 5, 2020.

23. Ho Ah Kow v. Nunan, 12 F. Cas. 252 (C.C.D. Cal. 1879).

24. Gyory, *Closing the Gate*, 32.

25. Edward McPherson, *A Handbook of Politics for 1876: Being a Record of Important Political Action, National and State, from July 15, 1874 to July 15, 1876* (Washington, DC: Solomons & Chapman, 1876).

26. Chy Lung v. Freeman, 92 U.S. 275 (1875).

27. Kerry Abrams, "Polygamy, Prostitution, and the Federalization of Immigration Law," *Columbia Law Review* 105, no. 3 (2005): 641–716; Eithne Luibhéid, *Entry Denied: Controlling Sexuality at the Border* (Minneapolis: University of Minnesota Press, 2002), 31; George Peffer, "Forbidden Families: Emigration Experiences of Chinese Women Under the Page Law, 1875–1882," *Journal of American Ethnic History* 6, no. 1 (1986): 28–46.

28. Luibhéid, *Entry Denied*, 31–37.

29. Abrams, "Polygamy," 701.

CHAPTER 3: WHATEVER HAPPENS, THE CHINESE MUST GO

1. Denis Kearney, *Speeches of Dennis [sic] Kearney, Labor Champion* (New York: Jesse Haney & Co., 1878), 3, 5.

2. Kearney, *Speeches of Dennis Kearney*, 18, 17.

3. Kearney, *Speeches of Dennis Kearney*, 6.

4. Kearney, *Speeches of Dennis Kearney*, 18.

5. *Congressional Record*, February 28, 1882, 1482.

6. Gyory, *Closing the Gate*, 3–4.

7. The party platforms are available as part of the American Presidency Project from the UC Santa Barbara Library, https://www.presidency.ucsb.edu/documents/republican-party-platform-1880, accessed November 9, 2020.

8. *Congressional Record*, February 28, 1882, 1482.

9. *Congressional Record*, February 28, 1882, 1483.

10. *Congressional Record*, February 28, 1882, 1483, 1487.

11. *Congressional Record*, February 28, 1882, 1486.

12. *Congressional Record*, February 29, 1882, 1515, 1517, 1523.

13. *Congressional Record*, February 29, 1882, 1548.

14. *Congressional Record*, February 29, 1882, 1546.

15. *Congressional Record*, March 6, 1882, 1638–39.

16. There were only thirty-eight states in 1882, so there were only seventy-six senators at the time. Because it was much harder to travel back and forth to their home states, during this era senators often paired up with each other on votes in which a member of one party would agree not to vote in order to account for the vote of another senator from the other party who was out of town, which resulted in a high number of senators voting present rather than yea or nay.

17. *Congressional Record*, March 9, 1882, 1753.

18. US Congress, *Congressional Record: Proceedings and Debates of the Congress*, vol. 32 (2012), 186.

19. LeMay and Barkan, *U.S. Immigration*, 43.

20. Jean Pfaelzer, *Driven Out: The Forgotten War Against Chinese Americans* (Oakland: University of California Press, 2007).

21. Gyory, *Closing the Gate*, 20.

CHAPTER 4: THE WHITE MAN, PAR EXCELLENCE

1. 8 USC Sec. 1405, "A person born in Hawaii on or after August 12, 1898, and before April 30, 1900, is declared to be a citizen of the United States as of April 30, 1900. A person born in Hawaii on or after April 30, 1900, is a citizen of the United States at birth. A person who was a citizen of the Republic of Hawaii

on August 12, 1898, is declared to be a citizen of the United States as of April 30, 1900."

2. Details from the *Ozawa* case are drawn from Shiho Imai, "Ozawa v. United States," Densho Encyclopedia, http://encyclopedia.densho.org/Ozawa_v._United _States, accessed November 5, 2020.

3. David Witherspoon et al., "Genetic Similarities Within and Between Human Populations," *Genetics* 176, no. 1 (2007): 351–59.

4. Josh Gabbatis, "Immigrants Have Been 'Moving and Mixing' Across Europe Since Ancient Times, Groundbreaking DNA Research Reveals," *Independent*, February 21, 2018.

5. Maya Krzewińska et al., "Genomic and Strontium Isotope Variation Reveal Immigration Patterns in a Viking Age Town," *Current Biology* 28, no. 17 (2018): 2730–38.

6. Trevor Noah, *Born a Crime: Stories from a South African Childhood* (New York: Penguin Random House, 2016).

7. Andrea Wulf, *The Invention of Nature: Alexander von Humboldt's New World* (New York: Knopf, 2015), 218, 7.

8. Nell Irvin Painter, *The History of White People* (New York: Norton, 2010), 213; Joel Dinerstein, "The Pernicious Myth of the Caucasian Race," *Los Angeles Times*, September 11, 2019.

9. The term "social Darwinism" was coined in Richard Hofstadter, *Social Darwinism in American Thought* (Boston: Beacon Press, 1944).

10. John Higham, *Strangers in the Land: Patterns of American Nativism, 1860–1925* (New Brunswick, NJ: Rutgers University Press, 1955), 133.

11. Daniel Okrent, *The Guarded Gate: Bigotry, Eugenics, and the Law That Kept Two Generations of Jews, Italians, and Other European Immigrants Out of America* (New York: Scribner's, 2019), 11.

12. Matthew Frye Jacobson, *Barbarian Virtues: The United States Encounters Foreign Peoples at Home and Abroad, 1876–1917* (New York: Hill & Wang, 2000); John Galton, *Natural Inheritance* (New York: Macmillan, 1889).

13. Higham, *Strangers in the Land*, 143–47.

14. Painter, *History of White People*, 213, 214.

15. Painter, *History of White People*, 227.

16. Higham, *Strangers in the Land*, 150–51.

17. Keith Murdoch was a member of the Eugenics Society of Victoria. For more details, see Tom Roberts, *Before Rupert: Keith Murdoch and the Birth of a Dynasty* (Brisbane: University of Queensland Press, 2015).

18. Grant, *Passing of the Great Race*, 9.

19. Grant, *Passing of the Great Race*, 226–29, 167.

20. Grant, *Passing of the Great Race*, 222.

21. Painter, *History of White People*, 287, 308.

22. Speech by Ellison DuRant Smith, April 9, 1924, *Congressional Record*, 68th Congress, 1st Session, vol. 65 (1924), 5961–62.

23. Stefan Kühl, *Nazi Connection: Eugenics, American Racism, and German National Socialism* (Oxford: Oxford University Press, 2002), 85.

24. Okrent, *Guarded Gate*, 2019.

25. Painter, *History of White People*, 286–87.

26. Painter, *History of White People*, 275.

27. There are some disagreements about how much of a role race played in the nativist movements, with some authors suggesting instead it was a class and economic movement. See, for example, Brian Gratton, "Race or Politics? Henry Cabot Lodge and the Origins of the Immigration Restriction Movement in the United States," *Journal of Policy History* 30, no. 1 (2018): 128–57.

28. Painter, *History of White People*, 323.

29. Chinese cases: *Re Ah Yup* (1878), *In re Hong Yen Chang* (1890), *In re Gee Hop* (1895). Hawaiian: *In re Kanaka Nian* (1889). Burmese: *In re Po* (1894). Japanese: *In re Saito* (1894), *In re Yamashita* (1902), *In re Buntaro Kumagai* (1908), *Bessho v. U.S.* (1910). Mexican: *In re Rodriquez* (1897). Native American: *In re Burton* (1900). Armenian: *In re Halladjian* (1909). South Asians: *In re Balsara* (1909), *In re Akhay Jumar Mozumdar* (1913), *In re Mohan Singh* (1919), *In re Thind* (1920), *In re Sadar Bhagwab Singh* (1917). Syrians: *In re Najour* (1909), *In re Mudarri* (1910), *In re Ellis* (1910), *Ex parte Shahid* (1913), *In re Dow* (1914), *Dow v. U.S.* (1915). Filipinos: *In re Mallari* (1916), *In re Rallos* (1917). Korean: *Petition of Easurk Emsen Charr* (1921).

30. Native American: *In re Camille* (1880). Chinese/Japanese: *In re Knight* (1909). Filipino: *In re Alverto* (1912), *In re Lampitoe* (1916). Japanese: *In re Young* (1912).

31. Takao Ozawa v. United States, 260 U.S. 178 (43 S.Ct. 65, 67 L.Ed. 199).

32. For details on Bhagat Singh Thind's life, see "Naturalization Saga: Saga in Summary," https://www.bhagatsinghthind.com/civil-rights/saga-in-summary, accessed November 5, 2020.

33. Ernest Knaebel, *United States Reports*, vol. 261: *Cases Adjudicated in the Supreme Court at October Term, 1922* (Washington, DC: Government Printing Office, 1923), 206.

34. Japan: *Sato v. Hall* (1923). South Asia: *U.S. v. Akhay Kumar Mozumdar* (1923), *U.S. v. Ali* (1925), *U.S. v. Gokhale* (1928), *Wadia v. U.S.* (1939), *Kharaiti Ram Samras v. U.S.* (1942). Philippines: *U.S. v. Javier* (1927), *De La Ysla v. U.S.* (1935), *De Cano v. State* (1941). Afghanistan: *In re Feroz Din* (1928). Arabia: *In re Ahmed Hassan* (1942), *Ex parte Mohriez* (1944).

CHAPTER 5: THE VERY FABRIC OF OUR RACE

1. Wiegard, *Papers of Permanence*, 141. Additional details gathered from the personal papers of V. S. and C. K. McClatchy at the Center for Sacramento History.

2. Avella, *Charles K. McClatchy*, 22.

3. *Sunday News*, March 7, 1897, viewed in McClatchy Papers at the Center for Sacramento History.

4. Wiegard, *Papers of Permanence*, 141.

5. Wiegard, *Papers of Permanence*, 140.

6. LeMay and Barkan, *U.S. Immigration*, 45.

7. After the Gentleman's Agreement in 1907, Japanese entries declined from 30,824 in 1907, to 16,418 in 1908, to 3,275 in 1909.

8. Immigration Act of 1882.

9. Mae Ngai, *Impossible Subjects: Illegal Aliens and the Making of Modern America* (Princeton, NJ: Princeton University Press, 2004), 18.

10. LeMay and Barkan, *U.S. Immigration*, 47, 42.

11. Higham, *Strangers in the Land*, identifies this coalition, 160–65.

12. "Klan Is Established with Impressiveness," *Atlanta Constitution*, November 28, 1915.

13. The KKK "always remained something of a racket," writes Higham in *Strangers in the Land*, 228.

14. Higham, *Strangers in the Land*, 204.

15. Leonard Moore, *Citizen Klansmen: The Ku Klux Klan in Indiana, 1921–1928* (Chapel Hill: University of North Carolina Press, 1991), 47.

16. Higham, *Strangers in the Land*, 96.

17. Henry Cabot Lodge, *Speeches and Addresses, 1884–1909* (Washington, DC: Library of Congress, 1909), 245, 259, 260, 262, 264, 266.

18. *Congressional Record*, 1915, House of Representatives, 63rd Congress, 33rd Session, January 28, 2481–82.

19. V. S. McClatchy, *Japanese Immigration and Colonization* (Washington, DC: Government Printing Office, 1921), 74, 2, 32, 98.

20. V. S. McClatchy, *Four Anti-Japanese Pamphlets* (New York: Arno Press, 1978), 41.

CHAPTER 6: KEEP AMERICA AMERICAN

1. Entry on Albert Johnson in the Biographical Directory of the United States Congress, https://bioguideretro.congress.gov/Home/MemberDetails?memIndex =J000114, accessed February 25, 2021.

2. Okrent, *Guarded Gate*, 317.

3. Okrent, *Guarded Gate*, 295.

4. Calvin Coolidge, "Whose Country Is This?," *Good Housekeeping*, February 1921; Calvin Coolidge, First Annual Message to Congress, December 6, 1923, https://millercenter.org/the-presidency/presidential-speeches/december-6-1923 -first-annual-message, accessed February 25, 2021.

5. John B. Trevor Sr. papers are held at the Bentley Historical Library at the University of Michigan.

6. Higham, *Strangers in the Land*, 314.

7. Okrent, *Guarded Gate*, 329.

8. Samuel Gompers, "America Must Not Be Overwhelmed," *American Federationist* 31, no. 4 (1924): 314–16.

9. Grand Dragon of South Carolina (KKK), "The Regulation of Immigration," July 1923, in East Carolina University Digital Collections, https://digital.lib.ecu .edu/text/11176, accessed November 5, 2020.

10. "Preserving the American Race," *New York Times*, April 5, 1924.

11. Daniels, *Politics of Prejudice*, 100.

12. Letter from Japanese ambassador Masanao Hanihara to Secretary of State Hughes on April 10, 1924, in John B. Trevor, *Japanese Exclusion: A Study of the Policy and the Law* (Washington, DC: Government Printing Office, 1925), 46.

13. *Congressional Record*, Senate, 1924, 6458.

14. Biographical details from Elbert L. Watson, "J. Thomas Heflin," Encyclopedia of Alabama, last updated May 26, 2017, http://www.encyclopediaofalabama .org/article/h-2952.

15. *Congressional Record*, Senate, 1924, 6544–45.

16. *Congressional Record*, Senate, 1924, 6355.

17. For the vote count, see GovTrack, https://www.govtrack.us/congress/votes /68-1/s126, accessed November 5, 2020.

18. Okrent, *Guarded Gate*, 346.

19. Morton Grodzins, *Americans Betrayed: Politics and the Japanese Evacuation* (Chicago: University of Chicago Press, 1949), 47.

20. LeMay and Barkan, *U.S. Immigration*, 130.

21. Proclamation by the President of the United States, March 22, 1929, https://www.presidency.ucsb.edu/documents/proclamation-1872-limiting-the -immigration-aliens-into-the-united-states-the-basis, accessed February 25, 2021.

22. LeMay and Barkan, *U.S. Immigration*, 153.

23. Okrent, *Guarded Gate*, 345.

24. LeMay and Barkan, *U.S. Immigration*, xxiv.

CHAPTER 7: THE ETHNIC MIX OF THIS COUNTRY WILL NOT BE UPSET

1. Adolf Hitler, *Mein Kampf*, vol. 2, chap. 3, http://www.mondopolitico.com /library/meinkampf/v2c3.htm, accessed February 25, 2021.

2. Okrent, *Guarded Gate*, 368.

3. Laughlin quoted in William Tucker, *The Funding of Scientific Racism: Wickliffe Draper and the Pioneer Fund* (Urbana: University of Illinois Press, 2002), 47.

4. Okrent, *Guarded Gate*, 371; Tucker, *Funding of Scientific Racism*, 47.

5. Tucker, *Funding of Scientific Racism*, 37.

6. Douglas Blackmon, "How the South's Fight to Uphold Segregation Was Funded Up North," *Wall Street Journal*, June 11, 1999.

7. Tucker, *Funding of Scientific Racism*, 43 (quotations), 53.

8. Carl Degler, *In Search of Human Nature: The Decline and Revival of Darwinism* (Oxford: Oxford University Press, 1991), 144.

9. Okrent, *Guarded Gate*, 359.

10. Scott Jaschik, "New Evidence of Racial Bias on SAT," *Inside Higher Ed*, June 21, 2010.

11. Reed, "America of the Melting Pot," 1924.

12. LeMay and Barkan, *U.S. Immigration*, 226.

13. Tucker, *Funding of Scientific Racism*.

14. Tucker, *Funding of Scientific Racism*, 132.

15. John F. Kennedy, *A Nation of Immigrants* (New York: Harper & Row, 1958), 77, 82.

16. Steven Gillon, "How a Little-Known '60s Congressman Unwittingly Upended U.S. Immigration," History.com, last updated March 25, 2019, https://www .history.com/news/1965-immigration-policy-lyndon-johnson.

17. These quotations are from documents in the Michael Feighan papers at Harvard University and are cited in Erika Lee, *American for Americans: A History of Xenophobia in the United States* (New York: Basic Books, 2019), 239, 234.

18. *Congressional Record*, 89th Congress, 1st session, 1965, September 22, 24778.

19. *Congressional Record*, 89th Congress, 1st session, 1965, August 25, 21759–60.

20. US Senate, Subcommittee on Immigration and Naturalization of the Committee on the Judiciary, opening statement by Sen. Edward Kennedy, February 10, 1965, 1–3.

21. *Congressional Record*, 89th Congress, 1st session, 1965, September 22, 24770, 24773, 24772.

22. *Congressional Record*, 89th Congress, 1st session, 1965, September 22, 24781, 24776–77.

23. Lyndon Johnson, *The Papers of the Presidents: Lyndon B. Johnson, 1965*, vol. 2 (Washington, DC: Government Printing Office, 1965), 1037–40.

24. US Border Patrol, Nationwide Illegal Alien Apprehensions Fiscal Years 1925–2019, https://www.cbp.gov/sites/default/files/assets/documents/2019-Mar/bp-total-apps-fy1925-fy2018.pdf, accessed February 25, 2021.

CHAPTER 8: PEOPLE, PEOPLE, PEOPLE, PEOPLE

1. Clyde Haberman, "The Unrealized Horrors of the Population Explosion," *New York Times*, May 31, 2015.

2. Rachel Carson, *Silent Spring* (Boston: Houghton Mifflin, 1962).

3. Paul Ehrlich, *The Population Bomb* (New York: Ballantine Books, 1968), 1.

4. Haberman, "Unrealized Horrors."

5. The details on Tanton's personal and professional life are gathered from his papers at the Bentley Historical Library at the University of Michigan. Older correspondence is open, but all of the documents about his anti-immigrant groups and his correspondence after 1991 are closed until 2035. There is an ongoing lawsuit by Hassan Ahmad that seeks to open it. Other sources are Tanton's 1989 oral history "A Skirmish in a Wider War," https://www.documentcloud.org/documents/4521027-A-Skirmish-in-a-Wider-War-an-Oral-History-of.html, accessed February 25, 2021, and a biography written by one his admirers: John Rohe, *Mary Lou and John Tanton: A Journey into American Conservation* (FAIR Horizon Press: Washington, DC, 2002). As this book went to press, some scholarly work on Tanton began to appear, including O'Connor's *Blood Red Lines* and a chapter by Carly Goodman, "Unmaking the Nation of Immigrants: How John Tanton's Network of Organizations Transformed Policy and Politics," in *A Field Guide to White Supremacy*, ed. Kathleen Belew and Ramón Gutiérrez (Oakland: University of California Press, forthcoming).

6. Tanton, "Skirmish," 7–8.

7. Tanton, "Skirmish," 9.

8. Tanton, "Skirmish," 12.

9. Letter to William McWhorter, September 11, 1981, John Tanton Papers.

10. John Tanton, "International Migration: An Obstacle to Achieving World Stability," *Ecologist* 6 (1976): 221–27.

11. *Congressional Record*, 1965, 89th Congress, 1st session, September 22, 24772.

12. Tanton, "Skirmish," 15.

13. Tanton, "Skirmish," 13.

CHAPTER 9: ON OUR SAME SIDE

1. "Ku Klux Klan Plans Border Patrol to Help Fight Illegal Alien Problem," *New York Times*, October 18, 1977.

2. See Our Campaigns, https://www.ourcampaigns.com/RaceDetail.html ?RaceID=55213, accessed November 5, 2020.

3. Brett Barrouquere, "White Shadow: David Duke's Lasting Influence on White Supremacy," *Southern Poverty Law Center Hatewatch*, May 17, 2019, https://www.splcenter.org/hatewatch/2019/05/17/white-shadow-david-dukes -lasting-influence-american-white-supremacy.

4. Associated Press, "Klan Border Watch to Continue 'as Long as It Takes,' Leader Pledges," *Prescott (AZ) Courier*, October 26, 1977.

5. Alex Horton, "'George Zimmerman on Steroids': How Armed 'Militias' Roam the Border in Legal Grey Areas," *Washington Post*, April 25, 2019.

6. Michelle Alexander, *The New Jim Crow: Mass Incarceration in the Age of Color-blindness* (New York: New Press, 2010).

7. Kathleen Belew, *Bring the War Home: The White Power Movement and Paramilitary America* (Cambridge, MA: Harvard University Press, 2018).

8. Belew, *Bring the War Home*, 4.

9. Seyward Darby, *Sisters in Hate: Women on the Front Lines of White Nationalism* (New York: Little, Brown, 2020).

10. Davis and Shear, *Border Wars*, 15.

11. The book was originally republished by the American Immigration Control Foundation in the 1980s with money from Cordelia Scaife May's Laurel Foundation. In the 1990s, Tanton's Social Contract Press began to publish it.

12. Rohe, *Mary Lou and John Tanton*, 69.

13. Tanton, "Skirmish," 22.

14. Tanton letter to John B. Trevor Jr., December 22, 1995, John Tanton Papers.

15. Tanton letter to John B. Trevor Jr., February 1991, John Tanton Papers.

16. Heidi Beirich, *The Nativist Lobby: Three Faces of Intolerance* (Southern Poverty Law Center, February 1, 2009), https://www.splcenter.org/20090131/nativist -lobby-three-faces-intolerance.

17. "Ties Between Anti-Immigrant Movement and Eugenics," Anti-Defamation League, February 22, 2013, https://www.adl.org/news/article /ties-between-anti-immigrant-movement-and-eugenics.

18. Tanton letter to Harry F. Weyher, March 21, 1988, John Tanton Papers.

19. Tanton letter to Harry F. Weyher, February 28, 1991, John Tanton Papers.

20. Tanton letter to Robert K. Graham, August 7, 1995, John Tanton Papers.

21. John Tanton letter to Otis Graham, April 2, 1991, and John Tanton letter to Marge Wilkinson August 29, 1991, both in John Tanton Papers.

22. Jared Taylor, "Africa in Our Midst," *American Renaissance* 16, no. 10 (October 2005).

23. Tanton letter to Jared Taylor, March 12, 1990, John Tanton Papers.

24. Jared Taylor, "Who Speaks for Us?" *American Renaissance* 1, no. 1 (1990), 1.

25. Tanton letter to Jared Taylor, October 10, 1990, John Tanton Papers.

26. Tanton letter to Greg Curtis, January 24, 1991, John Tanton Papers.

27. Jared Taylor, *Paved with Good Intentions: The Failure of Race Relations in America* (New York: Carroll & Graf, 1992).

28. Tanton letter to Dan Stein and other FAIR employees, April 20, 1998, stating that they should read *American Renaissance*: "I write to encourage keeping track

of those on our same side of the issue, but who are nonetheless our competitors for dollars and members." Quoted in Beirich, *The Nativist Lobby*, 6.

29. Jared Taylor, "Trump vs. the Squad," American Renaissance podcast, July 17, 2019, https://www.amren.com/podcasts/2019/07/trump-vs-the-squad.

CHAPTER 10: INVADED ON ALL FRONTS

1. Patricia Sullivan, "Cordelia May, 76: Mellon Heir Avoided the Spotlight," *Washington Post*, January 25, 2005.

2. Burton Hersh, *The Mellon Family: A Fortune in History* (New York: William Morrow, 1978), 393.

3. "Cordelia Scaife's Troth," *New York Times*, January 16, 1949.

4. List of richest Americans from *Fortune* magazine cited in "List of 76 Said to Hold Above 75 Millions; Preparing the Estimates," *New York Times*, October 28, 1957, 20.

5. Caitrin Keiper, "Conquering Polio," *Philanthropy* (Summer 2012), https://www.philanthropyroundtable.org/philanthropy-magazine/article/conquering-polio, accessed February, 25, 2021.

6. Jane Mayer, *Dark Money: The Hidden History of the Billionaires Behind the Rise of the Radical Right* (New York: Doubleday, 2016), 73–111.

7. Christopher Reed, Richard Mellon Scaife obituary, *Guardian*, July 7, 2014.

8. Robert McFadden, "Richard Mellon Scaife, Influential U.S. Conservative, Dies at 82," *New York Times*, July 4, 2014.

9. "The Lewis Powell Memo: A Corporate Blueprint to Dominate Democracy," Greenpeace, https://www.greenpeace.org/usa/democracy/the-lewis-powell-memo-a-corporate-blueprint-to-dominate-democracy/, accessed November 5, 2020.

10. Robert Kaiser and Ira Chinoy, "Scaife: Funding Father of the Right," *Washington Post*, May 2, 1999.

11. Iver Peterson, "In a Battle of Newspapers, a Conservative Spends Liberally," *New York Times*, December 8, 1997.

12. Kaiser and Chinoy, "Scaife."

13. Nicholas Kulish and Mike McIntire, "Why an Heiress Spent Her Fortune Trying to Keep Immigrants Out," *New York Times*, August 14, 2019.

14. "Mrs. Cordelia S. May Is Wed to Pittsburgh District Attorney," *New York Times*, November 7, 1973.

15. Kaiser and Chinoy, "Scaife."

16. Jennifer Latson, "What Margaret Sanger Really Said about Eugenics and Race," *Time*, October 14, 2016.

17. Margaret Sanger, "The Eugenic Value of Birth Control Propaganda," *Birth Control Review*, October 1921, 5.

18. Joseph Tanfani, "Late Heiress' Anti-Immigration Efforts Live On," *Los Angeles Times*, July 25, 2013.

19. Kulish and McIntire, "Why an Heiress Spent Her Fortune."

20. Colcom 990 forms.

21. Kulish and McIntire, "Why an Heiress Spent Her Fortune."

22. Kulish and McIntire, "Why an Heiress Spent Her Fortune."

23. Tanton letter to Cordelia Scaife May, September 29, 1980, John Tanton Papers.

24. Tanton letter to Roger Conner and Jim Hickey, June 29, 1983, John Tanton Papers.

25. Kathy Bricker letter to JT Biography file, March 6, 1983, John Tanton Papers.

26. Tanton letter to Don Mann, June 30, 1983, John Tanton Papers.

27. Tanton, "Skirmish," 32.

28. Rohe, *Mary Lou and John Tanton*, 74.

29. Marked-up copy of Simpson's op-ed, May 18, 1981, John Tanton Papers.

30. Simpson letter to Conner, May 23, 1981, John Tanton Papers.

31. Copy of Simpson's speech, November 1, 1981, John Tanton Papers.

32. Simpson's letter to FAIR, January 24, 1986, John Tanton Papers.

33. Tanton, "Skirmish," 60.

34. Francis Donnelly, "Mich. Man Who Led Anti-Immigration Fight Nearly Forgotten," *Detroit News*, March 15, 2017.

35. "Mellon Heiress Bequeaths Most of Estate to Foundations, Conservation Groups," *Philanthropy News Digest*, March 2, 2005.

36. In 2012, the Laurel Foundation, which Cordelia had established in 1951, merged into the Colcom Foundation.

37. Kulish and McIntire, "Why an Heiress Spent Her Fortune."

38. Rohe, *Mary Lou and John Tanton*, 2.

CHAPTER 11: HOSTILE TAKEOVER

1. Kenneth Weiss, "Sierra Club Members Vote to Stay Neutral in the Immigration Debate," *Los Angeles Times*, April 26, 2005.

2. Quoted in Joseph Taylor III and Matthew Klingle, "Environmentalism's Elitist Tinge Has Roots in the Movement's History," *Grist*, March 9, 2006, https://grist.org/article/klingle.

3. William Cronon, "The Trouble with Wilderness; or Getting Back to the Wrong Nature," in *Uncommon Ground: Rethinking the Human Place in Nature* (New York: W. W. Norton, 1995), 69–90.

4. Sierra Club board of director's policy statement, March 13, 1966, https://www.susps.org/history/scpolicy.html, accessed February 25, 2021.

5. Heidi Beirich, "Greenwash: Nativists, Environmentalism and the Hypocrisy of Hate," Southern Poverty Law Center, July 1, 2010, https://www.splcenter.org/20100630/greenwash-nativists-environmentalism-and-hypocrisy-hate.

6. Matthew Sussis, "A Brief Chronology of the Sierra Club's Retreat from the Immigration-Population Connection (Updated)," Center for Immigration Studies blog, August 14, 2018, https://cis.org/Sussis/Brief-Chronology-Sierra-Clubs-Retreat-ImmigrationPopulation-Connection-Updated.

7. The Carthage Foundation 990 forms show it donated $300,000 to Diversity Alliance for a Sustainable America between 1999 and 2008.

8. Tanton memo to Witan IV Attendees, October 10, 1986, John Tanton Papers.

9. Beirich, "Greenwash."

10. Tanton letter to Alan Kuper, February 27, 1997, John Tanton Papers.

11. Tanton letter to Richard Lamm, April 1, 1998, John Tanton Papers.

12. Tanton memo on Alan Weeden, October 28, 1999, John Tanton Papers.

13. Many of the details in this section are drawn from Beirich, "Greenwash."

14. Kenneth Weiss, "The Man Behind the Land," *Los Angeles Times*, October 27, 2004.

15. "Former Sierra Club Director Discusses Hostile Takeover Attempt by Anti-immigrant Activists," *Intelligence Report*, Southern Poverty Law Center, April 20, 2004, https://www.splcenter.org/fighting-hate/intelligence-report/2004/former -sierra-club-director-discusses-hostile-takeover-attempt-anti-immigrant-activists.

16. Felicity Barringer, "Bitter Division for Sierra Club on Immigration," *New York Times*, March 16, 2004.

17. "John Tanton Is the Mastermind Behind the Organized Anti-Immigrant Movement," *Intelligence Report*, Southern Poverty Law Center, Summer 2002, https://www.splcenter.org/fighting-hate/intelligence-report/2002/john-tanton -mastermind-behind-organized-anti-immigration-movement. This article will be cited by its commonly used title, "The Puppeteer."

18. Beirich, "Greenwash."

19. Brenda Walker, "Save the Sierra Club from the Treason Lobby—Act Now!" VDARE, January 8, 2004, https://vdare.com/articles/save-the-sierra-club -from-the-treason-lobby-act-now.

20. Beirich, "Greenwash."

21. Morris Dees, "Morris Dees' Sierra Club Candidate Statement Seeks Tolerance," Southern Poverty Law Center, January 22, 2004, https://www.splcenter.org /news/2004/01/22/morris-dees-sierra-club-candidate-statement-seeks-tolerance.

22. *Club Members for an Honest Election v. Sierra Club*, Court of Appeals, First District of California, no. A110069, 2006.

23. "Sierra Club Yearly Election Results," April 2004, Sierrans for US Population Stabilization website, https://www.susps.org/info/election_results.html, accessed November 6, 2020.

24. Felicity Barringer, "Establishment Candidates Defeat Challengers in Sierra Club Voting," *New York Times*, April 22, 2004.

CHAPTER 12: OUT-TANCREDO TANCREDO

1. Charlie Savage, "Congress Set to Pass Strict Driver's Licenses Bill," *New York Times*, April 27, 2005.

2. See maps page by Kenneth Madsen of Ohio State University, https://u.osu .edu/madsen.34/maps, accessed November 6, 2020.

3. *FAIR Newsletter*, Federation for American Immigration Reform, May 2005.

4. Mass Immigration Reduction Act of 2001, HR 2712, 107th Congress.

5. *FAIR Newsletter*, May 2005.

6. *FAIR Newsletter*, Immigration Special Report, Federation for American Immigration Reform, June 2007, 7.

7. *Lou Dobbs Tonight*, CNN, April 26, 2007, https://www.youtube.com/watch?v =a3jxCLR6lP0, accessed November 6, 2020.

8. "The Puppeteer."

9. David Folkenflick, "What's Behind Lou Dobbs' Leaving CNN?" *All Things Considered*, NPR, November 12, 2009.

10. Sarah Wheaton, "Bringing Fire, Shoes to Immigration Debate," *New York Times*, April 26, 2007.

11. Tanton Biography File Memo by Kathy Bricker, August 23, 1986, John Tanton Papers.

12. Numbers USA states that Roy Beck was the founder. That is true, but it was established with money from John Tanton and remained part of Tanton's U.S. Inc. for five years.

13. Colcom 990 forms.

14. Robert Pear, "Little-Known Group Claims a Win on Immigration," *New York Times*, July 15, 2007.

15. "The Puppeteer."

16. Davis and Shear, *Border Wars*, 15–16.

17. Matt Apuzzo, "Specter of Race Shadows Jeff Sessions, Potential Trump Nominee for Cabinet," *New York Times*, November 16, 2016.

18. Emily Bazelon, "The Voter Fraud Case Jeff Sessions Lost and Cannot Escape," *New York Times Magazine*, January 9, 2017.

19. Herbert and Kennedy quotations from NBC News Report on Sessions 1986 Confirmation Hearing, March 17, 1986, https://www.youtube.com/watch?v =tuxBiTwHNhU, accessed November 6, 2020.

20. Davis and Shear, *Border Wars*, 15–16.

21. Pear, "Little-Known Group."

22. For example, in the January 2006 FAIR Immigration Report they review Michelle Malkin's book *Invasion*, and in February 2006 they quote Rep. J. D. Hayworth of Arizona: "Many in Washington view illegal immigration as a political problem to be managed rather than an invasion to be stopped." See https://www .fairus.org/sites/default/files/2017-08/Feb06_NL.pdf.

23. *FAIR Newsletter*, Immigration Report, Federation for American Immigration Reform, October 2006.

24. *FAIR Newsletter*, Immigration Report, Federation for American Immigration Reform, January 2007.

25. Tanton letter to Dan Stein, November 7, 1990, and Tanton Biography File Memo by Kathy Bricker, August 23, 1986, John Tanton Papers.

26. Pear, "Little-Known Group."

27. Carl Hulse and Robert Pear, "3 Months of Tense Talks Led to Immigration Deal," *New York Times*, May 19, 2007.

28. Jason DeParle, "The Anti-Immigration Crusader," *New York Times*, April 17, 2011.

29. *FAIR Newsletter*, Federation for American Immigration Reform, July–August 2007, 3.

30. Julia Preston, "Grass Roots Roared and Immigration Plan Collapsed," *New York Times*, June 10, 2007.

31. Video of Tom Tancredo's statement, https://www.youtube.com/watch?v =wQ5xQS817ps, accessed November 6, 2020.

CHAPTER 13: THE WORLD JUST CHANGED

1. Tanton letter to Gregory Curtis, July 12, 1988, John Tanton Papers.

2. Zita Arocha, "Dispute Fuels Campaign Against 'Official English,'" *Washington Post*, November 6, 1988.

3. Tanton memo to Witan IV Attendees, October 10, 1986, John Tanton Papers.

4. Tanton letter to US English Board of Directors, October 17, 1988, John Tanton Papers.

5. Tanton letter to John "Jay" Harris, January 31, 1989, John Tanton Papers.

6. Tanton letter to Warren Buffett, March 8, 1989, John Tanton Papers.

7. DeParle, "Anti-Immigrant Crusader."

8. Donnelly, "Mich. Man."

9. DeParle, "Anti-Immigration Crusader."

10. "Ties between Anti-immigrant Movement and Eugenics."

11. Tanton letter to Roger Pearson, August 26, 1991, box 14, John Tanton Papers.

12. Brendan O'Connor, "The Eugenicist Doctor and the Vast Fortune Behind Trump's Immigration Regime," *Splinter*, July 5, 2018, https://splinternews.com /the-eugenicist-doctor-and-the-vast-fortune-behind-trump-1827322435.

13. Tanton letter to Peter Brimelow, December 15, 1995, John Tanton Papers.

14. Tanton letter to Peter Brimelow, June 25, 1997, John Tanton Papers.

15. Tanton letter to Cordelia Scaife May, October 6, 1997, John Tanton Papers.

16. Tanton letter to Garrett Hardin, December 10, 1993, John Tanton Papers.

17. Southern Poverty Law Center website, https://www.splcenter.org/20200318 /frequently-asked-questions-about-hate-groups#hate%20group, accessed November 9, 2020.

18. In response to an SPLC piece on him in 2002, Tanton wrote a long rebuttal on his website. He responded directly to criticism of publishing *The Camp of the Saints* by providing information on how readers could order a copy from him and included a link to the VDARE website as part of his defense so readers could judge for themselves. Even after his death in 2019, the website was still available online as of February 25, 2021. See www.johntanton.org.

19. Jerry Kammer, "Immigration and the SPLC," Center for Immigration Studies *Backgrounder*, March 11, 2010, https://cis.org/Immigration-and-SPLC.

20. Beirich, "Nativist Lobby."

21. Jason DeParle, "Immigration Opponent Withdraws from Group," *New York Times*, April 29, 2011.

22. Matt Schudel, "John Tanton, Architect of Anti-Immigrant and English-Only Efforts, Dies at 85," *Washington Post*, July 21, 2019.

23. Anti-Defamation League, "Funders of the Anti-Immigration Movement," January 27, 2014, https://www.adl.org/news/article/funders-of-the-anti-immigrant -movement.

24. Chris Rickerd, "Homeland Security Suspends Ineffective, Discriminatory Immigration Program," American Civil Liberties Union, May 6, 2011, https://www .aclu.org/blog/speakeasy/homeland-security-suspends-ineffective-discriminatory -immigration-program.

25. Suzy Khimm, "Kris Kobach, Nativist Son," *Mother Jones*, March/April 2012.

26. Arizona v. United States, 567 U.S 387 (2012).

27. Jeff Sessions, "No Surrender on Immigration," Politico, November 10, 2014.

28. Nate Cohn, "Why Did Cantor Lose? Not Easy to Explain," *New York Times*, June 10, 2014.

29. Marguerite Telford, "Support of Amnesty Leads to Republican Leader's Defeat," Center for Immigration Studies, June 11, 2014, https://cis.org/Telford /Support-Amnesty-Leads-Republican-Leaders-Defeat.

30. Johnathan Weisman and Jennifer Steinhauer, "Cantor's Loss a Bad Omen for Moderates," *New York Times*, June 10, 2014.

CHAPTER 14: IT'S TIME TO MAKE IMMIGRATION POLICY GREAT AGAIN

1. 2015 Katz Award Ceremony transcript, Center for Immigration Studies, https://cis.org/2015-Katz-Award-Ceremony-Transcript, accessed November 6, 2020.

2. Mike Spies, "Trump's Top Policy Advisor Was Once a Budding Democrat. Then He Read Wayne LaPierre's Book," *The Trace*, February 1, 2017, https://www .thetrace.org/2017/02/stephen-miller-donald-trump-policy-advisor-nra-president.

3. Jean Guerrero, *Hatemonger: Donald Trump and the White Nationalist Agenda* (New York: William Morrow, 2020).

4. Guerrero, *Hatemonger*, 121.

5. Guerrero, *Hatemonger*, 83.

6. Michael Brown, "Email from 2007 Ties Trump Advisor Stephen Miller to Neo-Nazi Richard Spencer," Electronic Intifada, February 1, 2017, https:// electronicintifada.net/blogs/michael-f-brown/email-2007-ties-trump-adviser -stephen-miller-neo-nazi-richard-spencer.

7. Josh Harkinson, "Meet the White Nationalist Trying to Ride the Trump Train to Lasting Power," *Mother Jones*, October 27, 2016, https://www.motherjones .com/politics/2016/10/richard-spencer-trump-alt-right-white-nationalist.

8. Julia Ioffe, "The Believer," Politico, June 27, 2016, https://www.politico.com /magazine/story/2016/06/stephen-miller-donald-trump-2016-policy-adviser-jeff -sessions-213992.

9. Stephen Miller, "Santa Monica High's Multicultural Fistfights," *American Renaissance*, July 19, 2005.

10. Ioffe, "Believer."

11. "Ties Between Anti-Immigrant Movement and Eugenics."

12. Dylan Byers, "Neil Munro, Reporter Who Heckled Obama, Out at Daily Caller," Politico, March 31, 2015.

13. "Blow-Out: Breitbart News Sets Traffic Records in July—192 Million Pageviews, 31 Million Uniques, 89 Million Visits," Breitbart News, August 7, 2016.

14. Michael Hayden, "Stephen Miller's Affinity for White Nationalism Re-vealed in Leaked Emails," Southern Poverty Law Center Hatewatch, November 12, 2019, https://www.splcenter.org/hatewatch/2019/11/12/stephen-millers-affinity -white-nationalism-revealed-leaked-emails.

15. Hayden, "Stephen Miller's Affinity."

16. Constance Grady, "Turns Out Steve Bannon's Favorite Novel Is Very, Very Racist," *Vox*, February 10, 2018, https://www.vox.com/culture/2018/2/10/16990428 /steve-bannon-favorite-novel-camp-of-saints-racist.

17. Robert Costa, "Trump's Latest Hire Alarms Allies of Ryan—and Bolsters Bannon," *Washington Post*, January 23, 2017.

18. Julia Hahn, "'Camp of Saints' Seen Mirrored in Pope's Message," *American Renaissance*, September 2015.

19. Guerrero, *Hatemonger*, 130.

20. Sean Trende, "The Case of the Missing White Voters," RealClearPolitics, November 8, 2012, https://www.realclearpolitics.com/articles/2012/11/08/the_case_of_the_missing_white_voters_116106.html.

21. Donald Trump, Conservative Political Action Conference meeting, 2013, https://www.c-span.org/video/?311543-1/donald-trump-remarks-conservative-political-action-conference, accessed November 6, 2020.

22. David Moye, "Donald Trump Appeared in a Playboy Softcore Porn Video," Huffpost, September 30, 2016.

23. Ashley Parker and Steve Eder, "Inside the Six Weeks Donald Trump was a Non-Stop 'Birther,'" *New York Times*, July 2, 2016.

24. Gregory Krieg, "14 of Trump's Most Outrageous 'Birther' Claims—Half from After 2011," CNN, September 16, 2016.

25. Andy Barr, "51% of GOP Voters: Obama Foreign," Politico, February 15, 2011.

26. Race was a primary factor in turning the election for Trump. See Anne Oberhauser et al., "Political Moderation and Polarization in the Heartland: Economics, Rurality, and Social Identity in the 2016 U.S. Political Election," *Sociological Quarterly* 60, no. 2 (2019): 224–44.

27. Political donations are searchable on Ballotpedia.com.

28. Jeremy Diamond, "Donald Trump: Ban All Muslim Travel to U.S.," CNN, December 8, 2015, https://www.cnn.com/2015/12/07/politics/donald-trump-muslim-ban-immigration/index.html.

29. Davis and Shear, *Border Wars*, 33.

30. Julian Routh and Rich Lord, "Colcom Foundation, Rooted in Environmentalism, Increasingly Focuses on Anti-Immigrant Groups," *Pittsburgh Post-Gazette*, July 3, 2009.

31. Ioffe, "Believer."

32. The list of appearances is available here: https://soundcloud.com/search/sounds?q=Breitbart%20stephen%20miller, accessed November 6, 2020.

33. Davis and Shear, *Border Wars*, 36.

34. Pema Levy, "Long Before Trump, Kellyanne Conway Worked for Anti-Muslim and Anti-Immigrant Extremists," *Mother Jones*, December 9, 2016.

35. Davis and Shear, *Border Wars*, 37.

36. Betsy Swan, "Trump Making 'Nativist' Group's Wish List a Reality," *Daily Beast*, March 13, 2017, https://www.thedailybeast.com/trump-making-nativist-groups-wish-list-a-reality.

CHAPTER 15: THE INVISIBLE WALL

1. Davis and Shear, *Border Wars*, 54, 66.

2. Rachael Bade et al., "Hill Staffers Secretly Worked on Trump's Immigration Order," Politico, January 30, 2017.

3. "Immigration Newsmaker: A Conversation with Chairman Bob Goodlatte," Center for Immigration Studies, December 9, 2018, https://cis.org/Transcript/Immigration-Newsmaker-Transcript-Conversation-Chairman-Bob-Goodlatte.

4. Interview with Hassan Ahmad, June 18, 2020. Ahmad posted live about the event on Facebook, https://www.facebook.com/hassanmahmad/videos/10158212699260626, accessed November 6, 2020.

5. Trump v. Hawaii, 585 US (2018).

6. *FAIR Newsletter*, Immigration Report, Federation for American Immigration Reform, December 2015–January 2016.

7. Davis and Shear, *Border Wars*, 77.

8. Dara Lind, "Jeff Sessions Gave Trump the Immigration Crackdown He Wanted," *Vox*, November 7, 2018, https://www.vox.com/2018/5/23/17229464/jeff-sessions-resign-trump-immigration.

9. Hayden, "Stephen Miller's Affinity."

10. Alex Pappas, "John Kelly Suggests Trump Wasn't 'Fully Informed' When He Promised Wall Across Entire Border," Fox News, January 17, 2018, https://www.foxnews.com/politics/john-kelly-suggests-trump-wasnt-fully-informed-when-he-promised-wall-across-entire-border.

11. Twitter, January 18, 2018. Donald Trump's Twitter account was permanently suspended, but his tweets are archived at https://www.thetrumparchive.com.

12. Lucy Rodgers and Dominic Bailey, "Trump Wall: How Much Has He Actually Built?" BBC, October 31, 2020, https://www.bbc.com/news/world-us-canada-46824649.

13. Davis and Shear, *Border Wars*, 93.

14. Lind, "Jeff Sessions."

15. Priscilla Alvarez et al., "Stephen Miller Ally Heads to the National Security Council," CNN, April 27, 2020, https://www.cnn.com/2020/04/27/politics/veprek-national-security-council/index.html.

16. Camilo Montoya-Galvez, "Hardliners Gain Key Posts at Trump's Citizenship and Immigration Services Agency," CBS News, November 21, 2019, https://www.cbsnews.com/news/trump-immigration-policy-posts-hardliners-including-officials-who-worked-for-a-hate-group-gain-key-positions.

17. Colcom 990 forms.

18. Swathi Shanmugasundaram, "Trump Cites Hate Group at Conservative Political Action Conference," Southern Poverty Law Center, March 4, 2019, https://www.splcenter.org/hatewatch/2019/03/04/trump-cites-hate-group-conservative-political-action-conference.

19. Sebastian Murdock, "*New York Times* Runs Anti-Immigration Op-ed by Noted Hate Group," Huffpost, January 17, 2020, https://www.huffpost.com/entry/new-york-times-anti-immigration-op-ed-hate-group_n_5e21d9d8c5b673621f752f9c.

20. Both Stein and Beck quotes are from Swan, "Trump Making."

21. O'Connor, *Blood Red Lines*, 56.

22. "Praise for the RAISE Act," White House, 2017, https://trumpwhitehouse.archives.gov/briefings-statements/praise-raise-act, accessed February 25, 2021.

23. Sarah Pierce and Jessica Bolter, *Dismantling and Reconstructing the U.S. Immigration System: A Catalog of Changes Under the Trump Presidency* (Washington, DC: Migration Policy Institute, 2020).

24. Immigration Policy Tracking Project, Stanford University, https://immpolicytracking.org/home, accessed February 24, 2021.

25. "Asylum Decisions," Trac Immigration Report, https://trac.syr.edu/phptools/immigration/asylum, accessed November 16, 2020.

26. "Ombudsman Alert: Recent Updates to USCIS Form Instructions," Department of Homeland Security, January 23, 2020, https://www.dhs.gov/blog/2020/01/23/ombudsman-alert-recent-updates-uscis-form-instructions.

27. Catherine Rampell, "Trump Didn't Build His Border Wall with Steel. He Built It Out of Paper," *Washington Post*, October 29, 2020.

28. Rampell, "Trump Didn't Build His Border Wall with Steel."

29. Stuart Anderson, "Trump Cuts Legal Immigrants by Half and He's Not Done Yet," *Forbes*, July 21, 2020, https://www.forbes.com/sites/stuartanderson/2020/07/21/trump-cuts-legal-immigrants-by-half-and-hes-not-done-yet/?sh=6aa4e5da6168.

30. Steven Camarota and Karen Ziegler, "Immigration Population Growth Slows: 'Trump Effect' Likely Explains Slowdown," Center for Immigration Studies *Backgrounder*, October 22, 2020, https://cis.org/Report/Immigrant-Population-Growth-Slows.

31. Muzaffar Chishti and Jessica Bolter, "The 'Trump Effect' on Legal Immigration Levels: More Perception than Reality?" Migration Policy Institute, November 20, 2020, https://www.migrationpolicy.org/article/trump-effect-immigration-reality.

CONCLUSION

1. Transcript of Press Briefing by Press Secretary Sarah Sanders and Senior Policy Advisor Stephen Miller, White House, August 2, 2017, https://trumpwhitehouse.archives.gov/briefings-statements/press-briefing-press-secretary-sarah-sanders-senior-policy-advisor-stephen-miller-080217.

2. Peter Brimelow calls it a myth that "infests U.S. Immigration history" in *Alien Nation*, and Otis Graham Jr. also dwells on the changing symbolism of the Statue of Liberty in his book *Unguarded Gates*. Peter Brimelow, *Alien Nation: Common Sense about America's Immigration Disaster* (New York: Random House, 1995); Otis Graham, *Unguarded Gates: A History of America's Immigration Crisis* (Lanham, MD: Rowman & Littlefield, 2004).

3. David Lehman, "Colossal Ode," *Smithsonian*, April 2004, https://www.smithsonianmag.com/arts-culture/colossal-ode-103151288.

4. Lehman, "Colossal Ode."

5. Lyndon Johnson, , May 11, 1965, https://www.presidency.ucsb.edu/documents/proclamation-3656-adding-ellis-island-the-statue-liberty-national-monument.

6. John Fritze, "Trump Used Words Like 'Invasion' and 'Killer,'" *USA Today*, August 8, 2019.

7. Steve Reilly and Kevin Crowe, "While Trump Condemns White Nationalists, Facebook Ads Talk Immigration Invasion," *USA Today*, August 6, 2019.

8. President's Commission on Migratory Labor, *Migratory Labor in American Agriculture* (Washington, DC: Government Printing Office, 1951), 69.

9. *Congressional Record*, Senate, 1924, 6461.

10. *Congressional Record*, Senate, 1882, 1487.

11. Remarks by President Trump to the People of Poland, White House Website, July 6, 2017, https://trumpwhitehouse.archives.gov/briefings-statements/remarks-president-trump-people-poland.

12. *Congressional Record*, Senate, 1924, 6461.

13. *Congressional Record*, Senate, 1882, 1487.

14. Reed, "America of the Melting Pot."

15. Julia Hahn, "Exclusive—Jeff Sessions: Obamatrade Can Be Killed," Breitbart News, October 5, 2015, https://www.breitbart.com/politics/2015/10/05/exclusive-jeff-sessions-obamatrade-can-killed.

16. Hayden, "Stephen Miller's Affinity."

17. Josh Dawsey, "Trump Derides Protections for Immigrants from 'Shithole' Countries," *Washington Post*, January 12, 2018.

18. Stephen Schmidt, "President Trump's 'Animals' Comment Points to a Dark History of Using Dehumanizing Language," *The World*, PRI, May 18, 2018.

19. Alex Nowrasteh, "Deportation Rates in Historical Perspective," Cato Institute, September 16, 2019, https://www.cato.org/blog/deportation-rates-historical-perspective.

20. Katie Rogers and Nicholas Fandos, "Trump Tells Congresswomen to 'Go Back' to the Countries They Came From," *New York Times*, July 14, 2019.

21. Doug Swanson, *Cult of Glory: The Bold and Brutal History of the Texas Rangers* (New York: Penguin Random House, 2020).

22. Pfaelzer, *Driven Out*.

23. The International Organization of Migration maintains a website that documents migrant deaths, https://missingmigrants.iom.int, accessed November 6, 2020.

24. Tim Arango, Nicholas Bogel-Burroughs, and Katie Benner, "Minutes Before El Paso Killing, Hate-Filled Manifesto Appears Online," *New York Times*, August 3, 2019.

25. Andrew Marantz, "The Poway Synagogue Shooting Follows an Unsettling Script," *New Yorker*, April 29, 2019.

26. Andrew de la Garza, "Pittsburgh's Synagogue Shooter May Have Targeted HIAS on Social Media. Here's What to Know about the Organization," *Time*, October 29, 2018.

27. Åsne Seierstad, *One of Us: The Story of Anders Breivik and the Massacre in Norway* (New York: Macmillan, 2015).

28. New Zealand shooter's manifesto, "The Great Replacement."

INDEX